Rites
of Love

Anastasia herself has stated that this book consists of words and phrases in combinations *which have a beneficial effect on the reader.* This has been attested by the letters received to date from tens of thousands of readers all over the world.

If you wish to gain as full an appreciation as possible of the ideas, thoughts and images set forth here, as well as experience the benefits that come with this appreciation, we recommend you find a quiet place for your reading where there is the least possible interference from artificial noises (motor traffic, radio, TV, household appliances etc.). *Natural sounds,* on the other hand — the singing of birds, for example, or the patter of rain, or the rustle of leaves on nearby trees — may be a welcome accompaniment to the reading process.

THE RINGING CEDARS SERIES • BOOK EIGHT PART TWO

8·2

Rites of Love

Vladimir Megré

Translated from the Russian by John Woodsworth
Edited by Dr Leonid Sharashkin

RINGING
CEDARS
PRESS

KAHULUI • HAWAII • USA

Mixed Sources
Product group from well-managed
forests and other controlled sources
www.fsc.org Cert no. SW-COC-002283
© 1996 Forest Stewardship Council

Printed on 100% post-consumer recycled paper

Publisher's Cataloging-In-Publication Data

Megre, V. (Vladimir), 1950-
  [Obr´i`ady l´i`ubvi. English.]
  Rites of love / Vladimir Megré ; translated from the Russian by John
Woodsworth ; edited by Leonid Sharashkin. — 2nd ed., rev.

    p. ; cm. — (The ringing cedars series ; bk. 8, pt. 2)

    ISBN: 978-0-9801812-8-9

1. Spirituality. 2. Nature—Religious aspects. 3. Human ecology. I.
Woodsworth, John, 1944- II. Sharashkin, Leonid. III. Title. IV. Title:
Obr´i`ady l´i`ubvi. English. V. Series: Megre, V. (Vladimir), 1950- Ringing
cedars series, bk. 8, pt. 2.

GF80 .M44 2008i
304.2   2008923354

Contents

Chapter One

Love — the essence of the Cosmos

All of a sudden a figure appeared on the roadway ahead. He was standing practically smack dab in the middle of the travel lane with his back to my oncoming jeep. I began braking at once, so as to carefully go around this strange-looking grey-headed figure.

When I got within ten metres of him, the old fellow quietly turned around and I instinctively pressed the brake pedal to the floor.

There in front of me on the roadway stood none other than Anastasia's grandfather. I recognised him at once. His grey hair and beard were a complete contradiction to his incredibly young, sparkling eyes — a discrepancy which immediately set him apart from many of his peers. And the long grey raincoat of indeterminate cut from goodness-knows-what material was also something I was able to recognise all too easily.

Still, I had a hard time believing my eyes. After all, how could this oldster from the Siberian taiga turn up here in the heart of Russia, on a roadway leading from Vladimir to the city of Suzdal?[1] How, indeed? By coach and horses? How could this Siberian recluse hope to master all the intricacies of our transportation networks? Add to that a complete absence of any kind of identification documents.

---

[1] *Vladimir* (pron. *vla-DEE-meer*), *Suzdal* (pron. *SOOZ-dal'*) — two of Russia's oldest historic cities, located not far east of Moscow. For further information see footnote 1 in Book 5, Chapter 6: "A garden for eternity".

Money, of course, he could have laid his hands on, by selling dried mushrooms and cedar nuts,[2] as his granddaughter
Anastasia had done. But with no identification...

Of course we have lots of homeless people without identification, and the police can't do anything about it. But Anastasia's
grandfather is far from resembling your average homeless person. Sure, he was dressed in old shabby clothes, but they were
always clean, and his appearance was well-groomed, his face
was bright and a light blush adorned his cheeks.

I sat there, unable to move, behind the wheel of the jeep.
He came over and I opened the half-door for him.

"Hi there, Vladimir!" the old fellow greeted me as though
there were nothing unusual about the circumstances. "You
heading to Suzdal? Can you give me a lift?"

"Yes, of course I can. Hop in! How did you end up here?
How on earth did you manage to get here all the way from the
taiga?"

"How I got here isn't important. The main thing is *why* I
came."

"Well, why did you come?"

"To take a tour into real Russian history with you, and
to dispel your resentment toward me. My granddaughter
Anastasia told me to. She said to me: 'Grandpakins, you are
to blame for his resentment.' So here I am, joining you on the
tour. That's why you're going to Suzdal, isn't it?"

"Yes, I want to go see the museum. And I really did feel
resentment, only it's gone now."

We rode for some time in silence. I recalled how frosty our
parting had been back in the taiga. In fact, we didn't even say
good-bye. It had happened like this:

---

[2] *cedar nuts* — referring to the fruit of the Siberian cedar (Siberian pine, *Pinus
sibirica*), known in the West as 'pine nuts'. This tree is akin to the European
stone pine — see footnote 4 in Book 1, Chapter 1: "The ringing cedar" (esp.
the 2nd edition).

Anastasia's grandfather had recommended I set up a political party. He suggested calling it the *Motherland Party*.[3]

The idea of forming a party based on Anastasia's ideas had actually been noised about for some time, by various people. Many believed a political party was essential to make it easier for people to acquire land for the building of family domains and head off any kind of encroachment on the part of government officials, since none of the existing parties, regrettably, had even considered such questions in their platform.

In view of the fact that there are some sort of powers opposed to Anastasia's ideas and that all sorts of attempts have been made to discredit not only the ideas themselves but also people who have been attracted by them, as well as Anastasia and me, it was suggested to draft the party's constitution without any reference in its "Aims and objectives" section to creating favourable conditions for the setting up of kin's domains. Nor should there be any mention of Anastasia's ideas, or the Ringing Cedars Series.

The would-be organisers were trying to persuade me that this would be the only way to get the party officially registered. And so I decided to consult with Anastasia's grandfather on this question, as well as on the topic of the party's structure, its primary aims and objectives. I surmised that since he was well acquainted with the acts of the priests who were constantly setting up all sorts of societal structures and religions which had lasted millennia, he must surely know about the secret organisational tenets underlying such longevity.

Besides, he himself was a priest of some standing.[4] Quite possibly, even stronger than the ones currently ruling the

---

[3]See Book 8, *The New Civilisation*, end of Chapter 12: "People power".

[4]Anastasia's grandfather inherited the priesthood when his own father, Moisey, passed on. The first reference to the family's priestly status comes in Book 7, Chapter 7: "A conversation with Anastasia's grandfather".

world. If so, then he must certainly be aware of the principles underlying the priesthood itself, which had turned out to be more resilient than religion.

Indeed, the priesthood was and is a suprareligious structure, since the priests took direct part in the creation of certain religions and secular institutions. This is clear from the history of Ancient Egypt and other countries.

It followed that Anastasia's grandfather would be able to set forth certain fundamentals for the Motherland Party, making it a most powerful, if not *the* most powerful, institution.

I sincerely wanted to hear what he had to say on this, and so I took advantage of what I thought was a moment when he was not immersed in his inner contemplations, and said:

"You were speaking about a party. My readers, too, have been talking about this for some time. But some of them are recommending that I don't include any mention in its constitution of Anastasia, or her ideas, or the books — so that the registration will go smoothly."

The grey-haired old fellow stood before me, leaning on his father's staff, without saying a word. It wasn't just that he kept his silence — he stared at me fixedly, as though seeing me for the first time. His eyes reflected more criticism than kindness.

And when he did start speaking again after a lengthy pause, his voice, too, betrayed notes of disdain.

"Registration, you say. So, you've come to ask my advice? To betray or not to betray?"

"What's this about betrayal? I came to consult with you on how to proceed so that the registration will go smoothly."

"Registration, after all, is not an end in itself, Vladimir. Even the party is not an end in itself. No ideas, you say, not even a mention? So how are readers going to realise that it's *their* Motherland Party, and not just some mercantile traitors' party? You've been asked to set up some kind of meaningless organisation — without any basis, idea, or symbols which would already guarantee leadership for centuries to come. And now you've come to ask me whether you shouldn't follow their advice. Don't tell me you couldn't see through even this simple trick?"

I realised I had got myself into a rather sticky situation, and so I tried to get out of it by asking another question:

"I only wanted to see if there were some principles you could recommend including in the draft of the party's constitution, its aims and objectives?"

What happened next nearly drove me out of my mind. As it seemed to me back then, the old fellow was not only refusing to answer my questions, he had started making fun of me in a high-handed way. First he looked at me wide-eyed, then he gave a kind of irritated chuckle and turned away, even taking a step back from me. But then he turned around again and said:

"Don't you understand, Vladimir? All the answers to the questions you raise should be given birth within yourself, and within everyone who joins you in creating the party's structure. Sure, I can give you a hint. But tomorrow someone else will give you another hint, and then a third, and you won't *act* — all you'll do is focus your attention on the hints. Go right, go left, you'll all go forward and then backward again or keep going round in circles because of the laziness of your minds."

I strongly resented this latter phrase. Over the years since my first meeting with Anastasia I've been stretching my mind to the limit day and night. Maybe it's starting to overheat from the constant stress of the work. I've published eight books now and have often taken to contemplating what is written in them myself. Sometimes I've found myself pondering the accuracy of particular phrases time and again. And surely the old fellow must know all about this.

Even though my resentment was starting to become in-flamed, I managed to restrain myself, explaining:

"Indeed, it seems as though everybody thinks and re-flects, and various political systems are set up — communist, democratic, centrist. But as someone once said, no matter what party we aim to create, it all ends up looking like the Communist Party's Central Committee!"

"That's very true. That's what I've been telling you — you're going round in circles because of the laziness of your minds."

"What's 'laziness of mind' got to do with it? Maybe it's simply that not enough information is available?"

"So, there's not enough information out there and you've come to me to get it, eh? But if your mind is lazy, will you be able to make any sense of it?"

I could feel my resentment increasing, but I endeavoured to conceal my irritation and continued:

"Okay, I'll try to make my brain work harder."

"Then pay attention. The party should be structured along the lines of the Novgorod *vieche*[5] — I mean, in its early pe-riod. You'll figure out the rest later."

This answer made me really angry. The oldster knew per-fectly well that documents on pre-Christian Russia were no-where to be found — they had all been destroyed. So nobody could ever tell how this Novgorod *vieche* worked, especially in

---

[5] *vieche* (also spelt: *veche*) — an ancient form of self-governance in which a circle of local residents collectively discussed and decided questions of importance by general consensus. In later times, the term *vieche* was used to describe an assembly of freemen which served as a governing council in a number of cities of Western Russia from the tenth to the fourteenth centuries, even longer in the city of Novgorod (about 100 km south of St Petersburg). Not unlike the *Ting* in Scandinavian (esp. Icelandic) com-munities, these latter assemblies had the power (among other things) to enact local legislation, appoint and dismiss princes, wage war and conclude treaties with other territories.

its early period. That meant he was mocking me. But why? What had I done to make him—?

Trying to restrain myself out of respect for his age, I apologised:

"Excuse me for disturbing you. You were probably occupied in something important. I'll leave you."

And I turned around to go, but he called after me:

"But the aim or objective of the Motherland Party should be the creation of favourable conditions for the restoration of the energy of Love to families. It is essential to bring back the rites and celebrations which can help find one's 'other half', one's *soulmate*."

"What?" I turned to face the old fellow again. "Love? Bring it back to families? I realise you don't want to talk serious with me. But why are you making fun of me?"

"I'm not making fun of you, Vladimir. It is you who are not capable of understanding what it's all about. If you don't train yourself to contemplate, it can take years to figure out."

"Figure out what? You have at least a rough idea what kinds of aims and objectives parties all over the world write into their constitutions?"

"I have a rough idea."

"Then tell me, if you know that. Tell me!"

"They claim they will definitely raise the standard of living for everyone, and will offer people greater freedom."

"Exactly. And in particular they promise industrial development, guaranteed housing and control over inflation."

"Nonsense. Utter nonsense!" the oldster chortled.

"Nonsense??? Yes, it *will* be nonsense if I follow your advice and put in as a basic tenet of the party's constitution: *The Party will work toward the goal of helping every individual find their soulmate.*

"And you can add: *The Party will restore to the people a way of life and rites capable of preserving love in families forever.*"

"What on earth are you talking about??!! You— you want to make a laughingstock of me in front of everybody? Questions like this — like searching for one's soulmate — this is what marriage agencies do, on a commercial basis. If I include statements like that in the party's platform, it'll end up being not a party but a dating service! And as for love in families, well, that's a personal matter for families, and nobody, no political party, has the right to interfere in family affairs. That's none of the State's business."

"But don't tell me your State isn't made up of families! Aren't *families* the basis of any State?"

"They are, they are! That's why the State is obliged to raise the standard of living both for families and for individual citizens."

"And what then?" the old fellow snapped. "By raising the standard of living in the country, will you then restore love to a great many families?"

"I don't know. But it *is* accepted that states should care about the welfare of their citizens."

"Vladimir, ponder for a moment what that word *welfare* means. Calm down and delve into its meaning. Now I'm going to say it just a little differently: *well-faring* or *faring well*, that is, a *state of well-being*. If you think about it, you'll realise that love alone is capable of raising any Man's well-being to the highest possible level — not money or palaces, but only the feeling given to Man[6] by the Creator — the state of *love*.

"Love is the essence of the Cosmos. Living, thinking, with an advanced intellect. It is powerful, and it's no wonder God

---

[6]*Man* — Throughout the Ringing Cedars Series, the word *Man* with a capital *M* is used to refer to a human being of either gender. For details on the word's usage and the important distinction between *Man* and *human being,* please see the Translator's Preface to Book 1.

was so excited about it, giving its great energy as a gift to Man. It is imperative to try to understand love, and not be shy about paying attention to it even on the national level.

"And when the nation is comprised of a multitude of families giving birth to their children in love and creating a Space of Love, it will not suffer from lawlessness or inflation. Such a nation will have no need to fight against criminal tendencies; they will disappear from society. And all the prophets with their cunning philosophising will be silenced. Whether they foolishly neglected to mention it or whether it was simply beyond their comprehension is unimportant, but they led people away from the most important thing to a place where there is no love.

"The priests knew about this, and consequently humoured the prophets.

"For centuries mankind had been creating rites in aid of life and love. Whether these rites were suggested by the Creator or the people's own wisdom had perfected them is unimportant. They, in fact, over the centuries, created a state of well-being and helped young people obtain love and joy in perpetuity. None of these rites was characterised by occult superstition, as today. Each one served as a school of higher learning, an examination by the Universe.

"Anastasia told you about the Vedruss[7] wedding rite that dates back centuries. You mentioned it in just one of your books,[8] but it deserves to be mentioned in every book. It is far from being fully comprehended by people living today, including you.

"If you remember, she also told you about ancient ways of searching for your one to love. But again, you today have not

[7]*Vedruss* —. referring to a people prevalent in pre-Christian Russia, from which Anastasia is descended — see Book 6, Chapter 4: "A dormant civilisation". *Ved* is a Slavic root signifying 'awareness' or 'to know'.

[8]See Book 6, Chapter 5: "The history of mankind, as told by Anastasia".

been able to make sense of them. My granddaughter said: 'I, apparently, have not created strong enough images.' She takes all the blame upon herself, but I claim that the laziness of your mind (or minds) is also to blame.

"Let the best learned men study the Vedruss wedding rite letter by letter. They won't — and you'd better believe me, Vladimir — they won't find a single occult or superstitious act. It is an act which is both rational and exactly suited to love's creation. Compared to it, you will see how absurd are today's wedding celebrations — traditions smacking of occultism and superstition.

"You must realise that Anastasia knows immeasurably more than she tells you. Her acts, her logic, her behaviour are not immediately understood even by the priests, who subsequently can only marvel at what my granddaughter has done.

"Enquire of her and inspire her with your question. Ask her what rite the Vedruss people had for childbirth.

"Don't count on her to bring the subject up. She takes care to talk to you only about what she thinks interests you. But you don't have the slightest idea of what tremendous hidden wisdom lies in the ancient rites. They are the creation of cosmic worlds.

"Any world that forgets the wisdom of its age-old forebears deserves derision. It makes no difference whether an individual has forgotten on his own or under the influence of the priests who have mastered the occult sciences.

"Enquire of my granddaughter and inspire her with your question. And summon your party to the creation of love. Until that happens, you are of little interest to me. You need to have the most obvious things explained to you at length. Show forgiveness to an old man. Go. I do not find it useful to talk and think of unpleasantries."

The old fellow turned and started slowly walking away. I stood there all alone in the taiga, feeling I had been spat upon. The resentment I had felt right from the start of our conversation prevented me from making sense of everything he said. But subsequently, upon returning home, I mentally went back to our conversation in the taiga, pondering it and analysing it. I very much wanted to prove — perhaps not so much to Anastasia's grandfather as to myself — that I had not become completely lazy of mind.

I wanted to either disprove or confirm what he said — within myself.

Back in the taiga, the oldster had told me that as long as people are content merely to listen to hints and not begin to think about the essence of life for themselves, society will never be free from its cycle of social upheavals. And Man will never be happy.

I guess that's the way it is.

He also talked about the existence of some kind of programme created by God. Now, what might that be? To what extent does the life of Man today correspond with this programme?

CHAPTER TWO

Do our lives correspond to the Divine programme?

A Man was born in the operating room on the second floor of a hospital. The doctors were surprised to see an absolutely healthy baby.

Days and months flew by like seconds. The child attended kindergarten, then school, then university. 'Wise' educators, teachers and professors instilled in him some kind of programme of life.

The Man decided that the most important thing in life was to have lots of money, which would enable him to feed himself well, have an apartment, a car and clothing. And he began to work hard, sometimes even taking two shifts a day.

Still, the seconds dragged out into years, and when he reached retirement he had been able to earn enough for a modest two-room flat and a used car.

Long before retiring, he fell in love, got married, divorced and re-married. His first wife bore him a child, but after the divorce the child stayed with his mother. A child was born from the second marriage, but he went off to the Far North. They talked on the telephone once or twice a year. Seconds counted down the years of the Man's old age. He took ill and died.

Such is the sad fate of the majority of people living on the Earth today.

There is a minority who manage to become famous entertainers, politicians, presidents or millionaires. Life for this category of people is considered to be more happy, but that is an illusion. Their cares are no fewer than anyone else's, and their end turns out exactly the same: old age, disease and death. Was such a fate included in the Divine programme for residents of the Earth? No!

The Creator could not predestine such a sad and cruel fate for His children. It was human society itself, under the influence of some kind of powers, that ignored the Divine programme and started down a path of self-torture and self-destruction.

Perhaps somebody doubts the existence of the Divine programme of human life? After all, it is not something our scholars or politicians talk about.

Religions propound God's design, but invariably through intermediaries and mostly in different ways. About the only thing they agree on is that God exists.

Philosophers and many scholars, too, believe in the existence of a higher, rational, intelligent being that has created the visible world and earthly life. It is impossible not to believe this. Everything comprising our world, after all, is too logically interconnected for it to be otherwise. Well, if that is the case, then a supremely rational being could create only in a meaningful way, create only that which is eternal, and predestine a joyful perspective for all living beings — first and foremost, His beloved Man, made in His likeness. Man, in other words, is offered a specific way of life on the Earth which allows him to become aware of himself and all creation — to learn about and continue to carry out the Divine programme, contributing his own marvellous creations thereto. God desires from His son, Man, conjoint creation and joy for all from its contemplation.[1]

---

[1]See Book 4, Chapter 2: "The beginning of creation".

There is no doubt that God's programme exists, and it is not just a select group that can become acquainted with this programme, but everyone who wishes to do so. The Divine programme is not set forth in letters or hieroglyphs on sheets of papyrus, but in living signs of Nature — Nature as God has created it— and which belong only to Him.

The minds and intellects of the people of the Ancient Russian period still allowed them to read the grand Book of the Divine. Out of the billions of such letter-signs, the majority of people living today are acquainted with but a few, and we must begin anew to study the Divine alphabet.

The book I am writing at the moment is not on a religious theme. It is not an attempt at sheer philosophising. This book is a call to research, to becoming aware of the Divine programme.

I am not about to teach anyone or preach anything. I only want to acquaint my readers with information on the culture of our forebears, through the rites perfected by the 'wise-men'[2] through careful calculation and designed to preserve family love, and to call upon everyone to disprove or confirm the arguments presented.

I was prompted to publish this material by the sayings and logical conclusions of the Siberian recluses, especially Anastasia.

Publication is needed in order to let the information seep through to the level of one's own feelings and, through collaborative efforts, to start to act according to the logic of life, as well as in the hope that our generation will begin to contemplate, and then accelerate the building of a new civilisation for themselves and their children.

---

[2]*wise-men* (Russian: *volkhvy*) — a reference to ancient 'scientists' with particular knowledge of the workings of Nature, often possessing exceptional powers. For further information, see footnote 13 in Book 7, Chapter 20: "Pagans".

It is possible that Anastasia has conceptually outlined just the first point in the programme of mankind's development, to wit:

Human society should study the Divine programme, using the materials God has provided, and transforming the whole planet into a marvellous Paradise oasis, thereby creating a harmoniously balanced society for all living beings. Man's attainment of this level of life will open up possibilities for the creation of life on other planets and in other galaxies.

Against the background of this grand concept, Anastasia first proposed the creation of family domains.

Let us too begin our research by examining commonly known and outwardly simple issues.

CHAPTER THREE

Why does love come and go?

Oh, how many poems and philosophical treatises have been devoted to this very feeling! In fact, it is hard to find a literary work where it is not touched upon to some extent. Nearly all religions talk about love. It is considered to be a great feeling imparted to Man by God.

The reality of our current human conditions, however, portrays the feeling of love as a most sadistic phenomenon.

Let's face the truth. Statistics show that sixty to seventy percent of marriages are doomed to failure. The failure comes after years of an uneasy coexistence on the part of two people who were once in love. Sometimes these years are marked by mutual insults, scandals and even face-smashing.

The original beautiful and inspired feeling vanishes, only to be replaced by years of anger, insults, hatred and, ultimately, unhappy children.

This is the sad result of what we call love today.

Could such a result be considered a gift from God! No way!

But perhaps it is we ourselves who turn aside from some kind of way of life inherent in Man, and that is why love vanishes, telling us, in effect: *I can't live in such conditions. Your way of life is killing me. And you yourselves are dying.*

Remembering my conversation in the taiga, I recalled how unusually the grey-haired recluse talked about love. "Love," he said, "is the greatest and most powerful energy in the Cosmos. It is never thoughtless. It has thoughts and its own feelings too. Love is a living, self-sufficient entity, a living being.

"By the will of God it is sent to the Earth, ready to bestow its great energy on every Earth-dweller and make their lives eternal in love. It comes to each one of them, endeavouring to tell them, through the language of feelings, about the Divine programme. If Man doesn't listen, it is forced to leave, not by its own will, but by Man's."

Love! A mysterious feeling. And even though almost every Man who has ever lived on the Earth has managed to experience it, love remains largely uninvestigated.

On the one hand, the theme of love is touched upon in most works of prose and poetry, and in most artistic genres. On the other, all the information these contain merely establishes the existence of such a phenomenon. At best, it describes but the outward manifestations of love and variations in behaviour on the part of different people under the influence of the feeling as it has appeared in them.

But is it really necessary to *investigate* the feeling of love, which everybody knows?

The extraordinary and brand new information I received in the Siberian taiga confirms that investigation is extremely necessary. We need to learn to understand love.

I believe one of the most accurate answers to the question as to why love fades is simply that it vanishes when it finds no understanding.

People in the past understood love.

Judge for yourselves: more than ten thousand years ago the Vedruss people possessed knowledge enabling them to carry out actions which not only strengthened love but made it everlasting. One such action was the Ancient Vedic wedding rite. After the description was published in one of my books, many academic researchers came round to affirming that this particular rite was capable of transforming an initially flaring feeling into a permanent one. Comparing it with the rites of various peoples both past and present, I began more and more to draw the conclusion that the Ancient Vedic wedding rite was a rational deed thought up by the wisdom of the people, which is capable even today of helping many family couples find lasting love. However, let's go through everything in order.

And let us begin with the most important thing.

Should we seek out our 'other half'?

'My other half' — 'my *soulmate*' — it's a popular expression. Let's see what it means, exactly. I think many people will accept the following definition: *a man or a woman close to you in spirit and their views on life, a pleasant communicator, someone you feel attracted to (including their appearance), someone capable of inspiring you to love.*

Should we seek out our soulmate, or let our 'other half' be found all on its own, through the will of destiny?

As many centuries of mankind's experience has shown, a determined search is essential. This is attested in multitudes of stories in which stout-hearted young men have set off on long quests in search of their intended.

There are a number of ancient rites which can aid this most important search of one's life.

There are ancient rites, too, which can help determine whether one has made the right choice. What if that 'other half' has come to you straight from the devil himself?

Some of these rites I have already described in my previous books. I did not touch upon well-known rituals, but mostly introduced rites that are not commonly known and have not been encountered heretofore. The present book focuses on the wedding rite and, at the same time, the rite for determining whether one has made the right choice of partner, which I shall go over again in a different context.

"Then get on with it — show us these miraculous rites," some of my readers may be thinking. "Why bother with all these expositions?" But the expositions are absolutely essential! We need a vision of our reality today, otherwise we shall not understand the tremendous signification of the wisdom of the people. Everything in the world is relative and, hence, comparisons are crucial.

So let's now take a look and see which life situations in today's world can facilitate a meeting and which may just get in the way.

Strange as it may seem, in our present so-called 'information age', situations favouring a meeting of two 'halves' are getting harder and harder to find.

People living in large, densely populated megacities are virtually cut off from each other by invisible barriers. Someone living in a modern multi-storeyed apartment block is often unacquainted with his next-door neighbour.[1] Passengers on public transport, even those standing jam-packed shoulder-to-shoulder in the aisles, are all absorbed in their own individual problems. Pedestrians walking along the same street have no reason to communicate with each other.

And in America, for example, you can't even look closely at a woman without being suspected of sexual harassment.

And so, just sitting in your flat or travelling to work or studies, there's practically no opportunity to find your soulmate.

Let's say your work involves contact with a lot of different people. Let's say you're sitting at a cash register in a large

---

[1]For a description of what this means in Russian apartment blocks, see footnote 1 in Book 8, Chapter 13: "A new civilisation".

supermarket. But none of the customers passing by you every day thinks of striking up an acquaintance with you. It's more likely they see you merely as an adjunct to the cash register.

A college or university where a whole lot of young people congregate, though it indeed offers opportunities for conversation and coupling, is not a place for general selection of one's soulmate, since an educational institution is designed with a completely different function in mind.

Today the most acceptable locales for meeting people are generally bars, restaurants, discotheques and resorts. But encounters here, even those which end in marriages, do not, as a rule, result in a happy life in love and harmony. According to statistics, ninety percent of such marriages end in divorce.

The principal cause lies in a false image. And what might that be? Well, here's an example.

False images

Back before I met Anastasia I took a two-week cruise on the Mediterranean Sea.

Each day in the ship's dining room my mealtime companions were three young people — two women and a man — who worked in a design institute in Novosibirsk. Each day the girls appeared in new and stylish clothing, with intriguing hairdos. It was a delight to chat with them. Nadia and Valia,[2]

---

[2]*Nadia* — an informal variant of the name *Nadezhda* (the Russian word for 'hope'); *Valia* — an informal variant of *Valentina.*

as they were called, were always cheerful and outreaching. One time I found their male companion in his cabin, and I asked him:

"What pretty and pleasant girls we have at our table! Maybe we can make some time with them?"

To which he replied:

"I have no desire to make time with riff-raff like that."

"Why 'riff-raff'?"

"'Cause I work with them in the same institute and I know what they're really like."

"And what are they really like?"

"In the first place, they're rowdies. Secondly, they're lazy and slovenly. It's only here that they try to keep up appearances and make people think they're nice and smart. It's quite clear they've come here specially to find themselves husbands among the wealthier class. You've noticed how they play up to the Armenian men on board."

I had an opportunity to see for myself the discrepancy he mentioned when I paid a subsequent late-afternoon visit to the design institute to see my table companions from the cruise ship. To put it mildly, they weren't nearly as impressive as they had been on board, and all their former cheerfulness and pleasantness had somehow vanished.

Which means that back on the ship they were putting on a false image.

Many men and women in the world today try to find their 'other half' with the aid of an external image which doesn't correspond with their real nature. Perhaps such a sad phenomenon is due to an obliviousness to other possible methods? In that case both parties end up being deceived.

A man will give flowers and expensive gifts to an image which has taken his fancy. He may go so far as to offer her his hand and his heart. Then, after marriage, all of a sudden he sees her real character, which doesn't appeal to him at all. He feels a sense of irritation and a yearning for the earlier image which has now vanished.

A woman all of a sudden sees that the suitor who only recently was so kind and attentive to her doesn't love or understand her at all. How did this happen? But he never did love *her* — he only loved the image.

The striking discrepancy between the artificial image and the real person is particularly evident in the case of entertainment celebrities, especially if you should happen to see them in their everyday lives.

A situation no less unfortunate arises from the fact that women often change their outward appearance after marriage.

When a man falls in love with a woman, especially at first sight, it is difficult to say what, specifically, has aroused the feeling of love in him. Perhaps it was the colour of her hair or the way she plaited her braid, or maybe her eyes. It is customary to think that the feeling of love is aroused by the whole gamut of external and internal traits. And when a woman changes her external appearance, she thereby takes away part of her appeal and weakens the love between them. Even if following a radical change of clothes, hairdo and make-up, everybody around tells her how beautiful and attractive she's become, and even if these compliments ring true, and even if her husband gets excited over his wife's new look, it may be only a matter of time before his love begins to fade or disappears altogether.

After all, he has glimpsed a great many beautiful women who are a lot more attractive than his wife at present. Still, he has fallen in love specifically with *her*, and with the appearance she had when they first met. And all of a sudden that previous image is no longer there. And you will, no doubt, agree that in falling in love with the new image, he thereby betrays the image she presented before.

Why were people in ancient times so cautious about changing their clothing? Perhaps they didn't have much in the way of a selection of fabrics? But they did. They imported silks from far across the seas, and they themselves knew how to weave cloth, either coarse or fine. They could do all sorts of designs on the cloth with different colouring agents, or embroider them.

Perhaps they were lacking in imagination or finances? They had plenty of imagination — an abundance, in fact. Practically every other person was a fine artist or designer. You only have to look at houses from those times — how they are all decorated with wood-carvings.

And every woman was a master of embroidery. As for finances, both people of modest means and even those well-off were very conservative when it came to changes of clothing or hairdos. They were extremely cautious about altering their own appearance, being careful to preserve their image.

The current fashion world, especially women, is wont to change their image like a kaleidoscope.

Such extreme fashion swings are extraordinarily profitable to the clothing manufacturing industry, when people throw out things that are still perfectly serviceable and buy new fashions in the hopes that they will bring something new in the way of a semblance of happiness. But no, it never comes. In its place appears only a new artificial image someone has created — an image people put on under the influence of aggressive propaganda.

In all the round of modern life I never have discovered any efficient system of measures designed to help people find a life-long companion. Not only that, but I have been getting more and more the impression that our modern living — indeed, our whole way of life — is designed in such a way that we shall never meet our true soulmate. Maybe this situation even works to somebody's advantage. A Man who is dissatisfied with life, who has no goals or meaning in his life, can be a profitable catch for many a man out to make money. Not to mention profitable to the powers that be.

As to the question of whether or not we are actually seeking out our 'other half', I think the answer will be: no, we are not. We don't know how to. And there are no favourable conditions to facilitate the search.

I attempted to discover sagacious hints on finding one's soulmate in the rites of bygone centuries. I shall cite a few typical examples of wedding rites. Let us examine just how sagacious — or primitive — they are. I shall include my own commentaries as we go along, but if you don't happen to agree with them, you can always cross them out, or white them out and write in your own, right here in the book.

I find myself tapping more and more into the feeling that Anastasia's grandfather is right: if we don't start thinking for ourselves, we'll go on accepting any sort of crap as the wisdom of life.

I shan't even name modern weddings. Apart from drunkenness, tripping around in cars and laying flowers at the so-called 'eternal flame',[3] there's precious little worth saying.

Let's take a closer look, then, at some earlier wedding rites.

---

[3] *laying flowers at the 'eternal flame'* (i.e., at tomb of the unknown soldier) — a common practice among Russian newlyweds which takes place shortly after the wedding ceremony.

CHAPTER FOUR

Wedding rites

I shall cite a typical rite from pre-revolutionary Russia with a view to examining it from the standpoint of social degradation in relation to love.

Courting rituals in Perm.[1] Weddings for the people of Perm involve a whole complex of preliminary operations. First, a father has to seek permission from the local authorities and from the parish priest before setting about courting a bride for his son. This kind of procedure invariably takes place without the participation of the groom, evidently according to ancient custom, and is limited to just the opinion of relatives and close friends called in to give advice. And these are the ones who will decide the fate of their closest relative's future well-being.

It happens that the groom first meets his intended only after the matchmaker has already reached an agreement with the bride's father, and sometimes not until the day of the wedding. Rarely does a young Permian have a chance to court his future bride on his own. The groom's father seeks out, on his son's behalf, a bride with a fair-sized dowry, a maiden of character and respectable moral standing.

Once the final decision had been made as to which girl is to be targeted, the courting itself begins, known as the *korasiom*. This task is always entrusted to the family elder or, in

---

[1]*Perm* — a major city in the Ural Mountains, founded in 1781, located about 1,000 km east of Moscow on the Kama River.

his absence, to the godfather or one of the older relations, or to someone who has had experience in such matters.

It is further explained how and what the go-betweens should say. But it seems to me the whole process is utterly absurd, since the primary principle is violated right from the start.

As we can see, there is not even a hint of the young people's love in carrying out this rite. Sad, too, is the fact that with this abusive attitude toward the energy of Love, they are implicating God.

In preparation for the groom's departure to bring back his bride, the groom's mother (or matron of the house) places on the tablecloth a loaf of bread intended for the blessing of the groom, along with salt, beer and *braga*,[2] and lights the candles in front of the icons.[3] The groom prays and bows low at his mother's and father's feet, seeking their blessing. After reciting Jesus' prayer, he takes up a position at the table as all the wedding guests approach, reciting the same prayer. One after another they reach out with both hands to present the groom with the gifts and goodies they have brought: a cooked shoulder or cut of raw pork, always with bread, and each one chants: "Accept these precious gifts, young prince", followed by the prayer "Lord Jesus Christ" and so forth. At this the groom replies to each one individually: "Amen to your prayer", before accepting (also with both hands) the gifts of food, placing each one first on his head and then on the table, and honours each wedding guest

---

[2] *braga* — a mild, home-made brew.

[3] *icons* — sacred paintings on wood. Every Russian Orthodox church features a multitude of icons, but at least one icon stands or hangs in a corner of the living or dining room in practically every Orthodox household, often with candles in front.

with beer and braga (on rare occasions, wine) as he recites Jesus' prayer and intones: "Drink this to your health, (name of guest)." This naturally meets with a response from each wedding guest the groom addresses with the words "Amen to your prayer". Taking the glass from the groom, he bows to the groom and intones: "May the Lord grant you long life, great happiness, good living,[4] may He grant you to attain happiness, cattle, a full stomach, and bread and salt,[5] obtain a young princess, accompany the princess to the church as her swain, retain a standing position beneath the golden crowns and maintain the law of God!" And then the guest takes a drink.

And here is some more intriguing information.

Permian women rarely preserve their virginity, but their grooms pay no special attention to this and do not avoid such women, but rather accept them eagerly, even those who are pregnant, anticipating the speedy arrival of another worker in the family. It is said that the fathers in some families, considering their daughters to be blameless, will resent any attempt at matchmaking, will swear and even chase away the go-betweens, sometimes even beating them, saying: "What, you're telling me my daughter is *penna?*" — that is, *guilty* (from the word *penya,* meaning guilt).

---

[4]*good living* — the Russian term here is *zhit' da byt'* (literally: "to live and to be"). This ancient expression indicates a distinction between *life* (which is given not only to Man, but also to plants and animals) and *being* (in the sense of existing in a space of conscious awareness —accessible only to Man). The now largely forgotten meaning of this phrase is a wish not only for a 'good life' but also for spiritual fulfilment.

[5]*bread and salt* (Russian: *khleb-sol'*) — a symbol of Russian hospitality (also found in other Slavic cultures), symbolising the earth (bread) and the Sun (salt).

So we end up not with a continuer of the family line, conceived in love, but a worker for the household.

There are, in fact, many characteristic features of wedding rites which portray our ancestors as wild barbarians. I should point out, however, that none of the rites we know of are traditionally Slavic, even though they're sometimes called 'traditional' in the literature on the subject. They stem from a period when the really traditional, wise rites were prohibited by the Church, with nothing rational offered in their place. So, for example:

Removing of boots. It happened (and in some places still happens), according to a native Russian custom, that a newly-wed woman is supposed to remove her husband's footwear. In ancient times this custom generally signified meekness, a servile attitude, even humiliation, since who would take off another's boots if she were not fully subordinate to the wearer of the boots? History teaches us that this custom existed at the time of Vladimir's reign,[6] along with the fact that the prince of Polotsk's[7] daughter was unwilling to remove her husband's footwear.

The same custom existed in Germany during Martin Luther's time: on their wedding night the young wife would take off her husband's boots and place them at the head of the bed as a sign of the husband's domination over the wife, the man over the (enslaved) woman.

Olearius and von Herberstein[8] observed from their stays in Moscow that even princes' and noblemen's weddings

---

[6]*Vladimir I* (?–1015) — Prince of Kiev (980–1015), who accepted Christianity for *Rus'* in 988. See footnote 4 in Book 7, Chapter 20: "Pagans".

[7]*Polotsk* — an ancient city in what is now Belarus, formerly under Polish and Lithuanian control, before the territory was absorbed into the Russian empire in 1772. The Polotskian princedom lasted from the 10th to the 14th centuries.

included the rituals of footwear removal along with three strokes of the whip (the whip was then placed, together with baked goods, in a special box). This rite was continued in Lithuania before the Jagiellonian dynasty[9] and is still preserved in peasant culture.

As we can see, the taking off of boots and honouring the bride's slave status is mistakenly passed off as a traditional Russian rite. But before the princes came along, Russia had no slavery at all. Hence this rite is not traditional for our people, but a transient custom not accepted by the people at large.

But there is one situation which strikes me as even more stupid, cruel and immoral — a situation typical of wedding rites among many peoples as late as the eighteenth or nineteenth centuries.

Directly the last food dish is placed on the table — i.e., the roast — the best man wraps up the dish, along with the bread and salt, in a tablecloth and takes it to a bed in the hayloft, to which the young couple are led immediately afterward. Whereupon the father of the bride, in handing over his newlywed daughter to her husband, stands in the doorway of the hayloft and offers her seemly advice

---

[8]*Adam Olearius* (born *Adam Öhlschläger,* 1603–1671) & *Siegmund Freiherr von Herberstein* (1486–1566) — Austrian and German diplomats, respectively, each of whom travelled to Russia in his time. Von Herberstein (sometimes spelt *von Herbenstein*), a German mathematician and geographer, visited Moscow in 1517 and again in 1526, setting forth his observations in a work entitled *Notes on Moscow affairs;* Olearius (also known as *Omarius*), a member of the Kaiser's council in Vienna, followed suit in the mid-1630s, and later published his *Description of my travels to Muscovy.*

[9]*Jagiellonian dynasty* — a royal dynasty that began in the Grand Duchy of Lithuania (1377–1392, 1440–1572) and spread to other East European countries, including Poland, Ukraine and even parts of Russia.

about marriage life. After the young couple have reached the bed, the wife of the master of ceremonies, wearing two coats at once (one in the normal fashion, the other turned inside out), showers them with grains, coins and hops, and feeds the young couple on their bed.

The next morning all the wedding guests show up at the hayloft and quickly remove the blanket so as to determine by well-known signs whether the newlywed girl has been chaste at the time of her marriage.

This part of the rite may be considered the most sinister and perverted, even if the newlyweds were in love with each other. In the sight of all the guests, the young people, having eaten and drunk their fill, were supposed to go to their room to consummate their marriage without fail, accompanied and encouraged by the lustful — one might even say, perverted — stares of the guests.

In the first place, after all the ups and downs of the pre-nuptial preparations, not to mention the wedding itself, the free-flowing libations of alcohol and the generous intake of food, it is best to hold off sexual intimacy for a period of time, so as to avoid the conceiving of a child in such a condition.

Secondly, why should newlyweds enter into intimate rela-tions the same day and, on top of that, be called to account for their actions in front of the guests? What if the bride happens to be having her period on that day? All-in-all, it is something resembling the imposed mating of animals, or even worse.

Nobody in their right mind would think of bringing a bitch to a male dog — or a cow to a bull, or a ewe to a ram — when the female is not in heat. But the attitude here is: you'd better get on with it, or you'll be put to shame.

The following story was told me by a seventy-year-old man upon learning that I was investigating various rites:

I was living in the country when I got married. They fixed me up with the one I loved. She was oh so quiet, and kind. Her name was Ksiusha.[10] She was nineteen then, I was twenty. We had been looking at each other for about six months, and were probably in love.

On the first night of our wedding, when everything was winding down, the two of us were sent to bed in a separate room. They placed a guard at the door, and the following morning they were supposed to hold up the sheet for all to see: was the blood of virginity there or not? The moment of decision for Ksiusha and me came. Maybe it was wedding jitters, or maybe something I ate, but I got the feeling nothing was going to happen between Ksiusha and me. She did this and that, and began awkwardly showing me her breasts, then she kissed me, and later got undressed completely.

Only there was no proper reaction in me to her caresses and undressing, and I got more and more embarrassed. I sat down on the bed, and turned my face to the wall. I felt Ksiusha's cheek press against my back, I could feel her trembling and her tears running down my spine. I too began weeping for sorrow. There we were both sitting on the bed, crying our hearts out. After that I told her:

"Don't worry, Ksiusha, I'll declare to everyone that it's my fault."

And she replied:

"Don't — they'll only make fun of you."

Before the dawn came, she did the piercing herself with her finger, and the blood came out. In the morning they showed off the sheet to the great amusement of the guests who were once more imbibing in an effort to counteract the effects of their hangover. They summoned us in their

[10] *Ksiusha* — an endearing variant of the name *Ksenia.*

half-drunk state, joking around and calling out *Gor'ko, gor'ko!*[11] before taking their next glass.

Ksiusha and I lived together for six months in the country, then moved to the city and divorced. Turned out I couldn't get anything to happen all those six months. I married again, and now I have four kids — three sons and a daughter — and grandchildren too. But that horrendous wedding I'll never forget my whole life long. And I still remember Ksiusha to this day.

---

[11]*Gor'ko, gor'ko!* (lit. 'Bitter, bitter!') — the traditional call at Russian wedding receptions for the bride and groom to kiss (and thereby sweeten the 'bitter' wine).

CHAPTER FIVE

Conception involves more than flesh

Those who have read my *Book of Kin* will remember that the Vedruss wedding rite I described ended with the loving couple, Liubomila and Radomir, conceiving a child.[1]

But back then I wasn't about to ask Anastasia whether there were any particular aspects of the Vedruss civilisation concerning the conception of children, or whether or not it was worth paying special attention to this topic in any case. But, as though anticipating my question, she said:

"The Vedruss people had a deep understanding of what was involved in the conception of their children. But for the moment I do not know how to talk about it in a way you will be able to understand."

Later on, after my conversation with Anastasia's grandfather and my search for various peoples' rites capable of preserving love in families, I obtained some information on conception and realised that it had nothing to do with Anastasia — *I* was the one who had not been ready to comprehend what she said. Even now this question has not been sufficiently researched by modern science.

Scholars have been attempting to clone Man, but it seems that even if they succeed, they will end up with an entity only superficially resembling Man. You see, it is not just the sperm and the egg that are involved in the act of conception, but something else besides — something invisible, something not tangible as matter.

[1]See the section entitled "A union of two — a wedding" in Book 6, Chapter 5: "The history of mankind, as told by Anastasia".

It is possible that any further exposition of the information I obtained will be shocking to some. I spent six months pondering whether it was something worth sharing with my readers or not. In the end, I decided that it was. Here is what it's all about:

Many families living on the Earth today are unknowingly raising children that are not their own in the fullest sense. This statement is supported by some weighty evidence.

The scientific world has a term *telegony*. In medicine it is called the *paternal impression phenomenon*. They try to talk as little as possible about 'telegony'. What's this all about?

The discovery began in England about a hundred and fifty years ago when Lord Morton decided to raise a new breed of horse with exceptionally resilient characteristics. At one point he crossed a thoroughbred mare with a zebra colt. But no offspring resulted, because of the genetic incompatibility of the two species.

Some time later this purebred English mare was crossed with a purebred English colt. Subsequently the mare gave birth to a foal, only... with marked traces of stripes, as with a zebra.

Lord Morton called this phenomenon *telegony*.[2]

---

[2]The 'zebra' was actually a quagga, an equine mammal of South Africa, with zebra-like stripes, which is now extinct. The experiment, conducted by a Scottish peer, the Right Honourable George Douglas, 16th Earl of Morton (1761–1827), was reported in a communication he wrote to the Royal Society of London in 1820 and described in many journal pieces of the past — for example, by J.C. Ewart of the University of Edinburgh in an 1899 article "Experimental contributions to the theory of heredity. A. Telegony" published in the *Proceedings of the Royal Society of London*, vol. 65 (1899), pp. 243–51; and later in Menia S. Tye's article "Pre-natal influences" in *The American Journal of Nursing*, vol. 7, n° 5 (February 1907), pp. 362–67 (see esp. p. 365; here, as in some other sources, the experimenter's titular name is misspelt *Marton*). Tye also mentions a female hybrid resulting from the first

Specialists in animal husbandry quite often encounter this phenomenon in their practice. Any dog-breeding club, for example, will dispose of even what was the most thoroughbred dam if it happened to mate with a mongrel. That particular dam would no longer produce thoroughbred pups, even if it were to be mated with the most thoroughbred sires.

Pigeon breeders will not hesitate to kill even the most precious purebred pigeon if it has been violated by a non-thoroughbred male pigeon. Practice has shown that it will never produce purebred offspring.

Scientists in various countries have done a great many studies showing that this phenomenon also extends to people. There have been instances where white parents have given birth to black children — where a black-skinned baby has come into the world as a result of a liaison between the grandmother or mother of the birthing woman and a black man. The cause of this phenomenon always turns out to be a previous relationship with a black man on the part of the girl or one of her direct progenitors.[3]

But these are clearly distinguishable cases. How many others are there that are not clearly distinguishable? After all,

---

union. And she subsequently observes (p. 366): "It would seem as though the Israelites had some knowledge of telegony, for in Deuteronomy we find when a man died leaving no issue, his wife was commanded to marry her husband's brother, in order that he might 'raise up seed *to his brother*'" (italics ours).

[3] While dozens of scientific articles on telegony were published in the 19th and the first two decades of the 20th century — by such luminaries, for example, as pioneer statistician Karl Pearson (1857–1936), subsequent acceptance of theories based on Gregor Johann Mendel's (1822–1884) 'laws of heredity' brought the concept of *telegony* into disrepute and many considered it "disproved". However, present-day genetics is far from being able to fully explain the mechanisms of heredity, and throughout the 20th century a great many prominent scholars have been conducting experiments and drawing conclusions quite at variance with the materialistic approaches of 'official' ('orthodox') science.

pre-marital relations are the 'in' thing today. That being the case, there's no point in blaming the woman if she is not a virgin when she marries. It is our society, our monstrous sex propaganda and sex industry that have made her that way.

In the West parents supply their school-age children with condoms, realising that they're no longer chaste. But what they don't know is that there is no condom that can counter the 'paternal impression phenomenon', or telegony. This is evidenced in concrete examples in the case of both people and animals.

Many ancient teachings and religions also speak about the phenomenon of telegony. Even though they may call it something else, the substance is the same. Both scientists and wise-men of old have determined that the first man in the life of a virgin leaves his imprint on her in spirit and in blood — a mental and physical portrait of her offspring to come. All other men who enter into intimate relations with her thereafter for child-bearing purposes have nothing to offer her but their semen and diseases of the flesh.

Isn't this what's behind the current massive lack of understanding of fathers and children? Not to mention the degradation of our whole human society of today?

A multitude of specific examples testifies to the involvement of some kind of energy in the conception of children. But if that is the case, then it is not just scientists but the public at large that should know about it.

It is probable that our recent forebears had some inkling of it. They tried to make sure that a girl entering into marriage was a virgin beyond the shadow of a doubt. It is possible that this is what lies behind the custom in many cultures of locking the newlyweds in a separate room, and subsequently hauling out and putting on display the blood-stained sheet in confirmation of the bride's virginity.

Earlier ancestors of ours, however, did not consider virginity in itself sufficient to qualify someone to be a continuer of the line. They maintained that if a woman was engaged in intimate relations with one man while thinking about another, the resulting offspring would bear resemblance to the one she was thinking about.

Such statements indicate that people of old assumed — and quite possibly knew for certain — that the most important factor in conception was *thought*. Or, more specifically, the *energy of thought*.

The phenomenon of telegony also testifies to this. A woman, perhaps sub-consciously, retains information in her memory about the first man in her life. As a result, a child is born who either fully or partially resembles *him*.

At first I hesitated to write about this subject for fear of provoking unpleasant questions among parents and their children, and between spouses — let them be happy in their ignorance. However, such happiness has not been all that noticeable. And perhaps one of the reasons it is not particularly noticeable is a lack of knowledge as to the culture of conception.

The question of sex education courses for children in schools has been an issue for some time now. People argue over whether they should be introduced or not. If such courses touch only upon the use of condoms, there's no point in introducing the courses at all. If, however, children are told about the woman's chief purpose, about the correct approach to conceiving children, in that case the subject is absolutely essential. For that, however, the instructors must have a thorough grounding in the very essence of the question, and have appropriate literature available. It is a subject that *must* be discussed, even though the mass media, unfortunately, serves up nothing but sex propaganda.

There is a lot of talk in so-called democratic countries about human freedom. But can a Man be called truly free when important questions of life are hidden from him, and in their place allegedly beneficial perversions are fobbed off on him through some kind of supposedly 'free' propaganda? In a situation like that it turns out that Man is 'liberated' only from a true and happy human life.

Still, I wouldn't have written about telegony if I hadn't learnt from Anastasia about how to correct this situation, even if the marriage-bound woman has already had a relationship with another man.

Not only that, but it turns out that the Vedruss people had a momentous rite through which 'stepchildren' could become one's own in blood and spirit.

Our pagan ancestors, the Vedruss all the more so, were very well acquainted with what is known in modern medicine as the 'paternal impression phenomenon'. And through the help of special rites they were able to protect their young people against it.

With the aid of particular acts or rites, wise-men, too, were able to erase the genetic code of the 'first sire' and make even girls who had been raped during enemy attacks absolutely clean. As proof of this, they were not afraid to let their sons take such women in marriage.

However, there is one 'but'. It is impossible to understand and reproduce pagan (and especially Vedruss) rites simply through a knowledge of their outward aspects. They must be experienced through *feeling*.

What's the use in just writing about it? It is essential to *love*, it is essential to prepare for the appearance of the child, it is important to give birth only at home, at the very place of conception.

"To preserve love in the family for ever, it is essential to combine — into one — three points, three feelings, three planes of being". But what's the point in simply re-stating the words? An intellectual understanding is far from sufficient — it must be felt. The philosophy of our forebears must be *felt*.

And the first essential act must be one of sheer repentance in respect to our forebears, who are now called pagans, who have been slandered and whom we have betrayed. We betrayed the traditional Slavic culture of our fathers and mothers — a culture that lasted for tens of thousands of years. Instead we started calling Christianity 'traditional' for Rus'.[4] But in Rus' it has been around for a mere thousand years. There's no way it can be classified as 'traditional'.

Why is *repentance* necessary? For the simple reason that if we go on thinking of our ancestors as wild, dull-witted barbarians (as we are urged to believe) but still adopt their rites, those rites will have no effect. After all, all such rites are founded on a knowledge of the Cosmos, of the designated purpose of the planets and on a knowledge of the power of mental energy, the power of thought.

Even if we try harnessing the tremendous energy of our thought with the aid of their rites, we shall not obtain any positive results, since our thought will be contradicted by another thought of ours — namely that the Vedruss people were ignorant.

Hence a paradox: you're an ignorant fool, but your acts are marvellous. The one excludes — or, at least, contradicts — the other.

Perhaps the culture of our forebears is being deliberately concealed from us? After all, a bunch of ignorant and disoriented people cut off from their roots are easier to control. Perhaps this is God's retribution to our civilisation? Popular wisdom says "What you sow, that shall you reap."[5] We have

---

[4]*Rus'* (pron. *ROOS*) — the name of the East Slavic state of the first millennium of the Common Era (A.D.). See footnote 5 in Book 7, Chapter 12: "The ultimate taboo".

[5]Compare Galatians 6: 7: " whatsoever a man soweth, that shall he also reap" (*Authorised King James Version*).

broken the ties with our forebears, and consequently the threads linking us with our children are also being broken.

We can get another glimpse of the elevated culture of our pagan forebears in the question of conception of children by examining the traditions that are even today preserved in modern China and especially Japan, where a man and woman about to enter into intimate relations for the purposes of conceiving a child undergo a special rite of purification. The beliefs of Ancient China, Japan, India and Ancient Greece — and these are traditionally ancient pagan countries — lay tremendous emphasis on the matter of conception.

So what, then, can anyone do who desires to bring forth good offspring? Should they first spend a lot of time studying the volumes of literature on this subject — besides spending a lot of time on studying treatises on choosing one's soulmate, and on the education of children?

I can tell you right off: there's absolutely no need to waste part of one's own life on such study. I myself spent several years — not *studying* such sources, but simply familiarising myself with them, and I came to the sudden realisation that the Vedruss people have condensed all their monumental works into a system of simple, cheerful and rational rites covering all events of one's life. It gives the impression that God Himself helped them in formulating these rites, as well as in understanding the essence of Man's existence.

Before attempting to apply the experience of our ancestors, we need to determine: which ancestors? I mean, how many years ago? And which territories of present-day Russia were settled by our forebears?

As is known, history textbooks, including those written in Russian, tell about people's lives in Egypt and Rome of five thousand years ago. These countries have carried out (and are still carrying out) archæological excavations, which draw huge crowds of tourists every year. *Russian* history, on the other hand, if we take the word of even our own history books, covers a mere thousand-year period.

That would mean our country's territory before that time was somehow home to a culturally backward people, or maybe there wasn't anybody there at all? Either that, or possibly somebody's been deliberately hiding our history from us? Indeed, they have. I have already written about this,[6] but now I should like to present some archæological data.

I shall tell you about Arkaim, a place which has a direct connection with the question of telegony. According to Anastasia's grandfather, it was there that three and a half thousand years ago a remarkable discovery was made.

---

[6]See, for example, Book 6, Chapter 5: "The history of mankind, as told by Anastasia".

Chapter Six

Into the depths of history

Arkaim — Academy of the wise-men

In 1952 satellites sent back to the Earth photographs of several unusual circles clearly delineated on the surface of the Southern Ural steppe. No one doubted that these circles had been artificially produced, though nobody could say exactly what they were.

A debate was raging in both scientific and occult circles of the time as to where one should look for the original Indo-European homeland. Not without some justification scientists posited that the many European peoples, as well as those of India, Persia and part of Asia, could be traced back to a single source — a mystery people known as *Proto-Indo-Europeans.*

Many researchers have dreamt of finding the remains of the land where once lived the legendary White Aryan race. Researchers have been attempting to reach the fringes of the lost ancient and precious knowledge which the ancient Aryans possessed.

When excavations began in the Arkaim Valley, archæologists announced to the academic world that an ancient city dating back more than forty centuries had been unearthed, and that it had been inhabited by people of the ancient Indo-European civilisation. The researchers started calling Arkaim[1] a city, a temple and an observatory, all at the same time.

Whoever is interested in the academics' hypotheses can read about them in specialised literature on the subject.

I shall pass on what Anastasia's grandfather told me about Arkaim. The logic of his thinking is much more accurate and intriguing than the logic underlying the scholars' scientific hypotheses.

He stated right off:

"Arkaim is not a city and not a temple. The part about the observatory is true, but that's not the main thing here. Arkaim is an *academy* — that's what it would be called today. It was in Arkaim that the teachers of the wise-men lived and worked. Here they engaged in research on the Universe; they also determined the interrelationship of celestial bodies and their influence on Man. Their tremendous discoveries were never recorded, nor did they make long speeches in public. Through their many years of research they worked out the rites, presented them to the people and subsequently kept track of how effective they were. They made corrections as required. They were able to sum up their lengthy researches in a brief word or two which signified the substance of their discovery.

"For example, there are some very early rites, such as the Saviour of the Honey[2] (14 July) and the Saviour of the Apple[3]

---

[1]*Arkaim* (pron. *ar-ka-EEM*) — located in the Chelyabinsk Oblast of Russia, near the border of Kazakhstan. For further information on Arkaim, see: Genadii B. Zdanovich, "Arkaim Archæological Park: a cultural-ecological reserve in Russia", Chapter 20 in: Peter G. Stone & Philippe G. Planel, *The constructed past: experimental archæology, education and the public* (Oxford & New York: Routledge, 1999), pp. 283–291.

[2]*Saviour of the Honey Feast Day* (Russian: *Miodovy Spas*) — a Russian Orthodox Church holiday (actually celebrated 14 August) to mark the beginning of the Assumption Fast. New gatherings of honey are brought to churches on that day for blessing before sharing with parishioners.

[3]*Saviour of the Apple Feast Day* (Russian: *Yablochny Spas*) — a Church holiday coinciding with Transfiguration Day, celebrated at the mid-point of the Assumption Fast (actually 19 August). On this day farmers take grapes to the churches — or, in their place, apples from the new crop.

(19 July). People did not use any new-crop apples until the Saviour of the Apple feast, or any new gatherings of honey until the Honey feast.

"Through their lengthy researches and observations the wise-men discovered that up until this date the apple does not give any significant benefit to Man, even if it is ripe. And this goes far beyond just the apple. Many berries, edible herbs and root vegetables beneficial to Man ripen before the Apple feast. If Man began to eat apples too soon, he would not have room left for the produce that was more beneficial to him at this very time.

"It was these wise-men who discovered that the particular sequence of fruit and vegetable ripening in Nature is no mere coincidence. It is this very sequence that constitutes Man's divine dietary régime, which the science of the centuries to follow would be searching for in vain.

"Volumes of treatises could be written about how they conducted their research. The wise-men, however, never compiled any, and did not burden people with the task of reading them. They imparted their conclusions to people — in ready-made form — in just a few words. And people believed the wise-men. Their advice invariably proved true in life.

"Besides, there is no comparison between the Vedruss wise-men and their counterparts in Greece, the Egyptian priests or today's acclaimed academic lights. The Vedruss wise-men never received any honours or rewards for their remarkable discoveries. They could not accumulate wealth or power that, say, the Egyptian priests enjoyed. And they were not given the kind of adoration showered upon many in church hierarchies today. The only thing a wise-man could expect upon arriving at a certain settlement was food and any replacement clothing or footwear he might need, as well as a place where he could lay his head, though some wise-men might decline the offer of shelter in favour of sleeping under the stars, in the open air.

"Beyond that he enjoyed the people's sincere, unfeigned respect. Over the centuries such an arrangement ensured the selection of only the best teachers and thinkers among the people.

"The receptive populace also showed their gratitude by building, according to the wise-men's own designs, complexes like Arkaim where the wise-men could retreat for meditation and a mutual sharing of thoughts. Here they would tell each other of their discoveries and describe the rites they had come up with based on their discoveries. It was something on the order of a supreme academic council.

"Most of the time ordinary people didn't even know who was behind any given rite, or whom they had to thank for a particularly insightful and effective rite.

"There was one wise-man, for example — an acclaimed philosopher, astronomer and psychologist — who devoted ninety years to the study of how to combat the phenomenon we know today as telegony.

"He discovered a cure and offered people an effective remedy, consisting of a rite of only fifteen minutes in duration. True, the preparation for the rite took a lot longer. Why don't you ask Anastasia, Vladimir — she might tell you about it.

"Only I'll say right off: this rite can be felt only through an understanding of the *feelings of love* possessed by our distant ancestors, the philosophy of their love. The further back you manage to go with your thought, the more you'll be able to make sense of the rite."

To be more thoroughly persuaded of the truth of what Anastasia's grandfather has said regarding Arkaim, let us take a look at its architecture.

Arkaim has the form of a circle with an exterior diameter of approximately 160 metres. As you can see, that's rather small for a city. But I shall still call it a city, as scholars at the moment are doing.

It is surrounded by a two-metre-wide perimeter trench, outside a massive exterior wall. The wall was five and a half metres high and five metres thick. There were four entrances in the wall, the largest facing south-west; the other three were smaller, located on opposite sides.[4]

All the entrances led directly into the only ring road, about five metres wide, which separated the dwellings attached to the outer wall from the inner ring of walls.

This ring road was covered with logs, under which, for the whole length of the street, ran a dug-out two-metre-wide ditch, which connected with the perimeter trench. Thus the city had its own storm-drainage system: surplus water would seep through the logs into the ditch and eventually into the perimeter trench.

All the dwellings attached to the outer wall, like lemon sections, had doorways on the main street. No more than thirty-five dwellings were discovered around the outer circle. That's not much, even for a village.

Next we see the mysterious ring of the inner wall, which was even more massive than the outer one. Three metres thick, it reached a height of seven metres.

According to the excavation findings, there was no entrance through this wall except for a small passageway at the south-east point. Hence, another twenty-five interior dwellings, identical to those around the outer perimeter wall, were practically cut off from everything by the thick, high inner wall. In order to reach the little passageway to the inner ring, one had to travel the whole length of the ring road. This had a hidden significance. Anyone entering the city had to travel the same path as the Sun.

Finally, Arkaim was 'crowned' by a central plaza almost square in shape, approximately 25 by 27 metres.

---

[4]*opposite sides* — i.e., north-east, north-west and south-east.

Judging by the traces of fires spread out in a particular pattern, this plaza was used for some kind of rites.

Thus we see the schematic figure of a Mandala — a square inside a circle. In ancient cosmogonic[5] texts the circle symbolises the Universe, the square — the Earth, our material world. Ancient men of wisdom, who had a perfect knowledge of the structure of the Cosmos, saw how naturally and harmoniously it was constructed. And so in building a city, it was like re-creating the Universe in miniature.

Arkaim was built according to a pre-determined plan as a single complex whole, oriented with extreme precision to celestial bodies. The design resulting from the four entrances in Arkaim's outer wall forms a 'right-facing' swastika, reflecting the clockwise movement of the Sun.[6]

The swastika (in Sanskrit, 'connected with good', 'the best success') is one of the most ancient sacred symbols. It is encountered as far back as the Upper Paleolithic period[7] in the cultures of many of the world's peoples — including those of India, Ancient Rus', China and Egypt, as well as of the mysterious Mayan people in Central America, to name but a few. The swastika may be seen in old Orthodox icons. It is the symbol of the Sun, success, happiness and creativity. Correspondingly, a backwards ('left-facing') swastika symbolises darkness and destruction — the 'night-time Sun' of the dwellers of ancient Rus'.

Both swastikas were used, as may be seen on ancient ornaments — in particular, on the Aryan jars found around

[5]*cosmogonic* — relating to cosmogony, the astrophysical study (or a theory or model) of the origin and evolution of the Universe.

[6]*clockwise movement of the Sun* — that is, as seen from the Northern Hemisphere.

[7]*Upper Paleolithic period* — a period of between 40,000 and 10,000 years ago (also known as the late Stone Age, particularly in reference to Africa), before the advent of agriculture.

Arkaim. This has a deep significance. Day takes the place of night, light the place of darkness, and a new birth takes the place of death — and this is the natural order of things in the Universe. Hence in antiquity there was no such thing as a 'good' or 'bad' swastika — they were perceived as a unified entity (like the energy of *yin* and *yang*[8] in the Orient).

Arkaim was outwardly beautiful: the ideal circular city marked by distinctive gate-towers, burning torches and a beautifully formed façade — probably featuring some kind of meaningful sacral pattern. Everything in Arkaim, after all, was fraught with meaning.

Each dwelling was attached on one side to either the outer or inner wall, and faced either the main ring road or the central plaza. In the improvised 'entrance-hall' to each dwelling was a special watercourse, which emptied into the ditch under the main street. The ancient Aryans were thus provided with a sewer system. Not only that, but each dwelling had its own well, furnace and a small cupola-shaped storage area.

From each well, above the water-level, two earthen pipes branched out. One led to the furnace, the other to the storage area. What for? Quite brilliant, actually. We all know that if you glance down a well, you will invariably feel a current of cool air. So, in the Aryan furnaces this cool air, passing through an earthen pipe, created such a strong draft that it was capable of melting bronze with no need for bellows. There was a furnace like that in every dwelling, and all the ancient blacksmiths had to do was to perfect their craft and compete with their artistic rivals! The other earthen pipe leading to the storage area ensured a lower temperature there.

---

[8] *yin, yang* — the two opposite (though complementary) principles of Chinese philosophy (see footnote 2 in Book 7, Chapter 23: "Significant books").

The famous Russian astroarchæologist Konstantin Konstantinovich Bystrushkin researched Arkaim as an astronomical observatory and came to the following conclusion:

> Arkaim is not just a complex installation, but it is subtle in its complexity. In examining its schematics, one can easily see parallels with the well-known Stonehenge monument in England. For example, the diameter of the inner circle of Arkaim is always reported as being exactly 85 metres. In fact, it is a circle with two radiuses — 40 metres and 43.2 metres. (Try drawing it!) Compare that to the radius of Stonehenge's Aubrey Hole ring,[9] which is also 43.2 metres! Stonehenge and Arkaim are positioned at approximately the same latitude, and both are at the centre of a bowl-shaped valley. The distance between them is almost 4,000 km...

Researchers have determined that on the basis of all the known facts, Arkaim amounts to a *horizon observatory*. Why a 'horizon' observatory, specifically? Because the measurings and observations made there are based on the moment of the rising and setting of the Sun and the Moon on the horizon. The recording of the moment of 'disengagement' (or 'touchdown') of the lower edge of the disc on the horizon allows the accurate determination of the place of this event. If we keep track of sunrises on a daily basis, we shall note that the actual point of sunrise shifts from day to day. Reaching its northern limit on 22 June, this point then moves south to its opposite apogee on 22 December. This is part of the cosmic order.

That means there are four visible points of observation of the Sun each year — two points of sunrise (on 22 June and

[9]*Aubrey Hole ring* — a ring of 56 pits ('holes') thought to have held posts forming a timber circle — named after the poet and antiquary John Aubrey (1626-1697) who discovered them in the seventeenth century.

22 December) and two corresponding points of sunset on the western horizon. Add to these two more points — namely, sunrise and sunset during the equinox (22 March and 22 September). This offered a sufficiently accurate determination of the length of a year. However a year is made up of a whole host of singular events, and these can be determined with the aid of that other celestial body, namely, the Moon. Regardless of the complexity involved in its observation, people of old knew the laws of its movement across the empyrean. Here are a few of them:

(1) The full moon which occurs closest to 22 June is observed at the point of the winter solstice (22 December) and vice-versa.

(2) Lunar events can be observed near the points of the solstice on a nineteen-year cycle ('high' and 'low' Moon).

As an observatory, Arkaim allowed astronomers to follow the events of the Moon. It is possible to note eighteen astronomical events just on these huge circular walls alone! Six of them are connected with the Sun and twelve with the Moon (including the 'high' and 'low' Moon). By comparison, researchers at Stonehenge were able to identify only fifteen cosmic events.

In addition to information about these amazing factual events, the following data were obtained: the Arkaim unit of measurement of length is 80 cm. The centre of the inner circle shows a displacement from the centre of the outer circle by a factor of 5.25 Arkaim units, which is close to the Moon's orbital inclination: 5°9' plus or minus 10 minutes. In Bystrushkin's opinion, this reflects the correlation between the orbits of the Moon and the Sun (for the terrestrial observer). Correspondingly, Arkaim's outer circle is dedicated to the Moon, its inner circle to the Sun. Not only that, but astroarchæological measurements have shown a link between some of Arkaim's parameters and the wobbling of the Earth's axis — this is getting into some pretty sophisticated science, even in terms of modern astronomy.

And so we see that by any stretch of the imagination Arkaim hardly falls under the category of 'city'.

Its extremely small rooms offer no accommodation for families, but serve as an ideal space for philosophical reflections. Historians know that in ancient times so-called 'wise-men' were considered to be scientists and teachers. Consequently, it is possible that Arkaim, as one of the most celebrated scientific centres, could have belonged exclusively to these 'wise-men'. There were simply no other scientists around in those times.

It is also known that the wise-men devised and adjusted their rites on the basis of their knowledge of the Cosmos.

The question is: what has become of these unique rites today? What kind of obscurantism has destroyed them or is concealing them from people's view?

What is the message of Sungir?

And now I should like to bring to your attention some even more sensational news, eclipsing that of even the pyramids of Egypt or the ruins of Ancient Rome.

This information is also needed, as Anastasia's grandfather said, in order to better understand the phenomena and knowledge of the Universe prevalent in our ancient forebears' time. And for that we have to delve as deeply as possible into history.

The Siberian recluse said, furthermore:

"If your thought can dig down to three thousand years ago, you will begin to gradually feel the knowledge of three millennia. If it can go as deep as five thousand years, then five millennia, though not everything you discover will be comprehensible to you. You actually need a minimum of nineteen thousand years."

This attempt to dig into our country's historical past seemed to me utterly unfeasible. I was already prepared to go off to India or Tibet where, it is said, one can learn more about our ancestors than here at home. But, as it turned out, there was no need to go anywhere. Everything was available right here, and now I invite everyone reading these lines to cast his thought about our forebears more than nineteen thousand years back in time.

The archæological finds I am about to describe were made (by mere chance) on the outskirts of the city of Vladimir, which, according to official sources, is approximately 1,015 years old.

In 1955, while excavating a clay pit mine for the Vladimir Ceramics Factory, Alexander F. Nacharov discovered in one of the buckets the bones of some very large animal, which had been resting at a depth of three metres. Archæologists were informed about the discovery.

The first excavations thereafter simply astounded the scientists. Buried on the site were the remains of people, jewellery, clothing ornamentation and everyday objects, all testifying to some kind of ancient culture. Further investigation confirmed that our ancestors had arrived on the banks of the Klyazma River[10] as early as the Old Stone Age, approximately 25,000 years ago.

---

[10] *Klyazma River* — a tributary of the Oka, which in turn flows into the Volga at Nizhny Novgorod east of Moscow. Vladimir is one of the major cities on the banks of the Klyazma.

Now somebody could be wondering whether they might have run about on all fours, dressed in home-made skins and carrying clubs! Not at all. The scientists were amazed by another finding.

On the skeletons themselves or close by were a whole lot of jewellery and ornaments which aided in reconstructing the appearance of the clothing worn by these ancient people — something similar to either overalls or a perfectly civilised dress.

The finding is such that if we are not going to relegate these remains to the category of buried extra-terrestrials, then we shall have to completely revise our whole historical outlook on the world.

In one of its halls the Vladimir State Museum of History and Ethnography mounted a special exhibition dedicated to these unique findings. It put out a booklet stating that the Sungir site is the most interesting archæological monument in Russia, and is known to archæologists the world over. It has hosted a number of international scientific conferences.

Sungir represents one of the northernmost settlements of Ancient Man in the Vladimir Region on the Great Russian Plain. In terms of richness of both objects and state of preservation of such ancient remains, it has no compeer anywhere in the world.

Thanks to the collaborative efforts of archæologists, geologists, paleontologists and paleobotanists, we have a fairly clear picture of how people lived back then, in this incredibly distant time-period.

Here, on the edge of a glacier, was where the tundra used to begin, dotted here and there with islands of fir, pine, birch and alder groves. The animal world was quite diversified.

According to the booklet, "ancient Sungirians hunted the reindeer, wild horse, Arctic fox, wolverine, bison, brown bear, wolf, Arctic hare; they also went after the black grouse, junglefowl and herring gull. And of course, they hunted the mammoth — a huge animal, now extinct, almost four metres tall and weighing six tonnes. This represented for them a much sought-after trophy: meat, skins (indispensable in constructing dwellings) and tusks (a solid and superb material for the preparation of both weapons and ornaments."

The inventory of objects made from bone and horn is most interesting: shaft adjusters, hoes, spearheads, arrowheads and beads from mammoth tusks, jewellery made from the fangs of the Arctic fox. A small silhouetted figure of a large-headed horse came to be recognised as a rare example of primitive art. This famous Sungir horse was decorated with tiny dotted ornaments and red ochre. The number of dots on the figure — a multiple of five — testifies to the use of a quinary counting system among inhabitants of the site. A seven-based system points to the knowledge possessed by people living 25,000 years ago. But it is the unique burial sites of these ancient people that have brought global fame to Sungir.

In 1964, in a heavy layer of ochre-coloured rock, was found the skull of a woman; lower still were the remains of an elderly man. On his chest was a pendant made from a pebble, while on his arms were twenty-five plate bracelets made from mammoth tusks. In addition, on the skull, all along the arms, legs and torso almost 3,500 beads were arranged in rows. The pattern of their arrangement on the skeleton allowed scientists to reconstruct the embroidered costume of this ancient Sungirian. It was reminiscent of the fur clothing worn by Arctic peoples today. At the bottom of the shallow grave they discovered a knife and some kind of scraper made of flint.

Just as much a treasure was the next burial site, unearthed some five years later.

This grave contained the remains of an adult body, but without a skull. Beside it lay a necklace of mammoth-tusk beads, a ring and a pair of reindeer antlers. But farther back, at 65 cm below the upper grave, were found two skeletons of children.

A boy of twelve or thirteen and a girl between seven and nine had been placed in the grave in a stretched position, their heads pressed tightly against each other. Children on their way to 'the next world' were accompanied by hunting weapons made from mammoth tusks: eleven darts, 3 daggers and two spears made out of split and straightened tusks, one 2.5 metres and the other 1.5 metres long. The grave also yielded mammoth-tusk 'rods', very expressive figurines of a horse and a mammoth, carved discs of an apparently ceremonial nature and connected with the worship of the Sun and the Moon. The children's clothing, too, was embroidered with thousands of little beads, and fastened across the chest with pins made of bones. The back of the costume had been outfitted with threads of beads in the shape of animal tails.

This finding testifies to the complex rite of burial and the developed religious beliefs of the ancient people of the Stone Age. One may confidently assume that they believed in the afterlife.

Multidisciplinary archæological investigations have been going on at Sungir, with a few interruptions, ever since 1956. For almost twenty years the project was under the supervision of the famous archæologist Dr Otto Nikolaevich Bader.[11] Anthropologist M.M. Gerasimov,[12] along with his students

---

[11]*Otto Nikolaevich Bader* (1903-1979) — an internationally recognised archæologist of Soviet Russia, accorded membership in the Italian Institute of Prehistory and the Society of Prehistoric Archæology in France. As early as 1924 he was appointed head of the Archæological Division of Moscow's Central Industrial District Museum, and, in 1931, Academic Secretary of Moscow State University's Institute and Museum of Anthropology. He went on to hold a number of other prominent positions in Russian academe.

[12]*Mikhail Mikhailovich Gerasimov* (1907–1970) — a prominent Soviet anthropologist, archæologist and sculptor, who specialised in the re-creation of the outward appearance of a human being on the basis of skeletal remains. He has created reconstructed portraits of historical figures such as Yaroslav the Wise, Tamerlaine, Ivan the Terrible and Schiller.

G.V. Lebedinskaya[13] and T.S. Surnina succeeded in reconstructing the external appearance of the ancient Sungirians.

As is known, anthropologists are often able to reconstruct a
person's face with sufficient accuracy on the basis of the skull.
This offered a rare opportunity indeed to gaze upon the faces
of ancient people — an opportunity I decided to take advantage of. A wise, intelligent-looking face on the adult male. A
slightly sad expression on the young girl's face, a thoughtful
one on the boy's.

And yet the presumptions about hunting, and especially
the mammoth, I believe, were not entirely accurate.

I brought Anastasia's grandfather to this unique exhibition
in the Vladimir museum. The old fellow slowly made his way
around the displays, without stopping at any of them. Then
he stood in the middle of the hall and bowed four times, each
time shifting his position by ninety degrees. When I told him
about the scientists' conclusions, he began to refute a good
deal of it, explaining:

"These people, Vladimir, never hunted mammoths.
Mammoths were their household animals, and a very great
help to families, also a way of transporting heavy loads. They
performed a greater variety of tasks than elephants do today
in India, which are controlled by *mahouts*, or drivers.

"Standing on a mammoth, the Sungirians could gather fruit
from very tall trees and store them in woven bags and baskets,
and then carry them to wherever they liked.

"In the domain glades, the mammoths cleared out young
underbrush from the forest encroaching on the glades or,
depending on the task assigned, would shake and then pull

---

[13]*Galina Viacheslavovna Lebedinskaya* (1924-) — a specialist in remains reconstruction. Following Gerasimov's death in 1970, she succeeded him as head
of the Waxed Reconstruction Laboratory at the Ethnographical Institute
of the Soviet Academy of Sciences.

up trees so as to enlarge the glade. Whenever people had to move from one place to another, they would load their belongings, utensils and food supplies onto the mammoth.

"This was a very kind and industrious household animal. Even a small child could put his fingers around the end of its trunk and lead it about at will. Indeed, children often played with the mammoth, making it suck up water into its trunk and then give them a shower. The mammoth took great pleasure in watching how the youngsters jumped and squealed with joy.

"The mammoth was especially delighted, too, when his wool was combed out and removed by a special, rake-like instrument. A Man would wash the wool, dry it and then use it for his own purposes, for example, in making a bed.

"There was absolutely no need for these people to *hunt* the mammoth. This can be deduced just from the information available in the booklet, which contains quite a few contradictory statements."

"Why contradictory?"

"Think about it. They list all sorts of wild game which could easily be caught in sufficient numbers with the aid of special traps. If a Man killed a mammoth, which weighs six tonnes, he could not possibly eat all its meat right off."

"But what if there were a whole lot of people?"

"There couldn't have been that many. Back in those times people didn't live packed tight together the way they do now in cities or towns. Each family tribe had its own lands. Each family had their own territory, their own home. On an area of three square kilometres might be living fewer than a hundred people. Even collectively, they couldn't eat a six-tonne mammoth in just a few days, even if they didn't consume anything but meat during that time. The rotting meat would start to decompose and attract a huge number of insects. It could have started an epidemic."

"But maybe they invited people from other territories to some kind of feast?"

"What sense would there be in travelling several kilometres just to eat meat which there was enough of at home?"

"But if you say the mammoth's decomposing carcass could run the risk of provoking an epidemic, the very same threat could be posed by a household mammoth when it died."

"Vladimir, a mammoth would never die in the family surroundings. When it got old and felt death approaching, it would walk a little ways from the house and trumpet three times, before heading off to a cemetery for mammoths, where it died. You should have known that yourself, as that is what wild elephants do in India today. Before they die they trumpet and then leave the herd."

"So that means we have a very distorted understanding of how the ancient people fed themselves?"

"Yes, that's right. Perhaps it's an attempt to justify your current barbarity in regard to the treatment of animals. The farther you go back into history, the fewer people you'll encounter eating meat. They had a sufficient supply of growing things to sustain themselves. As for animals, they took from them only what the animals themselves gave to Man — milk and eggs, for example. Meat could have been harmful to the stomachs of the first people.

"Another argument in favour of the premise that hunting was not a basic source of food for primitive people is its illogicality by comparison with other ways of obtaining food."

"What other ways?"

"From tamed, domesticated animals. Picture to yourself a Man whose household includes a female mammoth, a cow and a goat, all of which can be milked, yielding a daily supply of top-quality fresh produce. This Man's household also includes domesticated fowl: a goose, a duck, a chicken, all of which provide eggs with little effort on his part. He has the opportunity of gathering honey and pollen from bees, and a great many root vegetables and edible herbs are also at hand.

"Then all of a sudden it appears as though the Man is going out of his mind. He kills all his domestic animals — which, apart from everything else, have also been guarding him when he is asleep — eats them and begins hunting for wild game, thereby putting himself in danger without guaranteeing himself and his family a regular supply of fresh produce.

"In place of friendly surroundings and the love expressed to him by his household animals, he ends up with nothing but an aggressive environment in which it is virtually impossible, one might say, for his household to survive."

"But did the first people really begin right off to domesticate and train their animals? Maybe that came along at a later period?"

"There would have been no later period for Man if he had taken an aggressive stance from the start. You must be acquainted, after all, Vladimir, with situations where an infant alone in the forest may be fed even by carnivorous wolves — the very same forest where a pack of wolves could tear an adult to pieces. What would account for the discrepancy in their attitude toward Man?"

"I really can't say."

"Because in the first instance the infant Man has no aggression, while in the second we have aggression and fear which create unease in the surrounding environment.

"The first people had no sense of fear or aggression. It was love that was dominant in them, along with a genuine interest in the world around them. Consequently, it was no effort to domesticate or train animals and birds. Their primary concern was to determine the purpose of every creature they encountered on the Earth. This they did. As far as the animals go, you already know that they find their own highest benefit in Man's feelings of love and care for them.

"Meat was first consumed by a less-than-complete Man, one drained of the energy of Love. It seems that he either went out of his mind or was infected with the most terrible disease — a disease which has come down to the present day."

"But what connection can there be between *love* and Man's first consumption of meat?"

"There is a direct connection. A Man living in love is incapable of killing."

"Possibly. But can you determine why these children died 25,000 years ago? Why were they buried in such an unusual manner, head to head like that?"

"I could tell you, of course, but it would be a very long story. Besides, it is not important for you to know *why* they were overcome by death, but *for what purpose.*"

"For what purpose?"

"There you go again, Vladimir, constantly asking questions. Too lazy to think for yourself. Only don't blame me for speaking like this, the way you did back in the taiga when you let resentment take over. Think, instead, on the whole point of my telling you things. What I say will bring you more harm than good if you don't begin to think for yourself.

"I speak, and you listen, and instead of working out your own conclusions in your thought, you are merely taking note of mine. You have set yourself up a goal of finding conditions in the past under which love could remain with people forever, and then reintroducing them in this present day. That's fine, the path is correct, and the goal is the most important of all.

"You are trying to determine how many ages ago love began to dwell with people. Look: here is a date right before your eyes. Think about it. Right in front of you lie two child skeletons. Their death at such a young age is meaningless unless people can realise what important information is concealed in their burial.

"Their death will acquire meaning if you retrieve this information right now."

I didn't resent the old fellow for his remark on my laziness of mind. I had long realised that he was using some kind of methods of his own, trying again and again to teach me how to control my thoughts by alternative means. But I, after all, did not go through the same school as they, training their thought from childhood. I went to an ordinary school, which quite possibly serves to do just the opposite — to switch thought off.

So here I am standing in front of these child skeletons, straining myself mentally, without being able to grasp how I can look on them and learn at least something about the love that existed 25,000 years ago — if it existed at all at that time.

"It did exist," the old fellow suddenly said.

"What made you decide that? There's not a word about love on the museum signs."

"Not a word, but so what? Look carefully. Judging by the skeletons, these are children. The boy is twelve and a half. The girl, she's eight.

"On their skeletons are hundreds of bone beads. On the basis of their arrangement your scientists have determined what kind of clothing the children were wearing. But is that all the bone beads can tell us?"

"What else can they tell us?"

"That their parents, Vladimir, loved these children very much. They loved their children and they loved each other. Only loving parents could get involved in such time-consuming ornamentation of their children's clothing. We can also tell that they had more than enough free time for artistic pursuits and for designing and then making fine clothing.

"Note that the objects found in the grave include absolutely no weapons capable of killing."

"What about the darts? Aren't those weapons?"

"Of course not. And they're not even harpoons for catching fish, since there are no barbs on the ends. The end of the object they've called a 'dart' is not even sharp. A thin, lightweight dart like that could hardly kill or even wound any creature."

"Then what was this object used for?"

"For training and controlling animals. See how it resembles a stick animal trainers use today? Elephant drivers, for example, use sticks like that to control their charges."

"But why did they need to make them out of bone? They could have also taken a real stick and not wasted time straightening out the bone and putting ornaments onto it."

"A wooden stick couldn't last very long. Animals, on the other hand, get accustomed to a single object — its shape and even the smell it acquires from contact with the master's hand."

"Right, then — everything you say sounds rather convincing, but there are other objects which resemble arrowheads. And arrows were meant for killing."

"In the case of these specific people, who were not of the very earliest period of human life on the Earth, arrows were intended for scaring away carnivorous beasts when they attacked.

"There are also some objects that look like hoes. These, indeed, were instruments for planting seeds and digging up roots."

"But the jewellery? Look, this necklace is made from the fangs of an Arctic fox. And scientists assume that the clothing was made from leather. So, they killed animals after all!"

"Your scientists are right about their clothing being made of leather, but there was absolutely no need to kill any animals for this purpose. There were reptiles which shed their old skin on a regular basis. Reptiles might die for some reason, and then ants would eat out their insides, leaving the skin untouched, which turned out to be very useful for making clothing. Given such circumstances, it would be silly to waste time on killing an animal, cutting up the carcass, processing and drying the skin or softening it. What for? Since it was possible to acquire a ready-made skin in an ideal condition. In the Divine Nature all Man's needs have been provided for in advance. As for the necklace from a fox's fangs, it was a lot simpler to take them from a skeleton already worked over and dried by Nature."

At this point I'm going to interrupt, for a moment, Anastasia's grandfather's account about the archæologists' unique findings.

In the booklet put out by the Vladimir State Museum there are drawings showing two exhibit halls — the Sungir Architectural Park and the Sungir Museum Complex. It mentions that international conferences have been organised around these unique findings.

However, I would not advise any great haste to visit the excavation site of this ancient civilisation. There are no actual pavilions on the site — only the remains of unfinished construction. And the archæological work is not proceeding at any intensive pace. The State has no funds for such important projects. They are going ahead, one might say, thanks to the level of enthusiasm both of the scientists involved and of the local authorities.

I arrived at this unique place on a weekend. In one of the pits I saw two men taking soil samples from the side of the pit and carefully placing them into plastic bags. They turned out to be workers from the State Archæological Institute. They confirmed that Sungir is considered the richest archæological site for the study of Ancient Man anywhere in the world.

The Vladimir Museum exhibition is the only one of its kind in Russia. They said that tourists sometimes visited the Sungir excavation site, but mainly tourists from Japan, since there is an even fuller exhibition on Sungir at the Tokyo National Archæological Museum.

It seemed pretty strange that the people in the Land of the Rising Sun show more respect to our ancient forebears living on our country's territory than we do ourselves. Thank you, Japanese friends, for protecting the culture of our joint forebears.

We talk about Russia's lofty mission, about spirituality and the need to support the national image, but what support can we talk about if foreign tourists see our relationship to history through their own eyes?

Well, the only thing we can do is hope that possibly our more civilised descendants will learn what secrets still remain to be discovered in Sungir.

I managed to find out that 25,000 years ago our forebears were civilised people, who knew how to love passionately and preserve love forever.

A family-centred society[14]

To all appearances, in order to bring back lost effective traditions and rites capable of preserving love in families, it would seem necessary to obtain full information about the life of our forebears.

To this end we must delve even deeper into our historical past, right down to the family-community-centred society,

---

[14]Here and throughout this section of the chapter, the Russian term for *family* is *rod/rodovoi*, which refers not just to the *family* in any particular moment of time, but rather to the *tribe, clan* or *family line*, which includes all forebears in addition to the present generation and all future descendants. See also footnote 7 in Book 4, Chapter 33: "School, or the lessons of the gods".

when a husband and wife who loved each other created a friendly family community together with their children, grandchildren and great-grandchildren.

In today's world a husband and wife simply cannot hold on to even their closest relatives — their children. No sooner do their offspring approach adulthood than they try to get out from under their parents' wing. They go off to live in a university residence, or rent an apartment — often at considerable expense, but they still go.

And we're not just talking about children! Many couples separate even before children come along, or shortly after their appearance.

The family-community-centred society existed many millennia in Rus' before the princes came along. It was characterised by an absence of divorce and stronger family units, in comparison with subsequent social structures in our history. Only genuine love is capable of starting a family line. In the past it was much easier for grown children to leave the family than today. I'm talking about the early period in Rus', before the arrival of the princes.

If two young people who loved each other weren't happy with their relationships with their parents, they could leave home and set up their own dwelling on whatever territory they took a fancy to. They could start by nourishing themselves on what they found in the forest; then they would till the ground and establish a household. But they didn't go away. That means the founders of the family line treated them with understanding and love.

We need to study this period and from it draw into our modern way of life grains of logic capable of helping build strong families today.

But how, by what means can we access information about this era in people's lives, when Russian history describes only the Christian period?

Another factor necessitating an investigation into our people's historical past is the importance of determining whether the ancient rites and culture disappeared all by themselves, having outlived their usefulness, or whether the traditions of many millennia were deliberately destroyed.

If they disappeared all on their own, then there is no point in digging into the historical past, since the people themselves rejected their ancient culture, not seeing it as useful, which means it would not be accepted today either.

If, on the other hand, the ancient traditions were deliberately destroyed, then we must look into the question of by whom and for what purpose. We must seek them out, find them and present them to society for evaluation.

It is possible the ancient rites and traditions conceal within themselves such important secrets of human existence that without uncovering them we shall continue to move toward an abyss, die out and torment ourselves with family strife. We often talk about large-scale wars. Family conflict, however, is often more painful for each of its participants than news about war in Iraq or events in Israel.

Recalling everything I knew about Ancient Russian history, I decided that, strange as it might seem at first glance, the only thread leading through the vast labyrinth of historical falsehoods was the conqueror Genghis Khan[15] — in other words, the three-hundred-year period of the so-called 'Tataro-Mongol Yoke' in Rus'. Why? Because this period began shortly after the Christianisation of Rus', when the traditions of our ancestors had not yet been completely annihilated.

---

[15]*Genghis Khan* (Mongolian: *Chinggis Khayan;* real name: Temujin, 1162–1227) — the founder, reformer and unifier of the State of Mongolia (1206). After uniting the nomadic tribes of north-east and central Asia, he organised campaigns of conquest throughout Asia and Eastern Europe, thus forming the largest contiguous empire in world history.

Not only that, but Genghis Khan was just about the brightest, most interesting and enlightened personality of his time. It is not only that he and his descendants conquered half the world, but it is fascinating to see how they did it.

I can tell you right off that their army played only a secondary role in this process. We know from various historical sources that Genghis Khan sent expeditions to many lands, as far away as China and India, which supplied him with wisemen. He spent a great deal of time conversing with men of wisdom. He was attempting to determine the purpose of human existence on the Earth, and to find immortality. In other words, he was gathering the wisdom of various peoples and could well have possessed information about the social structure of Ancient Rus'.

And it turned out, in fact, that he did. I am convinced that it was thanks to this information that his family, his sons and great-grandchildren were able to hold the so-called élite of many countries in subjection over the centuries. And I mean exactly that — it wasn't countries or their peoples that he held in subjection, but their élites that were usurping the peoples of these countries.

Somebody might wonder what on earth the knowledge of ancient family traditions and love-preserving rites has to do with the successful subjugation of states.

You shouldn't be surprised — there is a simple direct relationship, and such knowledge is more powerful than millions of soldiers' swords or even the most state-of-the-art weaponry.

I shall not bother describing the whole three-hundred-year period of the Tataro-Mongolian hold on Rus'. I shall cite just one episode — albeit a very typical and interesting episode — the subjugation of the Vladimir-Suzdal principality, on which I have collected information from various sources. Let's try to arrive at some conclusions together.

A mysterious manœuvre

Chronicles, modern historical sources and church literature all talk about a mysterious and even secretive manœuvre on the part of Batu Khan[16], grandson to Genghis Khan, on the outskirts of the city of Vladimir in 1238. What is the mystery here? This is how the chronicles tell it:

"Having taken Riazan[17] in 1237, in the spring of 1238 Batu Khan and his cavalry pushed their way into the city of Suzdal..." As subsequently reported in a multitude of ecclesiastical sources, he burnt Suzdal, exterminated part of the population and took the remaining part captive. A lot is said in these sources about the "atrocities committed against the people".

Secular historians, on the other hand, describe the situation more accurately and impartially. Thus, for example, in the materials available in the Vladimir-Suzdal State Museum the event is described as follows:

---

[16]*Batu Khan* (also known as *Baty,* 1205-1255) — the son of Jochi and grandson of Genghis Khan, who inherited the leadership of the so-called *Golden Horde* (Mongolian: *Altan Ordyn Uls*; Russian: *Zolotaya Orda*) — part of the Mongol Empire that covered much of present-day Russian territory (along with Ukraine, Kazakhstan and the Caucasus) for almost three centuries, beginning in the 1240s.

[17]*Riazan* — a city on the Oka River south-east of Moscow (see footnote 6 in Book 5, Chapter 17: "Questions and answers").

The Tatars set up their camps at the city of Vladimir, while they themselves went and took Suzdal, and plundered the Holy Mother of God (cathedral), and burnt the prince's court, and burnt the monastery of Saint Dmitry, and plundered others; and the old monks and nuns, and the priests, and the blind, and the lame, and the deaf, and the labour-weary and all other people were slaughtered, while the young monks, and monks, and priests, and their wives, and the deacons with their wives, and their daughters, and their sons — all these were led away to the Tatars' camps, and they themselves went to Vladimir.

As we can see, Batu Khan did not take anywhere near the whole population captive. And he killed off the old high-ranking monks and took the young ones captive. He didn't burn and plunder the whole city, but only the prince's residence along with Suzdal's churches and monasteries.

And now let us try to solve a superhistorical mystery. Why (as the document says) did the Tatars "set up their camps at the city of Vladimir, while they themselves went and took Suzdal"?

Any military historian — as, indeed, any modern army commander — will tell you that this manœuvre completely goes against standard military tactics.

To establish a camp under the walls of a major fortified city and then leave it and move one's troops to a smaller target — that is tantamount to suicide.

The distance between the cities of Vladimir and Suzdal at the time was equivalent to 35 kilometres. With the roads rendered impassable by the spring rains, it was a good day's journey on horseback.

The taking of Suzdal required a minimum of several more days, and then a day's journey back.

It wouldn't have taken any more than a day for the soldiers defending Vladimir to go out of their fortified city on a foray and rout the defenceless enemy camp. All they had to do was seize the spare horses, the spare quivers of arrows, the supplies, the wall-storming ladders and stone-throwing devices, and they would have shorn the enemy not only of the possibility of launching an attack on them, but of their battle-readiness in general.

But they never went out. Why not? Perhaps they didn't know that Batu Khan's troops had left the camp? But they knew. They could have easily seen that from their battlements; besides, their scouts would have reported it.

Possibly Batu Khan's forces were in such great numbers that more than enough guards had been left behind to repel an attack on the camp?

This is the way historians initially explained it. They said the Golden Horde's troops numbered almost a million. Then they changed their minds and reduced their estimate to 130,000, some even to as few as 30,000.

Naturally it is tempting to explain one's defeat by citing the enemy's significantly superior numbers. More objective scholars have begun to say that moving a million-strong army at that time was an absolute impossibility.

A million swordsmen together with equipment would mean three million horses. If a herd like that were kept in one place, even in the summertime, they would die of hunger, since the grass all around would be trampled down. And in the wintertime no amount of feed supplies would be enough.

So the figure was reduced to either 130,000 or 30,000. A humiliating figure indeed. With a scant hundred and thirty thousand men Batu Khan quietly went about conquering Russian principalities and whole countries too.

But even this figure is inflated. To subjugate the Russian princes of that time using the knowledge left by Genghis Khan to his descendants, there was simply no need for even a fifty-thousand-strong army. All that was required was knowledge of the way of life of the Russian people, Russian families, and the proper strategy based on such knowledge.

After setting up camp at the city of Vladimir, Batu Khan did not go with a whole army to Suzdal, but sent a small detachment to take it. This is why the people of Vladimir did not leave their fortified city to rout the camp and destroy the enemy's military facilities.

Do you know how many days and nights it took for Batu Khan's small detachment to conquer one of Rus's spiritual capitals of the time, surrounded as it was by more than a half-dozen monastery fortresses — this legendary city of Suzdal?

No time at all. He simply arrived, entered the city and burnt the prince's residence. The prince, meanwhile, had fled together with his armed garrison. It was no effort to cut down every last one of the high-ranked clergy and take the young monks captive. And the Mongols later caught up with the prince and his garrison at the Sit' River and destroyed them too.[18]

How could that be? someone may wonder. Where were the brave Russian people, their indomitable and freedom-loving spirit?

I can tell you right off that there was nothing wrong with the Russian people and their spirit. Logic suggests that the people applauded Batu Khan's small detachment on its return journey from Suzdal. They served *kvas* and *braga*[19] to the warriors along the whole route back to their camp at Vladimir.

The reason is that the people of that time did not look upon Suzdal as *their* city. Rather, they viewed its royal inhabitants as traitors and its clergy as foreign aggressors and enslavers.

---

[18]This battle took place 4 March 1238. Prince Yuri Vsevolodovich was beaten and beheaded by the detachment commander Burundai, who later presented the prince's head to Batu Khan as a trophy.

[19]*kvas* — a Russian fermented drink made from rye bread or vegetables; *braga* — a mild Russian alcoholic beverage.

This led to the flare-up of a number of rebellions on the part of the people against unbearable oppression.

Documents at the Vladimir-Suzdal State Museum put it this way:

> By the end of the thirteenth century Suzdal had eight monasteries. Founded by the princes and representatives of the Christian religion, they played a major role in assimilating new territories and served as fortresses in the event of enemy aggression. ...

> In the late fifteenth and early sixteenth centuries the Church owned a third of the best lands in the country and was endeavouring to subjugate the power of the Grand Princes to itself. From the end of the fifteenth century on, the State made repeated attempts to limit the landholdings of monasteries and churches, along with attempts at secularisation (in other words, complete eradication). The question of land provoked two ideological tendencies within the Church: *Josephism*[20] and the *Non-Possessors Movement*.[21] The first defended the monasteries' property interests, while the second emphasised the idea of inner self-perfection and condemned the monasteries' acquisitive pursuits. The ideological leader of the Josephites

[20]*Josephism* (Russian: *Iosiflianstvo,* also known as the *Possessors Movement*) — a movement defending the ownership of land by the Russian Orthodox Church, led by Iosif (Joseph) Volotsky (or Volokamsky; secular name: *Ivan Sanin,* 1439–1515), later recognised as a saint. Not to be confused with the 20th-century use of the same term, designating a movement opposing the Russian Orthodox Church's kowtowing to communist authority following the 1917 revolution (in this case named after Metropolitan Iosif [Joseph] of Leningrad).

[21]*Non-Possessors Movement* (Russian: *nestiazhatel'stvo*) — an opposition movement to Josephism, rejecting church land-ownership, led by *Nil Sorsky* (secular name: Nikolai Fedorovich Maikov, 1433–1508) and a Greek immigrant, *Maxim Grek* (secular name: *Mikhail Trivolis,* 1475–1556).

was Father Joseph, abbot of the Volokolamsky Monastery, while the Non-Possessors Movement was championed by a monk of the Kirillo-Belozersky Monastery, Nil Sorsky. The monasteries and clergy of Suzdal, as major landholders, came down solidly on the side of the Josephites. However, in the sixteenth century the authority of the Grand Princes did not manage to carry out its intended secularisation of the Church's wealthy landholdings, which continued to increase, even though on a limited scale.

Quite a trick! A third of Russian lands ended up in the hands of the Constantinople-derived[22] clergy and its puppets. Monasteries were transformed into large-scale slave-owners. And it wasn't the monks who tilled the ground and raised cattle, but the peasant serfs.

The princes were already trying to reclaim part of the country they had lost. But that was by no means easy!

And just how was this 'enriching' the souls of the peasants, whose primordial family lands had now become monasterial property at one fell swoop? What was offered to people in exchange for their centuries-old traditions and rites, which were now labelled 'barbarian'? The same archival documents show what happened here:

Fees and penalties imposed on the peasant serfs of the Pokrovsky Nunnery in 1653

From each household — two altyns,[23] a chicken and lamb's wool from the first shearing.

---

[22] *Constantinople* (original name: *Byzantium,* now *Istanbul*) — the seat of the Greek Orthodox Church, from which the Russian Orthodox Church was derived.

[23] *altyn* — a mediæval coin worth three kopeks (derived from the Tatar word for 'gold'). A kopek is worth 1/100 of a rouble.

On the purchase of a:
Horse — 2 dengas.[24]
Cow — 1 denga.

On the sale of:
Grain, horses, cows, hay — 1 altyn for each rouble received.
Log houses — 1 denga per internal corner.

For settling disputes:
Regarding field-lands — 2 altyns, 2 dengas.
Regarding household lands — 4 altyns, 2 dengas.

Court fees:
For travel to the site of a dispute — 1 denga per verst.[25]
For travel in cases of acquittal — 2 dengas per verst.
From the guilty party — 1 altyn for each rouble assessed.
From the vindicated party — 7 altyns, 2 dengas.
For taking an oath — 4 altyns, 2 dengas.

Wedding fees:
From the groom — 3 altyns, 3 dengas.
From the bride for a table — 2 altyns, 2 dengas.
From a groom from outside the district — 2 grivnas.[26]

From holiday beer-making
for weddings or funerals — 1 bucket of beer.

---

[24]*denga* — a mediæval coin worth half a kopek. The plural of this word (*den'gi*) is the current Russian generic word for 'money'.

[25]*verst* (Russian: *versta*) — an old Russian measurement of length, approximately equivalent to 1 kilometre.

[26]*grivna* (also known as *grivennik*) — an old Russian coin worth ten kopeks.

Penalties:

For alcohol distillation for one's self without a permit, or for sale — 5 roubles, a beating with a cane, and arrest.

For consumption of wine except on holidays — 8 altyns, 2 dengas, and a beating with a cane.

And here is a description of the property of the highest-ranked church official:

List of people and property belonging to Metropolitan Illarion

16 elders, 6 overseers in charge of properties, 66 personal bodyguards, 23 servants, 25 singers, 2 sextons, 13 bell-ringers, 59 craftsmen and labourers. In total: 180 persons.

Weaponry numbering 93 pieces, silver dishes weighing 1 pood[27] 20 pounds, pewter dishes weighing more than 16 poods, 112 horses belonging to the Metropolitan's horse farm, 5 carriages, 8 sleighs and chariots, 147 books.

(From the inventory of the Metropolitan's household, 1701)

A most extraordinary document. It is free of any kind of historical inaccuracies. It simply provides an impartial inventory of the Metropolitan's household property. However, it also begs a great many questions.

What kind of properties did the Metropolitan have that required the services of six overseers? Why a whole twenty-three servants for one man? And were the ninety-three pieces of weaponry also intended for the conducting of church rites?

---

[27]*pood* (rhymes with 'food') — an old Russian unit of mass approximately equivalent to 16.4 kg. A pood was divided into 40 funt (pounds).

Note that none of this was the monastery's property — it was just the Metropolitan's personal effects. The monastery had its own.

Just who was such a large contingent of guards supposed to protect the Metropolitan from? He had more bodyguards than the first American presidents.

The large contingent of guards, like the high monastery walls, were designed to protect the Metropolitan from the Russian people, of course. The walls of the Suzdal monasteries had no strategic significance in terms of military policy.

But why then do almost all historical sources describe the high monastery walls with their embrasures as fortresses, designed to protect the people from the enemy? Why were not these so-called fortresses capable of holding out for at least a month?

Because they weren't at all designed for defence against any external aggressor, let alone a smart one.

For the soldiers under Genghis Khan's grandson, in any case, such fortifications were no more than a distraction. If the possessors of these mock fortresses had not acceded to the enemy's demand for immediate surrender, the Mongols would have thrown up an embankment a little higher than the walls and dragged their stone-throwing devices up onto it. There are many possible scenarios here. One of them involved putting a bag into the stone-launcher attached to a long rope, and launching the bag over the monastery wall. Before it hit the ground, the bag would become undone, showering the people hiding behind the wall with infected meat. After that, all they had to do was shoot the people as they attempted to escape through the main entrance gate.

The only thing that the high monastery walls served as a protection against was their own people, the peasant serfs — or, rather, the monastery slaves — who from time to time rebelled.

It was none other than the Constantinople clergy who applied their lofty 'spirituality' to the inculcation of serf law[28] in Rus'.

One document from the Suzdal Museum archives attests to the following:

> Church landholdings prevailed in Suzdal in the seventeenth century, as they had before. Monasteries and the Metropolitan's residence were major feudal landlords, with enormous financial resources at their command, not to mention the free labour of many thousands of peasants.
>
> Thus, the Spaso-Yevfimiev Monastery[29] placed fifth among all Russia's church-based feudal landlords. Its prosperity depended wholly upon land grants and contributions. In the second half of the seventeenth century the earlier established fiefdoms did not increase in size, as the inordinate expansion of monastery lands was held in check by the State. The peasants were subject to a double exploitation — first by the landowners (the corvée and tribute system) and secondly by the State (taxes payable in both money and kind).

---

[28] *serf law* (Russian: *krepostnoye pravo*) — a feudal system prevalent in Russia (as in other European countries), binding the peasants to the land, subjugating them to the will of the landowners, church and political authorities. In Russia it was introduced by the Law Code (*Sudebnik*) in 1497 and not officially abolished until 1861. Even after abolition, most peasants, being granted no land of their own, had no choice for survival except to continue in their servile relationship with the landowners. Slavery-like conditions persisted throughout the Soviet period: peasants could not leave their village without a special permission from the authorities, and were compelled to do unpaid labour.

[29] *Spaso-Yevfimiev Monastery* — one of Suzdal's principal monasteries, founded in 1352 by Boris Konstantinovich, Prince of Suzdal and Nizhegorod, as a fortress designed to protect the city from enemies both within and without.

Or take this quote from a similar document on the history of the Sviato-Pokrovsky Nunnery:[30]

> The full and free life enjoyed by the nuns was made pos-
> sible by the labours of peasant serfs and the enormous staff
> of servants; the landholdings of the Pokrovsky Nunnery
> grew, thanks to rich donations and grants on the part of
> Russia's most élite families, including princes and tsars.

So there we have it: more lands — more serfs and more wealth.

But let us return to the thirteenth century.

What, then, actually happened with the arrival of Batu Khan's detachment at Suzdal? And where do traditions and love enter the picture?

The population of Suzdal at that time was fewer than 4,000 inhabitants. It consisted mainly of the prince's armed garrison and servants, craftsmen and clergy with their host of unpaid servants, hiding from the people behind the monastery walls.

All around Suzdal and Vladimir lived tens of thousands of peasant families, who were the only ones capable of worthily resisting an aggressor. But they didn't do this, they didn't rise up in arms, they didn't go to the monastery walls to protect the clergy. To put it simply, they hated the clergy. Note that they didn't hate God, only their oppressors. The people loved and revered God.

---

[30] *Sviato-Pokrovsky* (lit. 'Holy Veil') *Nunnery* — situated close to the Spaso-Yefimiev Monastery, founded in 1364 by the then Prince of Suzdal, Andrei Konstantinovich (brother to Boris), in gratitude for protection from a violent storm. It received special attention from the Grand Princes of Moscow, including Vasily III and later Ivan the Terrible (the first to proclaim himself tsar).

It was for this reason that the people didn't rise to the defence of the city of Vladimir.

Batu Khan waited six days before storming Vladimir. He waited until the news spread that it wasn't the people he was taking captive, but their enslavers.

He waited and took the well-fortified city in a single day. It was to this end that he made the foray against Suzdal. The foray was of no military importance, but it served to deprive the authorities of support from the populace at large.

And then what did the Mongols do?

Realising that they could find no better overseers and tax collectors than the princes in collaboration with the clergy, they began to issue the princes licences to govern and the right to collect taxes from the Russian people, a portion of which was to be handed over to the Horde. Many monasteries were exempted from taxation.

All of this is confirmed by specific documents. Just so people don't go pointing the finger at me or the scientists or secular historians, let us turn directly to literature from the Church itself.

There is a fairly decent historical book published by the Sviato-Pokrovsky Nunnery — with the blessing of Evlogii,[31] Archbishop of Vladimir and Suzdal, which states:

Saint Fiodor, the first Bishop of Suzdal, was from a Greek family. He arrived in Rus' in 987[32] in the entourage accompanying Saint Michael from Constantinople.

---

[31] *Evlogii* (secular name: Yuri Vasilevich Smirnov, 1937–) — consecrated Archbishop of Vladimir and Suzdal in 1990. He is an author of two books: *Èto bylo chudo Bozhie* (This was God's miracle) and *Premirnoe sluzhenie* (A humble service).

[32] *987* — the year before the official 'Christianisation' of Rus' by Vladimir I of Kiev (988), through his baptism at the hands of Saint Michael of Kiev — see footnote 6 in Chapter 4: "Wedding rites" above.

Saint Michael baptised Grand Prince Vladimir at Korsun,[33] and subsequently became the first Metropolitan of Kiev.[34]

After the baptism of the Kievans in 988, the prince, who had been accorded apostolic status, travelled around the Russian cities together with his sons and Saint Michael, on a zealous proselytising campaign. Bishoprics were established in Chernigov, Belgorod, Pereyaslavl, Novgorod and Vladimir-Volynsk.[35]

As can be seen from these reports, as well as from other sources, foreign ideologists were descending upon Rus' en masse. Complete with hired bodyguards and the prince's own contingent, they began to travel around the Russian cities, breaking down foundations that had been in place for millennia, planting an ideology profitable to the Church and government of the day and establishing foreigners in charge of cities.

Many historical documents testify to how the people resisted, though it appears they were poorly organised, and they did not expect treason on the part of their own prince. It was this treason that was largely responsible for the massive foreign invasion that befell Rus'. The saddest part was that it was done in the name of God. What an incredible sacrilege!

What if Prince Vladimir and the bishops from Constantinople actually believed sincerely in Christ's commandments?

---

[33]*Korsun* (also known by its Greek name *Chersonesos*) — on the southern tip of the Crimæan Peninsula, in what is now Ukraine.

[34]St-Michael was appointed first Metropolitan of Kiev by Nicholas II Chrysoberges, who served as Patriarch of the Eastern Orthodox Church in Constantinople from 984 to 996.

[35]*Chernigov, Belgorod* etc. — names of major cities in Ukraine and Russia. *Pereyaslavl* is now known as *Riazan* (see footnote 6 in Book 5, Chapter 17: "Questions and answers").

But subsequent events show that their real masters were the exact opposite of God. They were the servants of this opposite, with the advanced ability to manipulate the people, to subjugate to themselves their spirit and their will. They suggested to Man: *you are God's slave,* actually meaning: *you are my slave.* And Man began to forget that God has not and cannot have slaves. Man is the son of God, His beloved son.

All the quotations reproduced in this book are taken from historical documents. I gained access to them not by going to some super-secret archives, but simply by paying 15 roubles[36] to get into the State Museum and 30 roubles for the right to take pictures. I photographed the displays set up for general viewing. One of them was entitled: *Monasteries as ecclesiastical feudal landlords.*

And that is by no means the only official State source. There are many of them.

One that exerts an immeasurably greater influence, for example, especially on the young, is a Grade 10 high-school textbook published by Prosveshchenie[37] in 2003 and recommended by the Ministry of Education of the Russian Federation. This is a high-quality publication under the editorship of A.N. Sakharov[38] and V.I. Buganov.[39] On page 63 it says:

---

[36] *15 roubles* — equivalent to approximately US$0.50 at the time.

[37] *Prosveshchenie* (lit. 'Enlightenment' or 'Education') — a general educational publishing house founded in 1931 (named *Uchpedgiz* up until 1964) as a state-controlled enterprise for the publication and distribution of textbooks and educational literature. The textbook in question is entitled: *Istoria Rossii s drevneishikh vremen do kontsa XVII v.* (History of Russia from the earliest times up to the end of the 17th century).

[38] *Andrei Nikolaevich Sakharov* (1930–) — historian, author of books on the politics, ideology and culture of Ancient Rus'. Not to be confused with the nuclear physicist and political activist Andrei Dmitrievich Sakharov (1921–1989).

Along with this the Church persecuted the old folk pagan culture and came out against the Roman model of Christianity, calling it 'Latinism' and apostasy. This damaged Rus's relations with countries confessing the Catholic faith, and contributed to Rus's isolation from Western European culture. Church facilities began to introduce slave labour. Some clerics and monasteries engaged in usury and victimised people. There were cases where prominent politicians active in the Church took part in political machinations. Thus there frequently arose a discrepancy between the words of the Church and its deeds, and this provoked a feeling of discontent among the people.

The textbook also mentions that Prince Vladimir, who baptised Rus' in 987, "...was the son of Sviatoslav[40] by a slave of his mother's named Malusha. Consequently he was accorded a secondary ranking among the Prince's sons".
It further states:

Vladimir spent more than two years in foreign parts, and when he was approaching Novgorod, he had with him a strong Varangian[41] contingent. He quickly took control of

[39] *Viktor Ivanovich Buganov* (1928–1996) — historian, author of books on the sociopolitical history of Russia from the 11th to 18th centuries. He has also published a number of chronicle manuscripts.

[40] *Sviatoslav* (?–972) — Grand Prince of Kiev, who brought many lands — as far away as the Oka River (near present-day Moscow), the Balkans and the Caucasus — under the control of Rus'. He also established alliances with the Hungarians and the Bulgars.

[41] *Varangians* (Russian: *Varyagi,* equivalent to *Vikings*) — Scandinavian (mainly Swedish) explorers and traders who used the Dnieper River through Russia and Ukraine as a conduit to the Mediterranean and Black Sea merchants. According to the Chronicles, they had significant interaction (and intermarriage) with the Slavs and took an active part in the political life of Ancient Rus'.

Novgorod and began preparing for his trek south. Along the way Vladimir conquered Polotsk, where he killed the reigning Varangian prince Rogvolod and his sons, raping Rogvolod's daughter Rogneda and forcibly taking her to wife.[42]

The textbook goes on to describe how the Kievan prince Yaropolk, Vladimir's brother, came to negotiate with him. "No sooner had he entered the hall than Vladimir's body-guards ran their swords through him."

We also read an account of the baptism and the imposition of a sacramental obligation to pay the Church 10% of the tribute collected from the people. It should be remembered that at that time the Church was in subjugation to the Patriarchate of Constantinople (Russia still did not have its own patriarch), which means that 10% of the tribute money collected from the Russian people was at the disposal of Constantinople.

Might it not be in historical facts like these that we uncover an answer to the question as to why the people didn't rise to the Church's defence when Peter the Great closed a third of all Russian monasteries and melted down church bells to produce cannon, or when Catherine the Great went about 'secularising' (i.e., confiscating) monastery landholdings, which meant that formerly wealthy monks were obliged

---

[42]*Rogvolod* (also spelt: *Rogvold, Rogvald, Rognvald, Ragnvald,* 936–982 or 920–978, depending on source) — Scandinavian-born Prince of Polotsk (on *Polotsk* — see footnote 7 in Chapter 4: "Wedding rites" above). *Rogneda* (also spelt: *Ragnhild,* 962–1002) — reportedly a descendant of the Ynglings royal family of Norway. She bore Vladimir four sons (including Sviatoslav the Wise) and two daughters. It is also reported that after being divorced by Vladimir she entered a convent and took the name *Anastasia*. Her story was the basis for composer Alexander Nikolaevich Serov's (1820–1871) opera *Rogneda,* which had its première in 1865.

to beg for food and live at the mercy of the tsar. Or, when the Bolsheviks started killing clerics and blowing up churches, why some of the people themselves participated in the plunder of church property.

My remarks on the subject of the Church are based on historical facts and documents. I have resolved to call upon sensibly-minded members of the Church hierarchy and its wise elders who I am sure are out there, to transform the modern Church into a highly spiritual institution, one capable of helping society escape from its economic and spiritual crisis.

Love and the State's military preparedness

But what link can there possibly be, readers might wonder, between the conquest of Russia and *love*? The connection is quite direct. After seizing Russian lands, enslaving the Russian peasants, prohibiting rites capable of leading to love, the Constantinople assault force thereby began to hinder the formation of strong loving families and especially family domains. This meant, in effect, the immediate imposition of serf law.

Love among slaves, as a rule, is a most unhappy love.

In order for the feeling of love ignited in young people to be preserved, one's own Space is required. If it is not there, love, as a rule, vanishes. And what Space could be possessed by slaves? None at all.

Let's think: why, over the many millennia before the princes came to Rus', was our territory never conquered? There was the Egyptian army, after all, and the Roman legions, but all these hosts with all their well-trained and well-equipped soldiers did not succeed in conquering our lands.

To answer this question, let us suppose that Genghis Khan's troops had launched an invasion of pre-Christian Rus'.

At that time, the territory of our present-day country was inhabited almost exclusively by people living in family communities. At the approach of any army, no matter what its size, the members of the community would hide part of their food supplies, take the remainder with them — along with their household livestock — and head off into the forest. Their horses and cows were loaded up with family belongings.

An invading army could move into a territory only so far as the provisions they carried with them allowed. But this was already an army on its last legs. The return journey would be impossible.

They couldn't go hunting in the forest, as that had to be done in small groups (any larger groupings would scare away the game), but once they penetrated the forest, small groups would quickly fall into traps and perish.

They ate, for the most part, the meat of their own emaciated horses, whose numbers kept rapidly decreasing, so that any kind of movement became exceedingly difficult.

Our ancestors would set up a whole bunch of clever traps all along the route of the foe's retreat, both in the forests and on the rivers. For example, they would sink a huge tree with prickly branches and stretch a cable tied to the tree across the water and fasten its other end on the shore. Whenever a boat approached the spot, the tree would float to the surface and catch the side of the boat in its branches, and then sink again, overturning the boat in the process. In the meantime the retreating soldiers would be met with a hail of arrows and harpoons launched from the shore.

But when the retreating soldiers stepped out on the bank, after gathering together the rest of the troops that had been spread out along the flotilla, there was nobody to be seen. The people annihilated any enemy that invaded their Motherland. After all, they had something worth protecting. This was no abstract Motherland defined only by a beautiful word with not even a clump of native soil to back it up. They had their own family land, the same land that their ancestors had called home, and now it was where they lived along with their families, children, grandchildren and great-grandchildren.

And there was love in their families. And they protected their dear mothers, fathers and children. They protected their love! And that was why they could not be conquered.

Chapter Seven

Russia erased

Anastasia's grandfather and I rode along in silence. As we approached Suzdal and could see its buildings in the distance, I said to him:

"Look, there's Suzdal! It's a city around a thousand years old. Part of the Vladimir-Suzdal Principality. In fact it was one of the religious capitals of that period."

"Why are you going there, Vladimir?"

"I want to pay another visit to the museum, and take a look at the ancient sites, so's I can get a picture of how people lived over the past millennium."

"Try to get a picture *before* going into the city. Everything that lies around it is worth immeasurably greater attention than the city itself."

"All around are just fields," I protested, "with the occasional dilapidated village here and there. No information to help with the picture."

"Vladimir, stop the car. We shouldn't be talking while driving."

"Don't be afraid, I'm a good driver."

"I'm not afraid. I know, and so I'd better be quiet."

I pulled over to the side of the road and stopped the car. After a few moments I realised that I couldn't really drive and have this conversation at the same time. The difficulty was that, just like Anastasia, her grandfather sometimes spoke with certain special intonations, so powerful that the listener could perceive visible images, almost like holograms in space. This kind of speech allowed the possibility of showing scenes of the past or future, or even on another planet, as Anastasia once did.[1]

It's hard to tell just what is behind this phenomenon. Possibly hypnosis, possibly some kind of mysterious abilities enjoyed by people of the priestly class. Or maybe it was something possessed by everybody living on the Earth back in ancient times. A talented actor on stage can also create all sorts of pictures and images for an audience with the help of intonations and his own emotions — albeit not as vivid and detailed as those of Anastasia's. Still, it is actors above all others who confirm, through their mastery, the existence of such possibilities in Man.

It turns out that people of long ago didn't need television, with its huge network of personnel and technology, including satellites even. It turns out that in losing his natural, God-given abilities, Man replaces them with awkward artificial substitutes which are far less perfect. And he even boasts about it, calling his inventions a significant achievement.

The saddest part is that mankind today is losing its capacity for logical thinking. This is more than just a sad state of affairs. It is a most frightful epidemic, capable of transforming modern humanity into a bunch of mad rodents, devouring one another and destroying their own living environment. Suicide-rodents.

What Anastasia's grandfather was to tell me in the field needs to be understood. It gives rise to the following conclusion: in losing the ability to think logically, the people of the Earth no longer are able to see and understand the unenviable situation they are being pushed into. Judge for yourselves.

I had stopped the jeep at the side of the road. The grey-haired oldster got out and headed into a field. I followed along behind. Before long he stopped and bowed low to the ground, saying:

[1]See Book 4, Chapter 22: "Other worlds".

"Health to your thoughts and aspirations, dear people!"

He uttered this greeting most sincerely and with such a tone that it seemed as though there really were people standing there in front of him. Then something happened that I can't put a name to, at least not for now.

At first there was some sort of stirring in the air, and a barely noticeable mist arose from the earth. It seemed to be congealing, and soon afterward I could clearly see the outlines of some kind of human figure becoming increasingly distinct. And, finally, there standing before us was an elderly man with a powerful physique. A headband encircled his light-brown hair. He had a calm expression on his face, with just a trace of despondency. Behind him, in the distance, I could see gardens, copses and beautiful wooden mansions. It looked as though the barren fields of a moment ago were now populated with a whole lot of families.

The man standing before us was speaking in inaudible tones to the Siberian elder. The vision lasted for several minutes. Then it slowly began to dissipate, as though being erased by an invisible hand. What was being erased was the genuine Rus', not a Rus' someone had simply thought up. The vision disappeared altogether when Anastasia's grandfather turned in the direction of Suzdal. He stood there silently staring toward the city, then turned to me and asked:

"What, do you think, Vladimir, was the original purpose of the city we see in the distance?"

"What's thinking got to do with it? Everybody knows this from their history: Suzdal was where the clergy was cloistered. The first Christian bishops lived here. The monasteries and the kremlin[2] where the élite lived are still preserved today. That's a historical fact."

---

[2]*kremlin* — the Russian word describing a fortress in the middle of a city, the most famous example being the Kremlin in Moscow.

"Yes, you're right, historical. But all Russia's ancient cities have two histories. The original history is more significant."

"I guess we'll never be able to rediscover the original history."

"We *shall* know, Vladimir. You will figure it out through your own logic and you will even be able to see it. But start by determining the reason these cities sprang up, along with their original purpose."

"I would say their purpose lies in the fact that they made it easier to live together and defend themselves against enemy invasion. For example, apart from the clergy and the élite, Suzdal was home to many craftsmen. They produced equestrian harnesses, carts, sleighs, earthenware pots, ploughs and harrows. They would sell these items and live off the proceeds."

"Who did they sell them to?"

"To the peasants, of course," I responded.

"That's it," the old fellow confirmed. "They sold or bartered their handicrafts for produce. And the produce came into the city from all the many outlying domains."

"Yes, of course."

"But which d'you think came first, which was primary in this place — the domains or the city?"

"The domains, I would say. The builders and the craftsmen would want to eat every day. If they started to build things in the open fields, there would have been nowhere to get their food from."

"Correct. So we've come to the conclusion that a little more than a thousand years ago the fields around this city were the site of marvellous, rich domains. And the place where the city of Suzdal sits now was the site of their *kapishche*."[3]

"What is a *kapishche*?"

"It's a place where people gathered together from all around for fairs, to exchange goods and procure household

[3]*kapishche* — pronounced *KAH-peesh-cheh*.

effects. They shared experiences with each other. They put on massive celebrations with singing and dancing, and some of which were designed to help people find their soulmates.

"This was also the place the elders of the families gathered for a *vieche*[4] and adopted unwritten rules for living. They could censure a wrongdoer for his crime, although such instances were rare. Their censure was even a more fearful sentence than physical punishment."

"And who was in charge of this whole land?"

"A hired hand. I really can't think of an alternative term. A hired hand was the administrator in the kapishche. But he wasn't really *in charge*. Rather, he carried out the decisions taken by the elders.

"For example, when they desired to put in a new tethering-post or a new road or build a big barn, it transpired that people from each domain would be assigned to carry out that decision. Sometimes the hired hand would be required to find other hired workers like himself.

"It was also his job to keep the whole kapishche clean and neat. Let's say they had a fair, and after it was over, people dispersed to their homes. Then the tethering-posts might have had to be fixed and the horse-droppings cleaned up all over the place. This task would be carried out by the hired hand and his assistants. If he performed his work carelessly, the elders could sack him from his job. And then either the hired hand would go and look for work at another kapishche, or he would stay where he was, but be demoted to a hired hand's assistant. It was difficult for the elders to maintain hired help, as just about everyone wanted to live in their own domains. Thus it might happen that hired hands for kapishches could be acquired from foreign lands.

---

[4]*vieche* — a council in ancient Russia. See footnote 5 in Chapter 1: "Love — the essence of the Cosmos" above.

"The Vedruss social order of Rus' before the princes rose to power lasted for many thousands of years. It was superior to all the state social orders we know today, and it extended to all the continents of the Earth.

"When the Earth was overcome by corruption, Egypt and Rome fell into slavery, but the Vedruss social order in Rus' still lasted five-and-a-half thousand years."

"But why did the Vedruss social order give way to corruption, too?"

"Which are you most interested in — Rome, Ancient Egypt or Rus'? Pretty much the same thing happened in all three."

"If they're pretty much the same, then let's go for Rus'. I already know that it was subject to external invaders, resulting in the destruction of the traditions and culture of the great Vedruss civilisation."

"There were invasions, but there's much more to it than that. The Vedruss social order underwent its first changes in other lands, back when there was no foe to invade. There were no armies. There were no wars or military campaigns, because there was nothing that could lead to them. The whole Earth at the time was made up of marvellous domains. People's culture and concepts were truly outstanding. Everybody knew that to take vegetables or fruit out of someone else's orchard by force or stealth was not only improper — it was useless and dangerous to one's self.

"Only through produce that was given freely and with desire could benefit be acquired.

"Neither was it considered proper to take household animals from someone else's domain by deceit or by force. A cow would not have let a stranger come close. And somebody else's dog might have shown itself to be not a friend, but a foe. And a horse might have taken the occasion to throw a rider if it were not its own.

"With concepts like these, who would dare invade? Such concepts made invasions absurd. Corruption, in the main, came from ignorance, or rather from treason or betrayal, even in little things, of the culture of one's forebears, their way of life. The family chain leads us to God. To betray one's forebears' meaning of life is tantamount to killing God within one's self.

"Yes, in Rus', of course, the people were deceived, through the priests' well-honed manipulative techniques — techniques which are still active in our own time. Back then the elders overlooked this subtle play, and their mistake is still being paid for by subsequent generations even today."

CHAPTER EIGHT

The elders' mistake

From a hired hand to a prince

At the beginning of the present era many countries were already ruled by emperors, pharaohs or tsars. The form of government under which a large state is controlled by one Man is unnatural. It has never brought and will never bring a good, happy life to a single nation on the face of the Earth. This form of government benefits the priests, who manipulate countries through their rulers. It is difficult, after all, to negotiate with all the people at once, a lot easier to deal with just a single individual.[1]

Only in Rus' they did not succeed in setting up a single ruler. Everyone there was guided by the tribal elders' council. These councils were not something that could be corrupted or forced, under threat, into a decision that would lead to the oppression of the people. Who would make such an obscene decision for one's children?

Several times, through various subterfuges in different places, the priests' assistants attempted to set up a princely authority, a single ruler over the people. In this particular area, for example, events unfolded as follows.

One day a stranger from afar arrived at the Vedruss kapish-che situated where Suzdal is now. Like the wise-men, itinerant minstrels, and craftsmen, he was offered food and lodging.

---

[1]The first section of this chapter, told to the author by Anastasia's grandfather, is presented without identifying quotation-marks.

The stranger stayed two weeks, but did not engage in any useful activity. The hired hand in charge questioned him:

"What useful contribution, stranger, can you make to our kapishche?"

And the stranger replied:

"None at all, but to you personally I can render an invaluable service. I have heard rumours that the elders are not happy with you. In a year, maybe even half a year, you will be let go. If you take *my* advice, on the other hand, the elders will be crawling on their knees before you. You can have your pick of girls from any domain to wife, whereas right now there's not a single one that would live with you. I can make it so that it will be your decisions, and not those of the tribal elders, that will be carried out."

The hired hand in charge of the kapishche (and part-time janitor) agreed. He listened to the stranger, an agent of the priests. And the stranger proposed:

"When people gather for a fair at the kapishche from all around and stay until the following morning, during the night you will cut your face with a knife, and leave the kapishche along with your trustworthy assistants, so that you can return in the evening with broken-winded horses. During the night I and my assistants (they are already here in the guise of artists and craftsmen), will take the horses away from their tethering-posts, and you will bring them back in the evening, saying you recaptured them from the miscreants.

"In your wounded state you will ask the elders for an armed garrison for their own protection. They will agree. You will take my companions into your garrison: they will all meekly obey your command."

The hired hand agreed to the criminal act. He did everything according to the stranger's proposal.

When the 'wounded' man returned toward evening with the herd of stolen horses, he learnt that not only had the stranger's henchmen stolen the horses — they had also killed three people, and burnt the smithy and a barn. The 'wounded' hired hand appeared before the elders. He told how he and his assistants had given chase to the miscreants, but they were outnumbered, and his assistants were beaten back. And then he began asking the elders for the resources to maintain a strong armed garrison. He asked them to grant him the authority to take decisions on his own in the interests of general security.

The elders were taken aback at the hideous crime and agreed to maintain the garrison, only they were unwilling to pull their own sons away from the domains. So it was decided to bring in strangers to form a garrison, and allot them a tribute from each domain. Other kapishches followed their lead and also began to create their own armed garrisons.

Indeed, since they now had power, the hired hands began transforming themselves into princes. They started waging war against each other, justifying this to the elders as a necessary preventative first strike.

The princes supposed they had achieved considerable authority. In fact, for centuries now, they have been strictly following the priests' advice, often without realising it. Such a system of authority came together all by itself. The hired hand remained a hired hand — he merely exchanged masters.[2] The new master was exceptionally cruel to his hired hands.

For thousands of years the priests' hired hands kept killing each other, conspiring and hatching their schemes, aspiring more and more lustily for power.

---

[2] In Russian, the word for 'prince', *kniaz'* (formerly spelt *koniaz'*), is derived from *kon'* (horse) and originally meant 'a herder in charge of horses'. This original meaning of *koniaz'* survived in parts of Russia until the 19th century. Also, a Russian proverb says: *iz griazi v kniazi* ('princes [are derived] from dirt') — preserving the memory of the fact that it was the most marginal members of the society that became the princes.

You surely know yourself from history how many deaths the path to princely power is strewn with. They even resorted to slaying their fathers and brethren. Pretty much the same thing came about in various countries, and little has changed, even today.

Thus the time of the princes had its start in Russia, too, just as it had in other lands long before. You know the rest of the story, I dare say. And the armed garrisons are still around today, still serving somebody's interests.

The armaments and weaponry may have changed, but the essence is still the same. And the crimes have not abated — they keep multiplying, and keep getting more and more sophisticated.

The elders made a mistake. It is a mistake which, if you form your own political party, you will not want to make again.

A mistake not to be repeated

"What, precisely, was the elders' mistake?" I asked. "Was it in forming the garrisons with foreign mercenaries? But the way things have turned out now, a state can no longer survive without a militia or an army."

"The garrisons here, Vladimir, are not the underlying cause. It goes a lot deeper, into the psychological.

"I don't know how to put it more clearly. It has to do with forgetting the precepts of our ancestors — God's precepts. Think about it: God gave each and everyone equal authority. Consequently, the only social structure that can claim

perfection is one where there is no centralised authority —
where every individual is endowed with equal power.

"When you give somebody your vote, you are not bestow-
ing authority on anyone. By voting for someone, you are simply placing them in subjection to the existing system, and vol-
untarily relinquishing the authority God has given you. And
over the centuries most people's minds have been perverted:
it is the job of the ruler and the government to deal with all important questions for us, they think. These people's thoughts
don't even touch the question of the order of life."

"So, that means that there's no longer any point in voting
at all? We'll never establish a party that way. By law, we have
to vote."

"Well, if you have to, then vote to make sure no one individual is able to control people's lives."

"If you're talking about the *vieche*³ gatherings they had in
Vedic Rus'," I said, "that's totally impossible today. People
can't keep constantly coming together from different parts of
the country. Besides, there's no way a party like that can ever
get registered."

"Why do they need to come together? Just turn all the modern inventions at your disposal to a good purpose. Use any
kind of communications link — the computer, for example.
As for registration, isn't that a bit ridiculous for a party of the
majority of the people? You ought to be registrars yourselves.

"Anyway, securing some kind of registration isn't the main
point at issue. The main thing is not to allow the setting up of
any centralised authority. Anybody working in the central appa-
ratus, if it is absolutely necessary according to your law, should
be strictly hired staff — with no access to financial control.
Besides, money should never be concentrated in one place."

³*vieche* — see footnote 5 in Chapter 1: "Love — the essence of the Cosmos"
above.

"But the law requires all parties to elect a central committee," I observed.

"So, elect all party members to it, or at least every tenth person in the party."

"There's something else to think about here. I got really angry at first when you said the party's main goal was the restoration of love to families. I thought you were making fun of me, that you were trying to make me into a laughingstock."

"I remember."

"But now, I've given quite a bit of thought to this question and have come to the conclusion that it really is not just *one* of the main goals, but *the* main goal. And that the question of finding one's soulmate requires specific conditions to be set up, special events to be organised. The rites of Ancient Rus' should be made public, and we need to get not only science but also culture and ideological propaganda involved in working out these questions. They need to be resolved on the state level. The degree of civilisation of any given state needs to be judged on the basis of the number of happy, loving families living therein."

"Congratulations!"

"On what?"

"On understanding that."

"Congratulations are still premature. I can't for the life of me think of a way to formulate this goal without people laughing at its constitution, or at me, or at our future party."

"So, let them laugh."

"What d'you mean, *let them*? If people start laughing, then I'll be the only member of a party with a constitution like that. It will end up being an unregistered party with a laughable constitution, supported by a single individual, and an ordinary member of the party at that."

"Why just a single individual? There'll be at least two. I shall be supporting it as well. And the two of us will raise some money and hire ourselves an executive secretary."

"You serious? What, you're going to join the party, too?"

"No. I shan't be joining it. Anyway, as you point out, I can't be registered under your law. But I'll be supporting the Motherland Party with my whole heart from right there in the taiga.

"And if you're concerned about there just being the two of us, remember that all great causes have always begun not with a mass of people, but with just a single individual. Years down the road, humanity will indeed laugh, but not at *you*. They'll be laughing at themselves, and they'll be happy."

"Okay, I'll try. I'll give some more thought to drafting the constitution. And I'll ask my readers to think about it, too."

"If I were you, Vladimir, I'd ask Anastasia to tell more about the wedding rite. In the Vedruss culture, after all, it began right at birth."

"How on earth could a wedding rite begin at a Man's birth?"

"Vedruss people considered the primary birth to be not the appearance of the body, but the illumination of love. Nobody in today's world can illustrate this the way Anastasia can. *Ask her to re-create a picture of life in a Vedruss family.*"

I shan't say where or how this meeting with Anastasia took place. I'll start right away to set forth her description of one Vedruss family's attitude toward love.

Whoever manages to make sense of it and feel the significance contained in the culture of their love, may also be able, perhaps, to figure out the great wisdom and cosmic dimension of the Vedruss rites.

CHAPTER NINE

The Creator's greatest gift

Childhood love

It was with childlike joy and inspiration that Anastasia began telling me about the Vedruss rite associated with the energy of Love:[1]

The activities of the Vedruss people amounted to a continuous learning cycle. It was a great and joyous school of conscious being.

All Vedruss celebrations could be described as tests of mind and skill. They all involved, one might say, reminders to the adults, as well as wise lessons to the young. But even during the days of intense harvest gathering, the Vedruss people worked with a joyous heart. Their work was imbued with meaning that went beyond material creations.

Look, Vladimir — see, it is haycutting time. A magnificent, clear day. The whole settlement, from the littlest ones to the greatest, is heading out to the meadows with the first rays of the Sun. See, there go two drays carrying a whole family. Only the elder family members have stayed behind to keep the household animals company.

But the guys — the young lads — are riding horseback, with only collar-bands on the steeds and long lengths of rope

---

[1]Anastasia's story of the Vedruss family over this and the following three chapters is presented without identifying quotation marks.

in their hands. On these horses they will use these long ropes
to cope with the task of dragging the stooks of hay over to the
main stacks.

The stately *muzhiks*[2] in the carts hold their scythes poised,
blades up, while their wives and older children sit beside them
with their rakes, ready to start raking up the hay the men will
be cutting.

Also riding on the drays are some very small children.
What for? Just for the fun of it, out of curiosity, to mingle,
frolic and play, and to observe the grown-ups on this day.

The people are by no means dressed in rags. See their clean
white shirts, and the women wearing flowers entwined in
their braids, and embroidered dresses. Why are they dressed
up in their best, as if going to a celebration?

The answer, Vladimir, is that they are under no constraint
to actually cut hay. They all have their own piles of hay back
in their respective domains. Though naturally it does not
hurt to have some community stacks in reserve.

The main thing, however — the tacit purpose behind all
the general activity — is to show themselves at work in their
neighbours' eyes. To steal furtive glances at each other, and
give a chance to the young guys and girls to get to know each
other in a common activity. That is why the young people,
even from outlying communities, are so happy to turn out for
the haymaking.

Now it has begun — look!

The scythemen are moving forward steadily, all in a row.
Not one of them must fall behind. Their wives are raking up
yesterday's cuttings to be dried, singing as they work. The

----

[2]*muzhiks* (English plural of *muzhik*, stress on last syllable) — the Russian
term for a hardy male peasant, or rural dweller. In modern Russian the
word is also used in a broader colloquial sense, roughly equivalent to 'guy' in
American English usage.

young people gather the dried hay into stooks. Those slightly older will build the haystack.

See those two guys standing on top of the haystack? One of them is eighteen, the other, twenty. They are piling the hay on the stack which those six smiling girls are handing up to them.

The guys have taken off their shirts. Perspiration is streaming down their tanned skin. But they are trying to keep up with the merry girls below.

There are two guys up top, and there ought to be four girls throwing up the hay from below, but it turns out there are six of them down there, laughing and joking, trying to drown the lads in hay.

The guys' father comes over to the haystack to get a drink of water. He has quickly sized up the whole situation. His two sons are trying to keep up with the six girls. They simply cannot afford to get done in. Besides, in the group of nimble, laughing girls below there may be two brides for his sons. After taking a drink the father calls up to his boys:

"Hey, there, boys! I don't feel like cutting any more for now. How about I climb up there and help you? Seeing as how there are six down below instead of four."

"Why, Father?" answered the elder son, not slacking off for a moment. "There are two of us up here stacking hay, my brother and I, and we haven't even got warmed up yet!"

"It's as though I'm still asleep!" added the younger, as he somehow inconspicuously wiped the perspiration from his brow.

Down below the light-headed girls took notice of his movements. One of them called out over the general laughter:

"Watch out, don't let the sleepyhead get wet!"

The father broke into a smile of contentment, before rejoining the row of scythemen.

The train of four steeds, which the young men were leading by the bridle, was on its way to the haystack from the farthest meadow. The last horse was led by the youngest, whose name was Radomir.[3] He had turned eight just before the start of the summer, and was now into his ninth year. But the boy Radomir was very well developed for his age.

But it was not only his physical height that elevated him above his peers. He had a quicker grasp of knowledge than did the others, and he excelled in festive games. And here at the haymaking he swelled with pride at having been given work usually assigned to kids just a bit older. He was in no way going to lag behind his elders.

He himself was trying to bind up the stooks as quickly as possible, and the horse obeyed him. Even though he brought up the end of the 'train', he was still not lagging behind.

Just a little distance away, a chorus of younger children could be heard in play, over by the edge of the forest. As soon as they took notice of the train of horses dragging the stooks, they rushed over to catch a ride on them.

The kids rushed headlong to their goal, only one little girl, barely four years old, lagged behind. The others had already reached the stooks when she took a mind to try a shortcut and anxiously started running across a swampy stretch of ground. This small swamp had almost dried up, but one could still find patches of elevated ground dotted around. The dear girl jumped from hillock to hillock, very close to the horses dragging the stooks. All at once, however, trying to jump to the next patch of ground, the girl slipped and took quite a fall, scratching her knee badly on a stick and getting her dress and her face all muddied in the process. She picked herself up,

---

[3]*Radomir* (pron. *ra-da-MEER*) — a name first encountered in the section entitled "A union of two — a wedding" in Book 6, Chapter 5: "The history of mankind, as told by Anastasia". See esp. footnote 2 in that chapter. The name *Liubomila* (with its endearing variants *Liubomilka, Liubomilochka* — pron. *liu-ba-MEE-la, liu-ba-MEEL-ka, liu-ba-MEE-lach-ka,* resp.) is encountered in the same chapter (footnote 4).

but fell back at once and started screaming at the top of her lungs, smarting with annoyance at her plight, just as the last of the stooks came by and began to recede into the distance.

The stately youth Radomir heard the little girl's cries. He brought his steed to a halt, and followed the sound of her cries to the swampy ground. Here he found a dear little girl with clothes and hands all muddied, sitting in the midst of a puddle, using her tiny fist to wipe away the tears, and bawling with all her might.

Radomir took hold of her under her arms, picked her up out of the puddle, set her down on a dry patch of ground safe from harm and asked:

"What're you bawling for, little one? Is it that bad?"

Still crying, she tried to explain through her tears:

"I was running, running — see — I was jumping from patch to patch, trying to catch up, only I took a bad fall. All the stooks had gone, and I was lagging behind. Now all the other kids are having fun riding on the stooks, and I ended up in this puddle."

"They haven't *all* gone," Radomir responded. "Look, I'm still here, and there's my stook. If you can stop your bawling, I'll give you a ride on it. Only you seem to have got so dirty all over. Now stop that screaming once and for all," he demanded. "It's making me deaf!"

Radomir took hold of the hem of the little girl's dress. Finding a clean patch of dress, he put it up to her nose and commanded:

"Come on, now, blow your nose!"

Completely taken aback by this move, the little girl let out a loud "Ow!" and covered the front of her exposed lower torso with her hands. Now she blew her nose hard — one! two! — and stopped crying. Radomir let down the hem of her dress, and stared with a critical eye at the filthy and dishevelled little girl standing before him.

"You'd better take your dress off altogether," he said.

"*Shan't!*" she declared firmly.

"Take it off, I shan't look. I'll rinse out your dirty dress in the lake. You can sit here in the tall grass while you wait. Here, you'd best take my shirt. It will go right down to your ankles — it'll be longer on you than your dress."

Radomir rinsed the little girl's dirty dress in the lake while she wrapped herself in his shirt and peeked at him through the tall grass.

As she sat there in the grass, the girl was struck by a piercing, frightening thought. She remembered once overhearing her grandfather telling her grandmother:

"A terribly scandalous act took place in the next settlement — some good-for-nothing lifted up the hem of a maiden's dress before marriage."

"If he lifted up her hem, it means he's crushed the poor dear's life," her grandmother had sighed.

The little girl decided that something must be crushed in her too, now that a strange lad had lifted up the hem of her dress. She examined her little arms and legs and, even though they seemed to be in working order, nothing crushed, her fear did not dissipate.

If grandfather and grandmother believed that lifting up a dress hem would crush something, then something of hers must be crushed, too.

The girl jumped up from the grass and called out to Radomir, who had been rinsing out her dress in the lake:

"You're a dirty good-for-nothing!"

Radomir straightened up, turned toward the girl standing in the grass wearing his shirt and asked:

"What're you carrying on about this time? I don't know what you want."

"I'm telling you, you're a dirty good-for-nothing. You dared lift up the hem of a maiden's dress before marriage. You've crushed everything of hers."

Radomir looked at the girl's mud-covered face for some time, then burst out laughing. After getting a hold of himself, he said:

"Well, you've heard the song but got it wrong! Sure, lifting up the hem of a maiden's skirt before marriage is a bad thing. But in my case, I didn't lift up the hem of a maiden's skirt."

"You did, you did! I remember, you lifted up the hem of my dress."

"*Your* dress, sure," Radomir agreed. "But then you're not a maiden, are you?"

"How come I'm not a maiden?" the girl asked in surprise.

"'Cause all maidens have protruding breasts, but you don't. Instead of breasts all you have are two little spots which are hardly noticeable. That means you're not a maiden."

"Then who am I?" the little girl asked distractedly.

"You're still a 'little one'. Now you just sit there in the grass and don't say a word. I haven't the time to talk with you."

Once again he stepped into the water, finished rinsing out the dress, then wrung the water out of it and laid it out neatly on the grass to dry. Then he called out to the girl:

"Come down to the water, little one. You need to get your face washed."

She came to him obediently, and stood quietly while he washed her face.

"Now let's go to the stook, and I'll give you a ride."

"Let me have my dress back first," the girl asked, almost in a whisper.

"It's still too wet. You can stay in my shirt for the time being. I'll bring your dress along with me. It will have dried out by the time we get to the haystack and you can change there."

"No! Give me back my dress!" the girl insisted. "Maybe it's wet, but I'm going to put it on anyway. It can dry on me."

"Have your own way, spruce yourself up," said Radomir, as he handed her the wet dress and headed over to his horse.

The little girl quickly put on her dress. She rushed to catch up to Radomir at the stook.

"Here I am," she said, panting away. "And here's your shirt back."

"Okay. You're my bad luck charm. All the other lads are heading back already, and here I'm stuck with you. Climb aboard!"

He helped the girl climb onto the stook. He took hold of the bridle and they started off in the direction of the haystack.

The little girl sat on the stook in her wet dress, jubilant as it whisked smoothly over the ground. She was riding the stook all alone, not in twos or threes like the other kids. She sat there all by herself. Her face was beaming with joy, as though she had suddenly been turned into a goddess. If only her girl-friends could see her now, not as part of a train, but all alone. He was carrying her all by herself.

She noticed the way Radomir led the horse by the bridle, and couldn't take her eyes off his back. Her little heart began to beat faster. She felt a sensation of warmth permeate her whole body. Naturally, she was still too young to realise what was going on: she was in love.

Oh for the love of childhood! It is the ultimate of puri-ty — the precious gift of God. Only why does it sometimes make an early start, and perturb a little one's heart? Why? What does it mean when it comes early like that? It turns out that there is truly great meaning in early love, something the Vedruss people well knew.

Upon arriving at the haystack, Radomir came back to the stook.

"Climb down, little one. Don't be afraid, I'll catch you."

Catching the little girl in his arms, he set her down on the ground and asked:

"Whose kid are you?"

"I'm from the next settlement. My name is Liubomila. My sister and I are visiting, helping our brother," she replied.

"Go on then, go to your sister," Radomir admonished, walking away. He did not turn back even once to look at the little girl.

She stood there, watching everything: how he untied the rope from the stook, climbed up onto a barrel from where he could leap onto his steed. Then he took off at a gallop to fetch a new hay stook.

Love as a fully fledged member of the family

Little Liubomilka returned home with her sister. It was already the family's supper-time. But Liubomilka didn't want to sit down to the table. Clinging to her grandmother's skirt, she begged:

"Can we go for a walk together in the garden, Grammykins? I want to tell you about a miracle — just you alone."

Upon overhearing this request, the father protested:

"It's not proper, daughter dear, to go off when the family's about to sit down to table, let alone take your grandmother with you..."

But when the father looked into his daughter's face, he broke into a smile. The Vedruss people knew the grace of childhood love. They knew how to treat love kindly, to embrace it as a heavenly gift to the family, to refrain from making fun of it and to respect its every trace.

They valued the grace of its great energy, and so the diverse energies of Love would come to them with great joy.

"You and your grandmother go for a walk in the garden and eat some berries," said the father, feigning an air of nonchalance.

Little Liubomilka sat her grandmother down in a far corner of the garden and right off began excitedly telling her story:

"Grammykins, I was playing with my friends there at the haymaking, and they ran off to have a ride on the stooks. I didn't feel like joining them. I was just minding my own business. All of a sudden this most kind and handsome young lad stops his horse and comes up to me. Yes, indeed, Grammykins, he comes just as close as you and I are right now. And he was so handsome and kind. Here he stands in front of me and says: 'Little girl, I invite you...' No, he didn't say that. He put it another way. He said: 'Little girl, not only do I invite you, I *beg* you to take a little ride on my stook.' And I had a ride. There. You see, Grammykins? Has something happened with him?"

"Something's happened with you, granddaughter dear. And what might his name be?"

"I don't know. He didn't say."

"First of all, my little Liubomilochka, tell me the whole story, and try to remember the way it *really* happened."

"The way it really..." Liubomilka hung her head. "The way it really happened? I took a fall into a puddle, he came along and washed out my dress, then he gave me a ride on his stook, but I guess he never told me his name. He called me 'Little one', and when he left, he never once looked in my direction."

Liubomilka finished her story and began crying. She continued through her tears:

"I stayed standing there, and watched him go away. Only he never looked at me even once, and what his name was he didn't say."

The grandmother gave her granddaughter a big hug, stroking her dark blonde hair, as though stroking the energy of Love within her. And she whispered, as though saying a prayer:

"O great energy from God! Turn and help my granddaughter with your grace. Do not burn her still immature heart. Give her inspiration to take part in co-creation!"

Aloud she said to Liubomilka:

"Granddaughter dear, would you like this very good lad to always have eyes for you alone?"

"Yes, I would, Grammykins. I would!"

"Then you should not let him come by or see you for three years."

"But why?"

"When he spied you, you were all dirtied by the mud. He saw you as a crying, helpless little girl. That is the impression he still has of you. In three years' time, if you yourself make the effort, you will be older, smarter and more beautiful."

"I shall try. I shall try the very best I can. Only tell me, Grammykins, how should I try — what plan should I follow?"

"I shall share all my secrets with you, granddaughter dear. If you earnestly try to follow them, you will be more beautiful than all the flowers on the Earth, and people will rejoice at your presence. You will not need to wait to be chosen, you yourself will have your choice of lovers."

"Tell me, Grammykins, and I shall do everything you say. Only tell me faster!" Little Liubomilka was trying to hurry her grandmother up, tugging impatiently at the hem of her dress.

And, slowly and solemnly uttering the words, the grandmother told Liubomilka:

"You need to get up earlier in the morning. You spend your mornings just lazing around. You should get out of bed, run to the stream and wash yourself with pure spring water. When you get home, have a little porridge to eat. But you always demand sweet berries instead."

"But Grammykins, why should I try doing this all at home if he's not there to see me?" Liubomilka asked in surprise. "He won't see how I bathe in the stream and eat my porridge each morning."

"That, of course, is something he won't see. But your efforts will be reflected in your outward beauty. And the energy will be made apparent within."

Liubomilka tried to follow her grandmother's advice. She did not always succeed, especially that first year. But on those mornings her grandmother would come to her, sit down on her bed and say:

"If you don't rise with the Sun and run down to the stream, you will not become more beautiful this day."

And Liubomilka began rising early. By the second year she had become accustomed to the new regimen, and easily went through the routine of washing in the morning and cheerfully eating her porridge at breakfast.

Now the three-year waiting period recommended by her grandmother was almost at an end — only one month remained. People were gathering at the kapishche[4] from all around for this season's fair. Liubomila and her elder sister Yekaterina watched as carriages regularly passed by their domain on the way to the fair. And all at once they noticed one carriage pull off the road and approach their gate, where the sisters were standing. And lo and behold, there in the carriage...

Liubomilka recognised him right off. There sitting with the other passengers and holding the reins was none other than her beloved Radomir, looking just a little older.

[4]*kapishche* — see footnote 3 in Chapter 7: "Russia erased" above.

The little girl's heart began trembling when the carriage came up to their gate and stopped. An older gentleman among the passengers, probably the father, said:

"Cordial greetings, my maidens. Please convey my respects to your father and mother, and all your elders. We would like a drink of your *kvass*. We forgot to bring our own along on the journey."

Liubomilka rushed into the house, calling out:

"They send all of you greetings. Where's the pitcher? Our pitcher with the kvass, where is it? Oh, yes, it's in the pantry, keeping cool." And off to the pantry she dashed, overturning a pail of water standing by the door in the process. Turning around, she rattled off to her grandfather and grandmother:

"Not to worry! I'll mop it up when I come back."

Grabbing hold of the pitcher, she ran out to the gate, where she stopped to catch her breath. Restraining her excitement, she opened the gate, walked out with stately stride and handed the pitcher of kvass to the gentleman.

While the father of the family was drinking the kvass, Liubomilka kept her eyes fixed on Radomir. But *he* had eyes for Yekaterina.

When his turn came to be handed the pitcher, he drank up the remaining kvass, then jumped down from the carriage and held out the pitcher to Yekaterina, saying:

"Thank you. This kvass was prepared by kind hands."

Liubomilka watched as the carriage drove off, then, running to the deep far corner of the garden, collapsed on the bench and began weeping bitterly.

"Why so sad again, Liubomilka?" Grandmother had come over and sat down beside her.

Through her tears the girl told her grandmother what had happened:

"They came to us and asked for kvass, and the boy was there who gave me a ride on the stook three years ago. He's even more handsome now. I ran and brought the kvass in a pitcher. They all took a drink, and said how good it was. He took a drink too, and then gave the pitcher to Yekaterina. Not to me, Grammykins, but to *her,* my rival, Yekaterina. And it was her he thanked, not me. She's a real dingbat, that sister of mine. She must have been chatting him up while I was getting the kvass. He looked back at her and even smiled. My own sister — a rival! A real dingbat!"

"Why are you blaming your sister? She's not at fault. You are."

"Why am I to blame, Grammykins? What have I done wrong?"

"Listen carefully. Your sister made a colourful embroidery pattern, which she neatly applied to the sleeves of her dress. You wanted to do everything yourself, too, but on *your* dress the sewing didn't come out straight.

"Besides, your sister can speak in verse, she's better than anyone at singing *koliadki,*[5] and you're unwilling to talk with any wise-men who can teach you to recite and compose verse. The boy you've chosen — no doubt he's a pretty smart lad, he has an appreciation of beauty and intellect."

"Does that mean I have to study another three years, Grammykins?"

"Three, perhaps. But it could be five."

---

[5]*koliadki* (pron. *kal-YAT-kee*) — songs traditionally sung during winter solstice celebrations, venerating the Sun and light which bring forth life and joy as well as bountiful harvests and family happiness. The term is derived from the ancient Slavic name of the winter solstice holiday — *Koliada* (from *kolo* = circle, annual cycle) — the beginning of the new solar-year cycle. (The Latin word *calenda,* signifying the first day of a month, and English *calendar* are derived from the same root.) As part of the Koliada celebrations, children went from one house to another offering good wishes to the families, who offered them holiday treats in return. It was expected that the children would make up songs on the spot for each particular family — an opportunity for them to demonstrate their creative abilities. In the Russian Orthodox Church the term was later applied to what we would call Christmas carols. *Koliadki* are still practised to the present day.

True love will most certainly be reciprocated

Ten years went by. One day Radomir was walking through one of the regular holiday fairs with his best friend, who had the unusual name of Arga.[6]

Arga had a flair for creating marvellous pictures and doing fantastic wood-carvings. He could fashion statues of clay that looked as though they were alive. This was a talent he had inherited from his grandfather. From his father was derived his blacksmith's art.

The two friends took little interest in the long rows of carts with their vast array of savoury offerings. Nor was the young men's attention attracted by the rows of assorted dishes and household utensils. In fact people did not come to the fair for any material acquisitions at all. The main attraction was talking with others, getting to know them, sharing their experiences with them.

The lads decided to head over to the place where they were getting ready for a colourful show by visiting performing artists. Suddenly they heard themselves being hailed:

"Radomir! Arga! Have you seen it yet?"

Radomir and Arga turned around to see who was calling to them. Three young men from among their community friends were standing a little distance away, engaged in animated conversation and beckoning Radomir and Arga to join them.

"Seen what?" asked Radomir as he approached.

[6] *Arga* — pron. *ar-GAH.*

"That extraordinary shirt," answered one of the three. "It's made from smooth fabric, and embroidered with very unusual ornaments. There's probably some secret meaning in them."

A second lad corrected him:

"The shirt's really good, but the girl selling it is much prettier. I've never seen a maiden like that at any fair anywhere."

"So, where do we find this marvel?" asked Arga.

The five boys headed over to the carts displaying jewellery and ornaments, marvellous handicrafts and fine clothing.

One cart in particular had drawn a bigger crowd than usual. Everybody was admiring an exceptionally beautiful shirt, hanging on a wooden hanger. The fabric was rippling lightly in the breeze, and people could see how different it was from the usual shirts made of coarse cloth, exuding, as it did, a feeling of lightness and tenderness. And the patterns embroidered on the collar and the sleeves were extraordinarily delicate and fanciful.

"A pattern like that is the mark of an accomplished craftsman," Arga said aloud in excitement.

"Never mind the pattern, squeeze your way through the crowd and see who's sitting beside it," said a neighbour from their settlement.

After making their way around to the other edge of the small crowd, the friends managed to approach the cart and catch a glimpse of the maiden.

Her eyes were blue as the sky, her dark blonde hair in a tight braid was tied. Her eyebrows were like two brown arches, her lips betrayed just the faintest hint of a smile. Her movements were gracious, but seemed to be entwined with some kind of energy. It was some time before the lads could take their eyes off the maiden.

"She's clever with her tongue, too," the tallest of them quietly observed. "She can speak in verse and comes up with witty sayings." Another added:

"She's kind of tender, but as aloof and inaccessible as a high cliff. Try talking with her."

"I can't," answered Radomir. "She's taken my breath away."

Arga spoke to her first:

"Tell me, fair maiden, are you the one who crafted this magnificent shirt?"

"I am," the maiden replied without raising her eyes. "I wove this shirt to while away the boredom, to make the winter nights shorter. Sometimes I would do some embroidery at dawn."

"And what kind of price are you asking for your handiwork?" Arga enquired, so that he could keep hearing the maiden's tuneful voice a little longer.

The maiden raised her eyes to look at the young lads and it seemed as though her gaze was carrying them away into heavenly heights. She let her gaze rest just for a moment on Radomir, thereby dissolving him, as it were, into the blue. From that point on he felt as though he were in some sort of unusual, unreal dream.

"What price again? Let me explain." The beautiful girl sitting on the cart went on: "I can give this piece without payment only to a kind and courageous young man. I shall ask only something trifling for myself as a souvenir — a colt, for example."

"What a beauty she is! And such a worthy reply, she's a true master!" Loud exclamations could be heard from the crowd. "'A colt,' she says — 'just a trifle'! Yes, a real beauty all right, no doubt about it!"

The exclamations went on, but the crowd did not move along. Then suddenly the whole throng divided into two halves. There was Arga, leading a dun-coloured stallion by a halter rope. The steed was unbroken and hot-tempered, and kept bucking and prancing on the spot. Whispers spread through the crowd:

"Now that is quite a horse! Such a marvellous steed! Could the fine young man have decided indeed to give it away?"

Arga approached the cart and said:

"My father gave me this steed. I offer it to you, my beauty, in exchange for the shirt."

"Thank you," the maiden calmly replied. "But I did say, and people heard me say, that the shirt is not for sale. I can only give it away to you, or perhaps to some other young man fine and true."

"Aha, the beautiful maiden is frightened!" Mocking voices rose from the crowd. "Of course, the steed is hot-tempered, and too flared up to handle for many a young man. A while ago she was expecting a tame and gentle mare, and now she's got cold feet! See, she's given up the game. So, anyone should be careful. It's a downright shame when a steed is unbroken and hot-tempered."

The maiden looked out at the crowd with an artful smile and jumped down from the cart with an amazingly lithesome style.

At this point all the exclamations from the crowd ceased at once. The girl's torso was absolutely stunning, as though refined to perfection by a master artist. She stood before everybody standing around in all her beauty, smiling at the steed. She took three steps in Arga's direction, seemingly floating toward him, barely touching the ground.

Completely taken aback, Arga suddenly let go of the halter-rope. The hot-tempered stallion reared on its hind legs. But the maiden managed to catch hold of the rope with her hand. And then...

And then, to everyone's amazement, her left hand deftly squeezed the stallion's nostrils. Letting go of the rope, she began caressing the steed's nuzzle with her right hand. And the hot-tempered stallion all of a sudden calmed down. She inclined his head toward the ground. At first he put up some resistance, but eventually began bowing to the ground — lower and still lower. And then the steed suddenly fell to its knees before the maiden.

A grey-headed oldster stepped forth from the crowd and said:

"Only the old wise-men know how to tame a beast like that, and not even all of *them*. But you are still a young maiden! What is your name? And whose girl are you?"

"I am Liubomila, from the next settlement. And whose am I? Nobody's. I am simply the daughter of my father. And here he comes, that strict father of mine."

"If only I *had* been strict!" said the father, who had just come back to the family cart. "What have you been up to this time, my little gal?"

"Nothing much. I've just been playing a bit with this little colt."

"A bit? I see. Let the steed go. It's time we got on the road home."

Love, too, was teaching in the Vedruss school

What had happened to Liubomila during these years? Where had she learnt such wisdom and agility all of a sudden? In the Vedruss school.

People studied their whole lifetime in this school, from their early childhood to their most advanced age. Every year they sat for exams. The school programme had appeared right at the beginning of creation in all its minute detail and then become further enriched over the centuries. The wisdom was imparted unobtrusively. The lessons were not at all like those in your contemporary schools.

You once told me, Vladimir, about a certain expression used in your society. When it turned out that a child is mischievous and rude and bad habits show up in him, people would say that he was brought up by the street, that he's been granted too much freedom.

The Vedruss people had no fear about granting freedom to their children. It was common knowledge that the system of festivals and rites was so intricately and skilfully thought through that all children were absorbed in preparation for them. Even though it seemed as though they were playing, they were actually teaching themselves various disciplines, often without the help of adults.

Examinations in the Vedruss school were like one festival or celebration after another. With their help the adults taught the children, and they themselves learnt from the children.

Take the Festival of the *Koliadki*, for example. During the festival days children walk about and sing koliadki to all their neighbours. The verses and melodies, along with the accompanying dance movements, were all composed by the children themselves.

Children started preparing for their performances long before the start of the festivals, eager to learn from adults, their families, their peers and the wise-men as to the best way of mastering verse composition, along with singing and dance movements.

Not all children had the same abilities, of course. Those that were not as quick to learn as others would ask their parents to tutor them. And sometimes parents found they could use their children's thirst for knowledge to draw them into helping around the house and grounds.

A little boy might badger his grandmother, for example:

"Grammykins, dear, read some verse to me. Please do read, I beg you. I don't want to fall behind and be worse than the rest. My friends might not take me with them to sing koliadki next time."

And the grandmother would answer:

"I've quite a bit to do. Perhaps you could help me, and then I would be able to read you some verse this evening."

The child would be eager to help all day long and afterward would listen intently to his grandmother, and try to memorise all her verses or songs, and implore her to teach him the appropriate dance moves. Then he might implore his grandfather, and perhaps his mother and father, too, to tutor him just a little bit more. And he would be grateful to his parents when they offered him a lesson.

Compare this approach, Vladimir, with the lessons children get in schools today — in literature, let us say.

You are right, there is absolutely no comparison. The Vedruss children aspired to become poets themselves, right from a very young age.

The parade of merry festivals in the Vedruss period was a system that helped people learn about the order of the Universe and in turn teach their children the simple wisdom of life.

The wise-men were itinerant teachers and sources of information in regard to what was going on in the world. The *bayans*[7] and bards, too, not only reminded people of events of the past, but gave portents of the future, commending the world of marvellous feelings or reprehending unworthy ones.

Such lessons were constantly taking place in every settlement, but nobody would ever compel their children to attend.

[7] *bayan* (pron. *bah-YAHN*) — see footnote 4 in Book 4, Chapter 33: "School, or the lessons of the gods". On the role of bards, see Book 2, Chapter 10: "The ringing sword of the bard".

It was felt that each teacher himself should attract children's attention to the stories of science he was planning to tell.

Over the centuries rules such as these helped perfect the abilities of the wise-men-teachers.

You asked, Vladimir, whether any wise-men-teachers, in an effort to attract children's attention, would simply play some sort of game with them instead of actually giving them a lesson in science or the arts.

Indeed, if such a thing were to occur, the wise-man would be relieved of his wise-man's status. In talking with their children at home, parents would perceive right off that the children had not been properly taught. News of his dishonourable conduct would be made known in other settlements, and no matter what community he thought to visit, he would probably be asked to leave.

Before the appearance of love within herself, the little girl Liubomilka made no attempt to attend the wise-men's lessons or listen to the songs of the bards and bayans. The parents would not have forced their children to attend, but might drop a surreptitious hint at an appropriate occasion.

It was Love that enfolded little Liubomilka in its energy. In Vedruss families the appearance of love was greeted as a new member of the family sent by God to help them. And they knew how they could, in harmony with Love, make the little girl's life marvellous. This was why the grandmother advised Liubomilka to go and study with the wise-men. Not just to study for the sake of studying, but with a specific purpose — to become the very best she could be for the one she loved. Liubomilka consented, and decided that the next time a wise-man presented himself who could teach people to sing songs with a beautiful voice, she would indeed go see him along with her friends.

But the wise-man they needed never came. Liubomilka decided she would simply go listen to the next wise-man that showed up. She did, and began to listen to his lecture. This wise-man began talking about the specific function of various plants, the fragrances these gave off, and about how plants could be used to treat Man's diseases.

"What do I need this for?" Liubomila thought to herself. "Indeed, this is neither here nor there — everyone knows how to treat: Mama, grandmother, sister — they all know. And even if I should learn more than anyone else about the various herbs, how will that be noticed by my intended? He'll never notice it."

So Liubomilka listened to the wise-man without paying too much attention. She sat there on the log simply for her girl-friends' company. And sometimes she would get up, walk out and wander about the little glade. She was glad when the wise-man ended his lecture and everyone made ready to go home.

Then all of a sudden the elderly wise-man turned to Liubomilka:

"Tell me, little girl, you did not find my presentation interesting?"

"It's just that it's really of no use to me, it does not fit in with my secret aspiration," little Liubomilka informed the wise-man, almost in a whisper.

The wise-man-teacher broke into a faint smile. The perspicacious old fellow knew all about little girls' secret aspirations, and remarked:

"You know, little girl, you may be right — I can allow that this knowledge has nothing to do with you right now. After all, you are still pretty young. But for older girls I explain how they can become beautiful and create a Space of Love for the one they love. When *he* sees this Space of Love, he will definitely want to know who was able to co-create such beauty. And he will be so excited to meet whoever steps forward as its creator. I shall also reveal to the maidens the secret of how to

weave a garland, how to prepare a tea of herbs for their beloved, and what to use in washing in the morning to make their
bodies smell flower-sweet. I shall further be explaining..."

Little Liubomilka listened to the elderly fellow and began
to regret more and more that she had not gone to his classes. He stayed in the settlement for more than a week. He
revealed to the maidens important secrets, which she knew
nothing about. And Liubomilka asked the wise-man:

"Are you going to be staying much longer in our settlement?"

"I shall be on my way in a couple of days," he responded.

"In a couple of days?" The little girl could not hide her
disappointment. "Hmm, in two days... Then I would kindly,
kindly beg of you to spend your last two nights with us."

"I have already accepted invitations to other homes," responded the wise-man. "But if it means so much to you..."

"Yes, I very, very much need to learn from you about the
different herbs."

Each evening the old wise-man spent his whole time talking with the love-smitten Liubomilka. He knew that the inspiration of love would help this little girl grasp the essence
of the subject in a day or so, while even a year might not be
enough for some others.

When it was time for him to leave, Liubomilka escorted
the wise-man to the outskirts of the settlement, and he told
her:

"After me another wise-man will be coming here. He will
be talking about the stars and the Moon in the skies, about
the Sun and about worlds invisible to our eyes. Whoever suc-
ceeds in understanding him will be able to light a guiding star
in the skies for her beloved, and that star will shine for them
both for ever.

"Then along will come a wise-man who knows how to
tame wild beasts — indeed, how to render even the most

headstrong steed obedient to your beloved and a faithful friend to him.

"A bard, too, should be coming to you. He knows how to write verse and come out with such songs that many people will fall in love first with the voice, then after that, everything expressed in the song. And he can also teach dance."

"Tell me please, which wise-men should I not bother going to hear?" Liubomilka suddenly said to the old fellow. "After all, I can't spend all my time listening to wise-men."

Once more the old fellow, cleverly concealing a smile, answered the girl in all seriousness:

"Yes, you are right. If you go hear all of them day after day, then there simply will not be time enough for play. You do not need to go and hear every single one. Why, for example, would you want to learn how to draw? Or embroider clothes with ornaments and imbue them with meanings that only your heart knows? Why would you need this kind of teaching, if you have an older sister and she, I believe, will turn out to be an unsurpassed master thereof?

"And why would you, for example, go and learn how to instil feelings of kindness in a shirt you sew — a shirt that will protect its wearer from many ills?

"Or learn how to make fresh porridge with love for your dear ones, which will satisfy not only their flesh but their soul as well? The taste of that porridge will be unsurpassed. But that is something that can be done to perfection by your sister's friend who lives next door.

"And when you want to obtain a beautiful dress or shirt to present to someone as a special gift — a gift that will arouse everyone's elation — you can always ask your sister and she will come up with a marvellous creation.

"And if, in the end, you want to treat someone to an extraordinary dish of porridge or kvass, you can always ask your sister's friend."

"*I shan't ask anybody!*" Liubomilka suddenly blurted out, even stamping her foot, quite forgetting herself. "Those are my rivals!"

"Rivals? In what way?" the old fellow asked in all seriousness.

And Liubomilka did not blush but responded:

"There's this boy — he's the best of the bunch, only he doesn't pay any attention to me, 'cause these dingbats managed to grow up ahead of me. They kept smiling at him all the time. I saw it when they danced the *khorovod*[8] at the kapishche. And I'm supposed to present him with a shirt my sister made? And kvass prepared by her girl-friend? No way! *Never!*"

"But why should it not be that way? You say he is the best of all the lads."

"He is the best. That I know for sure."

"Then answer me, why should not the best lad receive the very best shirt as a gift, and the best porridge, and kvass besides? And..." The old wise-man paused, and very quietly, almost to himself, he added: "I think it is only just for him to have the best bride of all."

"*Bride?*" Liubomilka's cheeks flushed.

"Yes, bride," replied the wise-man. "Indeed, should you not wish him only good? Let him have the best bride of all!"

Liubomila looked at the wise-man, not able to utter a word. She was filled with feelings which set her on fire. And

---

[8]*khorovod* (pron. *hur-a-VOT*) — a circle dance accompanied by choral singing, traditionally popular among Russians, Ukrainians and Belarusians. The *khorovod* is one of the ancient rites venerating the Sun. The dancers would almost invariably move clock-wise, symbolising the movement of Sun across the sky (as seen from the Northern Hemisphere). The dance, music and song served to put the participants into a trance-like state, so as to help them reconnect with the spiritual forces permeating the Universe.

suddenly she began running off. But after a short distance she stopped, turned around, and cried out to the wise-man:

"I agree. He *does* deserve to have the best bride of all. And that bride will be *me!*"

Liubomilka eagerly paid a visit to every wise-man that came to the settlement thereafter. She was always the first to arrive and the last to leave, and the wise-men could hardly believe the surprising questions she asked. She memorised in her head everything the men of wisdom said. In a learning situation this is possible only when a child not simply *attends* the classes, but actually *comprehends* where he will apply the knowledge received.

When instruction proves too gruelling for the pupil, it can be counterproductive. When a Man has a specific goal that can be mastered through the study of various disciplines, learning for him becomes an exhilaration, and the assimilation of knowledge proceeds a hundred times faster.

And when love enters into the equation, the resulting effect is unsurpassed. Love is capable of scanning the thought of any wise-man. Just a few words spoken by the teacher can be sufficient not only to explain the whole subject to the pupil in the blinking of an eye, but even beyond that, to further engage his thinking.

Love — a great energy, the gift of God — was paramount in Liubomilka's instruction.

Back at home the little girl followed her Mama and grandmother's dinner preparations with great eagerness. She had them explain all their actions in full detail, and tried her own hand at creating various dishes. And the little one came up with some rather unusual creations.

Once at *Maslenitsa*⁹ a group of relatives had come to join in a meal. Two stacks of pancakes stood on the table — one of them cooked by the girl's mother and grandmother, the other by little Liubomilka herself. The guests found *her* pancakes much tastier than the others. And this now-not-so-little girl watched from a far corner of the room as her stack of pancakes began disappearing faster than the other.

When the whole family sat down to the table on a weekday, Grandfather would be the first to taste the cabbage soup from a wooden spoon. And he would say:

"I know for certain who made this soup. It has a pleasant and tender taste that no one else can match."

"Hear, hear!" the girl's father added. "Not only does it contain flowers from unusual herbs, but there is *feeling* in it."

Little Liubomilka found learning the disciplines no chore at all. In her life she became a craftsman without peer. She herself blossomed into an extraordinarily beautiful woman.

From the first wise-man she had learnt without realising it the truth of great love: if you wish to be close to God, become a goddess yourself.

---

⁹*Maslenitsa* — a traditional week-long celebration in late February or early March, marking the coming of Spring and involving the ritual preparing and eating of pancakes (symbolising the Sun). Russia's Orthodox Church later incorporated the holiday into its calendar, known in English as *Shrovetide* — the week prior to the beginning of Lent. For further information please see footnote 1 in Book 7, Chapter 22: "The marvellous Vedruss holidays".

CHAPTER TEN

Pre-wedding festivities

The children grew up. The time came to search for soul-mates. Festivities were a great help to young people in this important undertaking.

Young Vedruss people would gather in the evenings at a designated place, usually just outside the settlement. They would light a bonfire, chat among themselves or sing songs. And once a week there would be a common festivity involving three or four settlements all told at one of their favourite spots, where they would similarly light a bonfire, sing songs and chat among themselves. But there were some festivities which were especially useful in helping young people find their soulmates.

While such festivities were outwardly quite simple, their simplicity harboured a great inner significance.

'Rucheyok'

There was a game called *Rucheyok*,[1] for example. Young people lined up in pairs, one couple after the other, took each other's

---

[1]*Rucheyok* (stressed on last syllable) — the Russian word for a small stream.

hands and raised them high, forming an arch overhead. To start with, boys were paired with boys, girls with girls. The first pair — or anyone left without a partner — would go to the end of the 'stream' and, bending over, pass under the arch of raised arms to the head of the line.

Those passing through the 'stream' were not supposed to look up. They were to slap somebody's arm at random, thereby selecting him or her as a temporary partner. Whoever was selected followed suit, and the two of them then stood at the head of the line of couples. Those left without a partner went to the end of the line and chose a new partner in a similar fashion.

The game was simple, but think about it, Vladimir: upon clasping hands for the first time, the young people could convey a great many feelings for each other without words: recognition, gratitude and love, or, on the other hand, revulsion. As the game went on, the couples switched, and it was easy to compare which pair of hands held the most pleasant feeling for you.

'Chastushka-govorushka'

This ancient wedding game was the most complex of its kind. Modern *chastushki,* which people still sing today, are derived from it.

The game, known as *Chastushka-govorushka,*[2] can be described as follows. Two rows of people stood facing each other. One row was made up of young men, the other of young maidens. The last girl in the row dedicated a four-line chastushka to the last chap in the men's row, standing opposite her. Her singing would be accompanied by dance movements. Directly she finished, the rest of the girls quickly stamped their feet twice and clapped their hands three times. And if the lad standing opposite her did not succeed in composing or recalling from memory a worthy response, the girl started singing a new *chastushka* to the next young man in line.

If the lad managed to come up with a worthy answer in the time allotted, the conversation would continue between them with the use of poetic witticisms. But that did not happen very often.

In spite of the fact that young Vedruss people knew a great many verses, still, not everyone was able to think up a worthy reply in the brief time available, especially since their rivals were trying their hardest to distract them from the sidelines by all their stamping and clapping.

At one of these get-togethers of young people from different settlements, Liubomila was present. Radomir's five friends who had caught a glimpse of this extraordinary girl at the fair kept stealing glances at her. His closest friend, Arga, could not take his eyes off her at all.

---

²*Chastushka-govorushka* (*che-STOOSH-ka ga-va-ROOSH-ka*) — The word *chastushka* (plural: *chastushki*) denotes a type of humorous, satirical or ironic four-line verse in trochaic tetrametre, sometimes sung to musical accompaniment. It is often compared to the limerick in English. The word *chastushka* is derived from the verb *chastit'* (to talk fast). In the name of this game it is paired with the rhyming word *govorushka*, a derivative of the verb *govorit'* (speak).

When the *Rucheyok* game began, the usually bold and deci-
sive Radomir walked under the couples' raised arms with the
full intention of taking Liubomila's hand and making her his
partner. But all of a sudden he got 'cold feet'. He could feel
her as he passed by between the two rows. He would have felt
her even if his eyes had been closed. But as he approached
the spot in the 'stream' where she was standing opposite her
girl-friend, he slowed down ever so little, and found himself
moving as in a dream. He ended up choosing a lad from a
neighbouring settlement.

His friend Arga, however, turned out to have more self-confidence. When it came his turn to pass through the 'stream',
Arga picked Liubomila right away, grabbed her hand and took
up a position with her at the head of the line of couples, much
to the envy of all the other young men.

Afterward they questioned him:

"What was it like when she held your hand? Did she
squeeze it tight or not?"

"I don't know," Arga replied. "I cannot remember aught.
It just seemed as though my hand caught on fire. Touch and
see for yourselves — it still feels hot."

"What a gal!" the fine young lads exclaimed in amazement
on the spot. "She's so hot with passion, it's as though she's
burning with a flame from some mysterious fire!"

Radomir in turn heard all of this without saying a word.
His own internal yearnings had been burning for some
time — ever since that day he first discerned this wondrous
girl at the fair. He had been thinking about her day after day,
first thing upon waking in the morning. She even appeared
to him in his dreams, but even there, it seemed, he could not
bring himself to touch her.

Always successful in any undertaking, Radomir had a reputation as a poet, but now all of a sudden even the simplest of
words to describe her utterly failed him.

When the *Chastushka-govorushka* game got going, he stood in the middle of the row of young men, next to his friend Arga. Liubomila was almost at the end of the maidens' row. When it came her turn to sing and dance the chastushki, she began her song with ease. At once it was clear to all that here was an extraordinary maiden indeed, impossible to beat.

She switched themes in a flash. She sang couplets no one had ever heard before. One after the other she won out over all the young men, even though she herself was the youngest of all.

When it came Arga's turn, he was still able to give a response to the crafty maiden, albeit not without a bit of a glitch. He replied to Liubomila with a quatrain, but she, without even waiting for the stamping and clapping, suddenly changed topic and offered up such a smooth new witticism in verse that Arga was completely thrown off the track and didn't even attempt to counter with one of his own.

Next it was Radomir's turn. Liubomila began singing to him, jauntily dancing to the rhythm of her verse:

> Bold and eloquent you are,
> Much you know, oh yes!
> D'you recall how in the lake
> You once washed my dress?

Some listeners laughed, thinking Liubomila was making a joke with her couplet. Some, including Radomir himself, could not figure out what it was all about. And, not being able to figure it out, he found it impossible to offer any kind of answer.

So Radomir could give no response to Liubomila. When the stamping and clapping came to an end, signifying the deadline for reply was up, he realised that his time had irretrievably gone by. This was something he could not allow. As

though completely forgetting himself, he now began moving toward Liubomila — first one step, then a second, then
a third. By this time he had come right up close beside her.
Everybody fell silent, wondering why the rules of the game
had been defied.

Radomir stood silently before Liubomila. And all at once,
against this background of silence everyone standing in
the rows heard Radomir utter, with audible aspiration, the
Vedruss declaration of love:

"With you, my marvellous goddess, I could co-create a
Space of Love to last forever."

Everybody waited with bated breath to hear what response
this fiery-tongued maiden would come up with.

But all of a sudden she became very meek. At first she def-
erentially lowered the gaze of her fiery eyes, but then raised
them again. Tears began rolling down her cheek and she
whispered:

"I am ready to help you in your grand co-creation."[3]

Finally Radomir recognised in the maiden standing before
him the same little girl whose dress he had washed in the lake
so many years ago. He recognised her, and took her by the
hand. As they walked along side by side, they no longer had
eyes for anyone else. The two rows of young people stood
facing each other in silence as they watched the couple's love
head into eternity.

[3]See the section "A union of two — a wedding" in Book 6, Chapter 5: "The
history of mankind, as told by Anastasia".

CHAPTER ELEVEN

The wedding rite

The Vedruss wedding rite, Vladimir, is something you already know about. You wrote about it in *The Book of Kin.*[1] Let me remind you of the essence of these great acts.

It was the lovers' task to jointly choose a place for their future domain. They would usually go out beyond the perimeter of the settlement where *he* lived with his parents, and then inspect the area around the settlement where *she* lived. And there was no need for the lovers to let their parents know of their intentions, as everyone in the settlements had an awareness and comprehension of the deed that this was leading to.

On their chosen plot of land, measuring a hectare or more, the lovers drew up plans for their real life together. Their task was to mentally envision a house and arrange a whole lot of plants so that every part worked together with each other in harmonious precision.

Liubomila and Radomir quickly found a spot for their future domain. As though by mutual agreement, they had each gone outside the boundaries of the settlement to a spot where there was a small grove of trees and a stream flowing by almost unnoticed from a small spring.

Radomir had been here before. He had sat here alone, dreamt about the future, about his future life together with his beloved.

[1] See the section entitled "A union of two — a wedding" in Book 6, Chapter 5: "The history of mankind, as told by Anastasia".

Liubomila had twice come by on her faithful fast-running horse without Radomir. She herself, without knowing why, had once halted her horse by the stream, walked over to the grove, let down her hair, put on a headband and stood for a long time by a goodly young birch tree.

Now the lovers stood on the spot together.

"I was really pleased when I came here on my own," said Radomir. "I would very much like to continue our family line here."

"And *I* like this place, too," Liubomila whispered.

Early the next morning, as soon as the dawn broke, Radomir brought to the place they had selected more than a dozen rods in a cart and long willow shoots, along with some small posts and a scythe. No sooner had he begun to cut the grass than he saw Liubomila approaching on her steed at a gallop. Radomir was absolutely delighted at the sight, and his heart started trembling. The beautiful girl leapt down from her horse, before it had come to a full stop, three metres short of the as yet unmarked boundary line of their plot, and dashed over to Radomir.

"I greet you with the dawning day, creator," she said to Radomir, smiling. "The day has turned out to be a fine one, and I decided to bring along some coloured ribbon to mark out the places for our future plantings."

"Thank you for brightening the day," replied Radomir.

The lovers did not kiss nor even embrace. According to Vedruss custom, anything like that was not seemly to do before the wedding. And there was a considerable significance to be perceived in this: they did not make a daily routine out of kisses and embraces before their children were conceived. And therefore, when the moment for conception arrived, their energies were at their peak potential. And they never set up dates for themselves.

Each one would visit the selected spot on their own whenever they wished.

Radomir was always the first to arrive with each day's dawn. Liubomila would follow suit on her steed.

Within a week Radomir had constructed a shelter resembling a magical little house. It was two-and-a-half metres wide and three metres deep. He dug the rods into the ground, made the walls out of interwoven branches, and covered it with a combination of rods and branches.

The lovers covered the whole thing with dried grass, and Liubomila spread a fabric cloth over the interior walls and ceiling. And she made two beds with straw on the bottom, hay on top, each bed covered with a cloth.

When the magical little house was ready, the lovers would often rest and spend the night there, but they did not enter into intimate relations. Such intimacy before the wedding, before creating the 'nest', was considered an affront to their future children.

Besides, the young people had a lot to keep them busy. Radomir brought a large board, on which he carved the plan for their plot, indicating all the points of the compass, including the rising and setting of the Sun and the risings of the Moon. Wind-speed and direction for both daytime and nighttime were also recorded.

Liubomila would often go to the perimeter of the plot, where she would stand for a long time, picturing in her mind their future plantings. She would also check with Radomir's plan to make sure they would not have any harm from the wind or shade.

When winter came, Liubomila made less frequent visits to their love domain. She would spend her days weaving fabric in her parents' home, and embroidering a shirt for Radomir with love.

But Radomir came again and again to their future domain. He continued to obtain and note down information on wind movements, and memorised how the snow lay in the plain.

This is how the Vedruss people over the years made a weather calendar. Every Vedruss family had boards inscribed with such plans and were able to accurately describe the weather to come for a year in advance — two and three years ahead, even. It might seem as though it would have been easier simply to copy a calendar like that from one their parents had made, but it would not have been entirely accurate. The landscape would be just a little bit different, and a copse or a hillock might be able to protect a plant from the wind. The wintertime snowdrifts, too, could be different.

By the time spring arrived, the design was already complete in Radomir's and Liubomila's thought, and in early spring they began once more to live in their little house. The task now before them was to mark out all the planting areas with posts, ribbons and branches, and harmonise their ideas with each other. Radomir also had to dig a well and fence off the waterspring.

There were only two weeks left until they could put the seedlings into the ground, and the lovers began preparing for the wedding.

First they went to the settlement where the groom lived, and then to the bride's. They would pay a visit to every house, inviting its residents to their wedding. In every house their arrival was eagerly anticipated. Everyone wanted to see their love and decide on a gift for their future living home. When the young couple visited a garden, a house or a household courtyard, they would speak briefly to the residents. Just a sentence to each one — something like *Oh, what a splendid apple tree you have! Your cat has a knowing look!* or *Your bear is a real worker, very considerate!*

To any resident hearing the lovers praise a tree growing in the garden or the household cat, this was a sign of appreciation of the resident's worthy life. It also indicated that the young couple, too, would like to have a plant or an animal like that.

The couple was not invited into the house nor given any-thing to eat. This was not just a random practice on the part of the Vedruss people. It would not have been deemed con-siderate for the young lovers to refuse an invitation for a visit and a meal, but if they had started making extended visits, they would not have had enough time to go round to all the families before the wedding.

Arga, who had known Radomir from childhood, broke the rules slightly. When the lovers paid a visit to his house and began talking with his father, Arga suddenly ran off and fetched a marvellous colt from the stable — the one that had earlier caught the fancy of the whole settlement. He started talking excitedly:

"Please, accept this steed as a present from me. Just as be-fore, he has not let anyone near him since Liubomila made him submit that day at the fair."

The father gave his son a sly smile and said:

"Perhaps, Arga, you are not letting any horse-breakers near your steed? For some reason you don't seem to want to break him in yourself."

Arga replied, slightly embarrassed:

"I haven't been breaking him in. I decided to leave this stallion forever free. But now I've changed my mind. Take this steed as a present from me." And he handed the reins to Liubomila.

"Thank you," replied Liubomila. "But I cannot accept this steed, seeing as he is already accustomed to another. But if he has a colt, we shall gratefully accept it indeed."

When the young couple had completed the round of the domains, and the wedding day that had been announced to all finally arrived, young and old began hastening at daybreak to the designated spot.

People lined up along the perimeter of the plot of land which the young couple had staked out with dry branches.

Right in the centre, next to the shelter, a little mound rose out of the ground, decorated with flowers. Radomir mounted the hillock, and excitedly outlined the plan for the future domain before the gathering.

And each time the young man pointed to a spot where some sort of plant was to grow, someone would step forth from the circle of listeners and go over to the place Radomir was indicating. And this Man held in his hands a seedling of the plant Radomir had named. And each contributor who stepped forth was accorded a bow from the people in turn. After all, each contributor had earned the young couple's praise during the visits to the domains for having been able to grow a marvellous plant. This meant that he was worthy of the praise of the Creator, the Father of all, the all-loving God.

After announcing their design, Radomir came down from the mound and went over to the spot where his Liubomila was following the whole procedure with excitement and trembling. He took her hand and led her solemnly to the little mound, where the lovers now stood together before the whole gathering.

Then Radomir once again addressed the crowd:

"I was not alone in creating this Space of Love. Here beside me, and standing before you, people, is my marvellous inspiration."

The girl — or, more properly, a maiden — initially lowered her gaze before the gathering.

Every woman has her own beauty. But there can be moments in every woman's life when she shines above the rest. Such moments are absent in our modern culture. But back then...

Now Liubomila raised her eyes to focus her gaze on the assembly.

The excitement of the whole throng before her merged into a single exultation. The girl's face shone with a radiant smile, not of impudence but of courage. She was filled to overflowing with the energy of Love. Her cheeks were aflush with a brighter than usual glow. The people and the whole Space around them were captured by the warmth radiating from her luxuriantly healthy body and her sparkling eyes. For a moment everybody froze in rapture.

The young goddess stood before the people, shining in all her beauty. The people, in turn, could only admire the most delightful vision.

This was why the maiden's parents waited before beginning their solemn procession, accompanied by the elderly and younger members of the whole family, to the mound where the loving couple was standing.

Stopping at the mound, the family first bowed to the young couple, and now the mother asked the maiden, her daughter:

"All the wisdom of the family line lies in you, my daughter. Tell me, do you see the future of the land you have chosen?"

"Yes, Mama, I see it," replied Liubomila.

"Tell me, daughter dear," the mother continued, "do you like everything about the future you have been shown?"

"I really do like the design. But still I should like to add just a little something."

Quickly jumping down from the mound, Liubomila all at once ran through the crowd to the edge of her future garden, where she stopped and said:

"Here is where an evergreen should grow, with a birch beside it. When a breeze blows from that direction, it will first meet the branches of the pine, then the birch, and after that the breeze will ask the trees of the garden to sing a tune. It will not be repeated exactly the same way each time, but it will always be a delight to the soul. And here," the maiden added, running off a little to one side, "here flowers are to grow. First there will be a flush of red, then over here, a little later, violets will spring up, and burgundy over there."

Liubomila, all aglow like a fairy, started dancing around her future garden. And once more the people remaining in the circle set themselves in motion, hurrying about to carry the seeds in their hands to the spots on the ground the high-spirited girl had pointed out.

Upon finishing her dance, she once more ran up to the mound. Here, standing next her chosen one, she said:

"Now the Space here will be splendid in its sheen. The earth will produce a most marvellous scene."

"Tell, my daughter, for all to hear," her mother once more addressed her, "who will be crowned to reign over all this marvellous Space around? Of all the people living on the Earth, upon whom could you bestow the crown?"

Turning to her fiancé, the bride responded:

"He is worthy to wear the crown whose thought is able to create a future that will be splendid all around."

With these words the girl touched the shoulder of the young man standing beside her. He got down on one knee before her. And the girl solemnly placed on his head a most beautiful crown, a garland woven from nice, sweet-smelling grasses by the maiden's own hand. Then, running her fingers thrice through her fiancé's hair with her right hand, she took hold of his head with her left and drew it a little closer to herself. Then Radomir, now crowned, stood up, while Liubomila ran down from the mound and bowed her head ever so slightly before him in a sign of meekness.

Now, as was the custom, the young man's father, accompanied by his whole family, made its way over to the mound. As they approached, they stopped in respect, and the father asked his son, who was standing over the whole assembly:

"Who are you whose thought is capable of creating a Space of Love?"

And Radomir replied:

"I am your son, and I am the son of the Creator."

"A crown has been placed upon your head, a sign of a great mission to come. You who are wearing the crown, what will you do as you reign over your domain?"

"I shall create a future that all around most splendid will remain."

And the father asked again:

"Where will you gain the strength and inspiration, my son, and crowned son of the Creator?"

"In Love!"

Another question:

"The energy of Love is capable of wandering through the whole Universe. How will you manage to see the reflection of universal love on the Earth?"

"There is one girl, Father, and for me she is the reflection of universal love on the Earth."

With these words the young man came down to where Liubomila was standing, took her by the hand and led her back up to the mound. Whereupon the two families merged into a single group, sharing hugs and jokes and laughter.

Then the young man thanked everyone, and they all began to plant their living gifts in the spot Radomir had indicated earlier. Those not assigned a specific spot set about to walk around the perimeter of the plot which had already been marked out and to the sound of the *khorovod* threw the seeds they had brought with them into the ground. Within the space of a few minutes a marvellous garden had been planted.

Once again the young man wearing the crown held up his hand, and, when all was quiet, said:

"Let all the creatures given to Man by the Creator live together with us in friendship!"

And those who had brought animals as gifts approached the shelter, carrying a kitten or a puppy or a wee calf on a lead, or even a bear cub. Arga, Radomir's friend, gave them the colt he had promised.

Then people quickly fashioned tree branches into a wicker fence to attach animal pens to the shelter. And soon the dwelling which just a short time ago had been used by people as sleeping quarters was now filled with animals, who were similarly young. And there was tremendous significance in this. For in mixing with each other this way, these animals would forever live together in friendship, caring for and helping each other.

After accepting the gifts, the young couple once again thanked everybody, and then a joyful celebration with songs and khorovods began. The young people, however, withdrew with their families each to their own house. They would not see each other again until after two nights and one full day had passed.

During this time the best craftsmen of both settlements carried the pre-built framework of a log-house to the new domain, put a roof on top, laid down the floor and filled all the seams with moss and grass. And the women placed their best fruits of their harvest in the new home. The two mothers covered the bed with a linen counterpane. And by the second night every last one of the visitors was gone from the domain. The energy of Love lingered over it in anticipation of the young lovers' coming.

"Look what happens, Vladimir," said Anastasia, after finishing her account. "The Vedruss family, in this case little Liubomila's family, accepted the appearance of the feeling of love in the little girl as the gift of God. And they treated the appearance of this feeling as that of a new member of their family, sent by God, as a helper in the raising of their little girl — perhaps as the primary helper. As a result, the girl's grandmother helped her understand what the great energy of Love wanted of her, pointing to concrete actions in a simple language comprehensible to a child.

"The little girl was inspired to start learning various disciplines, the pristine wisdom of being, and worked to perfect her own spirit and body.

"Who was primarily responsible, Vladimir, for Liubomila's success — her grandmother, the wise-men-teachers, the girl herself, or the great inexhaustible energy of Love?"

"I would say that if you took away the energy of Love, then all the other participants in the girl's upbringing would hardly be capable of getting even half of that done. But without them, the energy of Love would have a hard time setting the girl on the right path all by itself."

"So then, what happened was a joint creation, and joy was shared by all from its contemplation! Well, that is precisely what God wants of Man."

"I agree. The wedding rite itself is a festive masterpiece altogether unsurpassed in beauty, significance and rationality. If you compare it to modern wedding rites, it looks as though we've all transformed ourselves into a bunch of occult idiots. What are young people left with today, after a modern wedding? Memories of gadding around in a car, for some reason, to the 'eternal flame',[2] a drunken spree in a café or restaurant, cries of *Gor'ko, gor'ko!*,[3] and public kisses wasting energy that

---

[2]*'eternal flame'* (i.e., at the tomb of the unknown soldier) — Such a visit shortly after the wedding ceremony is a common practice among Russian newlyweds.

[3]*Gor'ko, gor'ko!* (lit. 'Bitter, bitter!') — the traditional call at Russian wedding receptions for the bride and groom to kiss (and thereby sweeten the bitter wine).

should be saved for the conception of a child. Whereas after the Vedruss wedding rite the couple is left not with just
memories but with an actual house built with joy by the finest
craftsmen, a garden with a multitude of growing things planted by the hands of relatives as well as friends and neighbours
who contributed to the young lovers' design."

"In reality, Vladimir, they are left with an actual Space of
Love. A sacred, living, truly Divine nest, where the conception of a child may subsequently be expressed.

"The witnesses at a Vedruss wedding rite comprise not just
two friends, as happens today, but all the relatives from the
whole area, and they create designs not on pieces of paper but
in a living creation on the earth.

"The young people in turn sit an examination together, describing their design for their future domain in front of the
whole community. I would say their presentation is on an in-
comparably higher level than today's doctoral dissertations.

"Of course the materialisation of living Space — the house,
the homestead, the beauty of the actions used to create these,
all play an undoubtedly important part. But there is one incredible aspect that is just as important. See who actually
marries the young couple. Not the parents, not some random
official in the Civil Registration Office or a priest whom they
often see for the first and the last time.

"Liubomila herself places the crown on Radomir's head, in
front of the whole gathering! This is an act that God's children are indeed entitled to fulfil. It is a psychological factor
that is not as simple as may seem at first glance.

"A Man who lets his love be registered by some random person is already relieving himself, on a subconscious level, of the
responsibility for the subsequent fate of his family. Liubomila,
by contrast, takes this responsibility upon herself.

"There are many formalities placed between modern couples registering their marriage and God. These include the

blessing by the parents, the registration at the Civil Office and a priest in the church. By contrast, nobody stands between the Vedruss couple and God. Consequently their marriage can be blessed only by God Himself.

"And even before the crowning, He really makes this into an actual manifestation. He sends them mutual love. The Vedruss people knew how to accept it and make it eternal.

"And what happened, one might ask, *before* conception in the Vedruss period?"

CHAPTER TWELVE

Conception

The wedding rite had now taken place. But the young people did not simply hop into bed to engage in the wedding-night activities we know about today, following a drunken spree. Their relatives did not make them lie in bed and then display the bloody sheet to the wedding guests the next morning, as has been done in many wedding rites, especially in the Caucasus.[1]

The young lovers went off, each to their respective parents' homes. They slept, and then made their ablutions. And in the execution of this whole custom there is a great significance.

The excitement associated with the approval of the domain's design quickly passed. The excitement associated with the wedding itself, where their attention was totally occupied with each other in a climax, may have had a pleasurable dimension, but it was still accompanied by a degree of nervous tension.

At their parents' homes they rested and slept off the excitement, while of course still thinking about each other.

Two days later they experienced their first encounter as husband and wife. And by this time everything was ready for the conception of their child. It was not just a question of material benefits. The house, the warm enclosure for their animals, the vegetable garden and the orchard were all very important, of course. But equally important was the mental and physical state of the young couple.

---

[1]Once more, this chapter is a continuation of Anastasia's narrative.

Radomir awoke before dawn. And without a word to anyone, he put on his garland and picked up his shirt that had been hand-embroidered by his mother. Then he headed off to the spring-fed stream.

The moon illumined his path through the pre-dawn darkness, while garlands of stars twinkled in the heavens. After washing in the stream, he put on his shirt and quickly made his way to his sacred creation. The heavens began to brighten.

And there he stood alone on the spot where the two villages recently celebrated their joy — the place he created through his dream.

The power of the feelings and sensations within a Man at such a moment can scarcely be comprehended by anyone who has not experienced them at least once for himself.

It can be said that these sensations and feelings are Divine in nature. And they have increased in quivering anticipation of the first ray of dawn, in which... *There she is! His most marvellous Liubomila!* Illumined in the dawn's rays, she ran to greet him and their co-creation.

The vision incarnate ran to meet Radomir. While perfection, of course, knows no real limit, it seemed as though time had suddenly stopped for the two of them. Enveloped in the mist of their feelings, they entered their new home. The table was spread with delicacies, and a tempting fragrance of dried flowers wafted from the embroidered counterpane on the bed.

"What are you thinking about right now?" she asked him in a heated whisper.

"About *him* — our future child," and Radomir gave a quiver as he looked at Liubomila. "My, how beautiful you are!" No longer able to contain himself, he very tenderly touched her shoulder and cheek.

It was not just that Liubomila and Radomir felt a joy in their hearts, they kept looking at each other in silent delight.

My husband, Liubomila whispered to herself without making a sound. *My husband, I thank heaven and the whole Universe. O righteous God, what happiness You give to people — the happiness of living a life in love!*

My wife, Radomir thought as he looked at Liubomila. He closed his eyes and opened them again so as to see her all of a sudden afresh. As though she were the best vision in the world. As though the most important goddess in the world had appeared before him. But it was not just 'as though' he saw the goddess Liubomila before him. Radomir saw a goddess in real life.

The warm breath of Love enveloped the twosome and carried them away to heights unknown.

Nobody in a million years would ever be able to describe in detail what occurs between *him* and *her,* when people merge together into one for the purposes of co-creation and bring forth the image of themselves and of God in a mutual impulse of love.

But the god-people of the Vedruss culture knew for certain that when two people are joined together by an unexplainable miracle, each of them subsequently maintains his or her individuality. At the same time, the Universe shudders at that unexplainable moment upon seeing the vision of the infant's Soul tripping barefoot through the stars, making its way to the Earth, thereby embodying in itself the twain — plus a third — in one.

The dawn progressed into a happy day. And the Sun was rising over the Earth. It shone more brightly with its delicate ray on the spot where the gods stood on the Earth. And the energy of Love, God's gift to the earthly gods, illuminated them with a light greater than the Sun, invisible, radiating blessings. And the energy of Love celebrated in joy!

Is this energy intelligent? It is! Like all feelings — particles of mind — it was considered by God to be the most important of all. When the grand creation of the Earth was given birth by God, he told Love:

"Hasten, My Love, hasten, do not stop for rational contemplation. Hasten with your last spark. Envelop them with your great energy of grace — all My future sons and daughters in your embrace."[2]

And now, when Liubomila and Radomir's conception took place in love, Love called out to God:

"You are invisible, Great Creator. But Your children are visible. I too was invisible. Now my reflection on the faces of Your children I see. They are Yours and, in a way, mine to be. I want to nurse their children and understand how You, Great Creator, were able to foresee when you gave to them, as a gift from You, the whole of me. How You could likewise foresee earthly grace. Show Yourself in all Your beauty and grandeur for all Your children to see."

God responded to Love in a whisper of a barely noticeable breeze:

"I Myself would not presume to distract My children from their grand and inspired co-creation. And I beg you, My Love, do not burn these young hearts in an impulse of your own delight. I remember how with the grace of your energy you once set Me alight. I feel you are also burning our children with your delight."

"My God, I do not burn, I only warm them. When You said 'our children', I gave just a little shudder, and for a moment my energy in turn increased in me. But I restrained them, I declined to burn them. You distinctly said 'our children', which means they must also be, at least a little bit, mine."

"Those who are born in love will understand who their mother and father are."

[2]See Book 4, end of Chapter 6: "First encounter".

It might not be easy, Vladimir, to understand, but you must try. The intimate relations involved were by no means the lead factor in the Vedruss conception of children. What people do in bed today, calling it 'love-making', is a mere mockery of Love and a debasement of God. The satisfaction of fleshly needs lasts but for a moment, and I would venture to say that it cannot compare with even a hundredth part of what has been determined in God's plan for Man.

The Vedruss people did not see each other as an object of fleshly desire. They saw something quite different altogether.

When the desire came to Liubomila and Radomir to create a child, they did not see him as being separate from themselves. The culture of feelings was quite different in those times. The husband and wife, in their love, saw in each other their own child. And, consequently, their caresses were quite different from today. People were not drawn to each other by the passion of copulation, but by the grand aspiration to co-creation.

And Radomir embraced Liubomila almost as his own child. He tenderly stroked her hair with his hand, touched her supple breasts, gently caressed her shoulders and kissed the palms of her hands. Her hands touched his face and his shoulders. She tenderly clasped him by the neck and drew him to her breast as though comforting a child...

There are many treatises in the world which try to teach the subject of intimate copulation. But there never has been, and never will be, a treatise capable of outlining the Vedruss approach to conception.

The lovers' bodies were not the focus of attention. The bodies simply carried out people's will and desire. People at that moment found themselves living in a different dimension. When the great and worthy act was accomplished, they returned to the Earth. The satisfaction they derived was no fleeting fancy. It remained with them eternally, as though lifting Man one step higher in the direction of Divine perfection.

At the actual moment of conception, Radomir seemed to be in a state of oblivion, as though he had not yet returned from a dimension he had never known before. He kissed Liubomila as though she were his own child, and fell asleep in a blissful dream. Men cannot help but fall asleep, perhaps because of an innate desire to return there once again.

But Liubomila did not sleep. She felt within herself, or so it seemed, an extraordinary particle of being. She rose from the bed and went over to the window, where the Sun was streaming through, dividing the windowsill into bright and shady sections.

Liubomila ran over the line with her finger where the light and dark met. She took off the flaxen ribbon encircling her wrist and put it on the same line. The Vedruss people always marked the day and moment of conception.

Then on the spot where the wedding took place they planted a tree whose trunk would be sure to grow straight. A second tree was planted at the moment when the border between light and dark coincided with the flaxen ribbon marking on the windowsill. The second tree was planted in the shadow of the first. This act allowed them to forever remember the moment at which they conceived the child. A horoscope calculated from this point will always be more accurate. The Vedruss people knew about the positioning of the planets and their influence on the flesh; nevertheless, in spite of the planets, they were able to accomplish successful deeds, since it was a great energy that they possessed.

Subsequently they poured the birthing water there, and buried the placenta there in the earth. And when he got older, a Man would go to sleep in the same spot on the anniversary of his conception. The position of the planets slightly varied from year to year, and a Man could feel all the information coming from the Cosmos on the night of such a sleep — not with his mind, but rather with his feeling, in his subconsciousness — right up to God's creation of everything earthly. And if there were any sorrow or disease, the dream could eliminate it on the spot with ease. But only very rarely could any disease of the flesh affect the Vedruss people.

The place of conception served them as a place to sleep and to become consciously aware of the whole order of the Universe.

CHAPTER THIRTEEN

Telegony can be overcome

"Anastasia, I heard that the wise-men knew how to overcome the phenomenon of telegony, i.e., the consequences of previous relationships. If a woman has had a prior relationship, then the first man, as is now known, will undoubtedly exert an influence on the appearance and character of a child fathered by another man — the woman's husband, for example.

"If they go through the wedding rite you spoke of, does that mean that the consequences of the woman's previous relationship will be eliminated once and for all?"

"Vladimir, the child does not always have to resemble the previous partner. When the new events in the woman's life and the sensations of her feelings are sufficiently bright, the information about prior unsuccessful relations will be erased. Still, the Vedruss people had a rite which could help erase old, unwanted information. It purifies both the man and the woman, and three thoughts must participate. Whose thoughts those are, try to guess on your own."

"It would be better for you to tell me yourself, Anastasia. My brain is overtaxed as it is from too much information."

"Fine, I shall tell you. But it is very important that people learn to draw the conclusions they need for themselves."

"At some point they will learn, but for right now *you* had better explain it, seeing as how the question is so important."

"Then give me a full formulation of a question as to what interests you."

"What d'you mean, a 'full formulation'?"

"Vladimir, you are aware, are you not, that this phenomenon touches not only women, but, in equal measure, men.
A man's previous relationships can also exert an influence on
his future children. And the most upright and chaste girl can
bear a child which is not her own, if the man is not a virgin.
You know about that, Vladimir?"

"Yes, Anastasia, unfortunately I do. I read how one soldier
on his way home from army service had too much to drink at the
railway terminal and slept with an Asian prostitute. He came
back to his village and married a girl who had been waiting for
him. They produced a child who had swarthy skin and slanting
eyes. Everybody started blaming the girl, but there wasn't a
single Asian anywhere in the vicinity. I thought, though, that it
wasn't really that necessary to bring up the subject of men."

"It is *vitally* necessary to talk about men too. They are to
play the principal role in the rite.

"The rite consists in this. The man must set up their bed in
the open air under the stars on the spot where the couple live
in natural surroundings. He should prepare the bed for himself and the woman. They should fast for three days and sleep
three nights under the stars. And before they go to sleep, each
time the man should wash the woman and himself with spring
water. The man should rub the woman down with flaxen fabric, but not rub himself down, just get the water drops off
himself with his hands. The man should be still wet when he
lies down in the bed with the woman. During those three days
they should not let themselves indulge in intimate relations.

"While they are falling asleep under the stars, on the first
night they should forgive each other for all past transgres-
sions and right away, right from that very first night, visualise
their future child.

"The man should think about how their child should be
like the woman, and the woman about how the child should
resemble the man.

"After these three days have gone by, they are free to engage in fleshly intimacy, while the planets will erase all the information they might be harbouring about the past, about children that have never been conceived.

"But before entering into intimate relations, the man has an obligation to place a garland upon the woman's head. In the normal Vedruss wedding rite this is done by the girl: she places the crown on the head of her chosen one, but in this variant it is the man who is to crown the woman.

"This rite does not necessarily pertain to couples who have jointly sought out and found their own domain and have started to live in it."

"Why not?"

"The search itself, and the first three days of preparing the site, will purify them if they spend three days thinking of their future child without actually conceiving it... "

"Anastasia, what about the third thought? You did say three thoughts had to take part at the same time."

"Yes, I said that, and in the case we are looking at there *were* three thoughts. By the third night, while the man and woman were sleeping under the stars, they were already receiving help from the thought of their future child."

"And where might he have been?"

"Where all children await earthly embodiment before conception.

"So here, Vladimir, is the whole rite which a great wiseman came up with and freely offered to people. He himself rejoiced at how effective the rite proved to be, and there was a subsequent increase in the number of happy families.

"Did you understand everything, Vladimir, and can you now try your hand at telling people about this rite?"

"Of course, I understand, and I shall tell it all in time."

"And you will not add anything to this account of mine?"

"No, I shan't."

"Then I can say that the rite will not be effective."

"In what way? Why not?"

"There is no participation on the part of our ancestors' thought."

"Yes, I remember your grandfather saying that we need to apologise to them.[1] I shall remind my readers of this. Although it's still not entirely clear to me why it is up to our generation in particular to apologise. After all, *we* were not the ones responsible for hiding their culture from people's eyes, or for its demise."

"Of course one could think that '*we* are not to blame'. But it would be better if a different thought came to mind."

"A different thought? What kind?"

"Upon our generation has fallen the great honour and grace of restoring the culture of our forebears, to bind up the torn threads that have remained, linking us with them. Only then will great discoveries begin to take place among mankind. Only then will their thoughts be able to help ours. For now, their thoughts — in view of our lack of understanding — feel constrained to withstand us.

---

[1] See the reference to 'repentance' in Chapter 5: "Conception involves more than flesh" above.

CHAPTER FOURTEEN

The psychology of Man's genesis and appearance in the world

In regard to this question, I have to say right off that according to Anastasia's information, the process of conception and carrying a child — as well as its appearance in the world as a Man — is not primarily a physiological, but a psychological one. It is the highest form of joint creation between a man and a woman. It is the apex of achievement of their thoughts, feelings and intellect.

Initially such an affirmation met with some scepticism on my part, as, indeed, I think, on the part of many of my readers. So I shall reproduce here my more detailed dialogue with her on this topic.

"Anastasia, how can you say that it is mainly psychological? After all, it's a real material fœtus that develops in the mother's womb. The woman experiences actual physiological sensations, sometimes even painful ones. There have been lots of popular scientific books written on the subject of carrying a child and its appearance in the world, and these often go into great detail about what a pregnant woman should do, how she should act on a physiological level. When you come right down to it, physiology is primary, after all."

"Yes, sadly, such an opinion has indeed been thoroughly rooted in human society. It means that the principal component of the human self has been either relegated to the background or eliminated completely. The result is that people have come into the world who are, in essence, quite the opposite of God's likeness.

"Think about it, Vladimir: the fœtus in the mother's womb lives and develops not because someone has written a bunch of treatises on the subject, but because this was the original thought of the Creator — indeed, of Nature. To interfere with this eminently perfect process is tantamount to replacing what is natural and perfect by something that is artificial and less perfect.

"The *physiology* involved in the formation of human flesh was pre-programmed by the Creator and is quite capable of developing all by itself, without bothering the mother or father with a need to control this process.

"On the other hand, the *psychology and philosophy* of birth — a process on an immeasurably higher level — is wholly dependent on the mother and father. It is a joint creation by Man and God.

"The appearance of pain at the moment of birth is a sign of an erroneous psychological approach to the birth process on the part of the parents.

"Many, many animals give birth to their offspring in natural surroundings and none of them perish or experience suffering. Nor did the Creator come up with any thought of pain for His most beloved creation, Man. Just as loving parents would never conjure up the thought of pain for their children.

"As she fulfils her highest purpose — that of co-creating God's Man — the woman who has carried the Divine child within herself receives a reward ordained by the Creator. This reward is the feeling of bliss and the chain of joyful ecstasies during labour, but certainly not pain. Quite to the contrary, the process of giving birth to a Man should be a joyful and pleasant one.

"It is Man himself, deceived by the occult sciences and suggestions from the dark side, who by his own intrusion has made childbirth painful for the mother and a fatal shock for the baby."

"What's this about a shock, Anastasia — a shock fatal for the baby at that? The baby just gets born."

"Yes, it gets born, but it does not understand why it is being so rudely torn out of its pleasant and perfect Space and why its mother suffers and experiences pain. The mother's pain occasions untold mourning on the part of the child."

"What, is it possible for a mother to give birth without any pain at all?"

"Not only is it possible without pain, but with a supreme and most pleasing joy and delight!"

"You know, Anastasia, our modern medicine is equipped to do just that — it can guarantee an almost painless childbirth with the help of anæsthetics."

"Anæsthetics can lessen the mother's physical pain, Vladimir, but they increase the mental pain for the infant, since anæsthetics cut him off from contact with his mother. Such a state instils in him fear and a lack of self-confidence, which continue even into adulthood, even into his most advanced years. They prevent him from being born again."

"But why does something like that happen?"

"When a Man is living in his mother's womb, he feels a coziness there — he feels comforted, cared for, peaceful. On the physical plane his needs are completely met. He is free of the problems plaguing Man in everyday life, he is allowed to experience the whole order of the Universe.

"Over the nine months all the information about the marvellous order of the Universe, about Man's purpose right from the beginning of creation, is imparted to him.

"The world he knows inside his mother's womb is vast and marvellous.

"And then all of a sudden, something rudely tries to thrust him out of this world of supreme grace. Every woman knows: this means the labour has begun — an inevitability, or so it seems — and hence people do not think about the effect it

might have on the infant. Few women in today's world realise that they do not have to frighten their baby — on the
contrary, they can caress their child during labour, talk with
it, express their thoughts to it, invite it to be born into the
world. And this need not be accompanied by any sensation
of stress or pain.

"After hearing the call of his mother and father, the child
will perceive the labour contractions as a caress — an invitation to make his appearance of his own free will, to explore a
world that is brand new to him.

"*To be born of his own free will* — that is an indication of great
and extraordinary significance. All the information imparted
by God during a birth like this will be preserved in him.

"When the woman experiences fear over her labour, this
fear is felt by the child in the womb.

"When the woman experiences pain from her labour trou-
ble and has thoughts only for herself, the child in the womb
experiences *double* the amount of pain. He feels abandoned,
and, above all, helpless and defenceless. Such feelings are
harmful, and they are lasting. They wipe out the information
the child has earlier received about the grand Creation, since
they are in contradiction to it. In this kind of birth, the child
feels for the first time in his life that he is not the master of
the Universe, but a worthless nonentity, subject to some kind
of external forces.

"His body is born, but the spirit of mastery and of a kind
creator is not born in him. Such a Man will not become the
likeness of the Divine. A mere slave of some other entity he
will remain, and he will try his whole lifetime to free himself
from slavery, but in vain.

"Earthly tsars, presidents, along with their bodyguards and
service staff, are likewise the slaves of circumstance. They
think they are deciding something of importance, and try to
make their life a happy one, but life for them only becomes

more and more unhappy and hopeless, like the ever deeper blackening of both the air and the water.

"This thought of hopelessness suggested at the birth by pain, interferes with human society's ability to make the right decisions."

"Yes, Anastasia, a birth like that presents a very scary picture. Maybe that's why some women today opt for a Cæsarean section? That would prevent something like that from happening, eh?"

"It still happens. One could hardly explain such a procedure as the birth of a Man — it is more like a routine operation. Who is thereby causing the Man to emerge into the world — the mother, who has not given birth to the child, or the surgeon, who has torn the fœtus out of the mother's body?

"The infant, who has not yet appeared in the world, suddenly loses contact with his mother and, consequently, with the whole order of the grand Creation. Then he is forcibly torn from the womb. What for? Whereto? And why so rudely? And why is he not in charge of anything himself? The whole world crashes before him!

"People believe a child is born into the world, while he, at the moment of birth, feels himself forlorn. And while it seems as though this infant Man has thrived, what has remained alive, in fact, is only his flesh. He will try to use what paltry remains he can reclaim of his spiritual substance to search for his Divine self throughout his life. And for this only his father and mother are to blame."

"Anastasia, as I understand it, it is on the women and on the way they carry and birth their children that the whole future of their offspring, not to mention the future of human civilisation, depends. Is that true?"

"Yes, it is true, Vladimir. But no less — in fact, in equal measure — does human birth depend on the *men,* on the fathers."

When a man brings a child into the world...

"Hold on, hold on there, Anastasia. Explain what you mean when you say 'a man brings a child into the world'. After all, men cannot actually give birth. They are physically incapable of giving birth."

"There is a trap hidden in there, you see, Vladimir. In accepting the suggestion that birth is mainly a physiological procedure, the majority of people have thereby excluded the Great Spirit, the Father-Creator, from the birth process. More specifically, they have excluded God the Father from the birthing mother's labour. It was God's absence that first got reflected in the woman in the form of labour pains, and subsequently of general human suffering."

"Can you explain in more detail the *man*'s role in the labour? And why is excluding him tantamount to excluding God? Should the father, or the man, attend to his wife's labour?"

"It is quite unnecessary for the man to *attend* to the labour. It is sufficient for him to be by her side, but that is not the father's main purpose."

"But what, then, *is* his main purpose?"

"To comprehend that, you must realise that the mother's womb nourishes the flesh of the fœtus conceived in her from her beloved male partner. It feeds the flesh, and that is important indeed, but it is not *the* most important factor.

"The fœtus reacts to the condition and feelings not only of the mother, but in equal measure to those of the father.

"When a husband talks with his pregnant wife, the fœtus conceived does not understand the parents' words, it does not really comprehend the meaning of the words uttered to their full extent, but acutely perceives the *feelings* of the parents.

"Sometimes a man is led by an impulse of tender feelings to caress his pregnant wife's tummy or to put his ear to it and hear the baby's movements. Caresses like that are pleasing to the woman, but the fœtus inside her, it would seem, does not perceive them physically, but it feels them on an immeasurably greater level.

"The feelings of the baby's mother and father come to him in a flood. He receives them with great joy, with supreme bliss.

"On the level of feelings, the fœtus takes account of *thoughts* as well. When parents wait for their child in love and harmony and keep thinking about him, then from the very moment of conception he constantly dwells in the father's and mother's energy field, and this is very pleasing to him.

"It is through the mother's and father's feelings that the child feels the surrounding world outside his mother's womb.

"If a father at his pregnant wife's side hears and exults in the song of a nightingale, the fœtus in the mother's womb will feel both the song and the father's joy. After he is born and grows up, he will continue to delight in the nightingale's song, just as he did in the womb.

"If the father or mother suddenly takes fright upon beholding a serpent, the child, once born, will be frightened at the same sight, too. In the womb, of course, he could not actually *see* the serpent, but through what his parents see, the information about it will be stored in his subconscious throughout his life.

"When a father, Vladimir, skilfully sings songs to his pregnant wife, their infant will sing no worse than his father as he grows up. If a father starts contemplating the stars in his mind, their offspring after birth will show an interest in the stars."

"I have also heard, Anastasia, of how a certain composer played the piano for his pregnant wife, repeating over and over again a tune he had composed which had caught his wife's fancy. But later the composer divorced his wife before the birth of their son.

"When the child had grown a bit, his mother put him in a music school. And one day she heard him performing his father's tune. The amazed mother decided that her son had somewhere discovered an old musical score, since this tune had never been performed at any concert, and the score had never been published. But upon entering the piano room, she saw that he was playing without any score at all. She asked her son:

"'Who taught you to play this piece, son?'

"'Nobody,' the boy replied. 'I just heard it somewhere, but I can't remember where. I like it. What about you, Mama?'

"'I like it, too, very much,' replied the woman, and asked her son how he could have memorised it, since in school he had never started playing new works right off, even from a score.

"'No, never right away, but this one took hardly any time at all to learn by heart, for some reason. It just seemed to be inside me. I want to continue it, and add to it in the same key.'

"The boy continued to develop his father's melody which he had heard in his mother's womb. Like his father, he too eventually became a composer."[1]

---

[1] A very similar experience is recounted by Boris Brott, former conductor of the Hamilton Symphony Orchestra in Ontario (Canada), who as a young musician found himself able to play certain pieces sight unseen. It turned out these were pieces his mother, a professional cellist, had played during her pregnancy. His experience is cited by Toronto psychiatrist Thomas Verny in his book *The secret life of the unborn child* (New York: Random House, 1981), pp. 22–23.

"That is a good example you cited, Vladimir, and it is by no means the only one. Many examples point to the fact that child-raising effectively begins right from the mother's womb. And even a little bit earlier, before the conception even takes place."

"What d'you mean, earlier? Prior to conception, after all, there isn't anybody there yet."

"Remember, you were telling me about telegony, Vladimir, about how a child born to a woman may resemble the first man in her life, rather than the father with whom the material conception took place. This very phenomenon attests to the fact that someone who is not yet conceived, but just waiting his turn in the conception queue, can 'read' information about the father."

"Is there really such a thing as a conception queue?"

"There is. Just as soon as intimacy occurs between a man and woman, a spirit is born in space, ready for a material embodiment."

"What, even if they're just having sex for fun, without any thought of childbearing?"

"The spirit appears whenever the man experiences satisfaction."

"You mean, orgasm?"

"I do not like that word, Vladimir. It implies information which gives a false impression of the essence of the act."

"Okay, let's just call it satisfaction. But is there any way you can prove the existence of this spirit?"

"You yourself can find the proof, Vladimir, if you wish. After all, one person may grasp the essence of this phenomenon from just a few words spoken, while another may require years, even after being presented with a multitude of examples, and even then may still be reluctant to understand."

"Well, can modern science offer at least indirect proofs of what you are saying?"

"Of course."

"What kind of science — biology, genetics? To tell the truth, I need to know, so that I can more easily search for proofs."

"You will easily be able to find them in physics, Vladimir."

"In *physics*? What's physics got to do with it? You were talking about the spiritual — maybe I could try esoterics, but *physics*?"

"In physics there is a law of conservation of energy."

"And what's that law got to do with it?"

"During intimacy with a woman an unusually powerful energy builds up inside the man, and the moment comes when he releases it. According to the law of conservation of energy, it cannot simply disappear without a trace, but is capable of mutating from one state into another. In the situation we are talking about, it is precisely the man's colossal energy and the lightning speed at which it is released that forms a spirit."[2]

"Yes, I can agree with that. But at the same time it's sad. How many spirits have men formed that haven't ever obtained a material embodiment! They probably number many times more than the population of the Earth!"

"Yes, many times more."

"Do they suffer, or do they just stay as senseless energy?"

"They have feelings. Their suffering is monumental."

"What about the spirits that are conceived? Do they begin right off to feel their parents?"

---

[2]One of the most prominent scientists to study energy released during orgasm from the physical standpoint was the Austrian-American psychiatrist Wilhelm Reich (1897–1957). He named this universal life force *orgone* (from *orgasm*) and was even able to build working apparatuses capable of accumulating it and using it for therapy. In 1956 he was arrested and thrown into prison, where he died the following year. His orgone accumulators were destroyed by the US government and his books burnt, including his monumental work *The function of the orgasm: Discovery of the orgone* (New York: Farrar, Straus and Giroux, 1986).

"Yes, right away. And they feel their father and mother in equal measure.

"Over the nine months in the mother's womb the parents can teach the living child a great deal. Such lessons need no repetition. The child will instantly memorise, with life-long retention, any information imparted by his parents.

"A father who possesses a thorough knowledge can 'carry' or shape, as it were, his child's spiritual and intellectual self.

"It is the father in particular who is responsible for the higher-level components of Man, and in this his role is indeed Godlike in nature.

"It is the father who gives birth to the Man's spiritual component. Fathers should spend the whole gestation period compiling the programme which shapes the spirit, character and intellect of the future Man."

"You are talking, Anastasia, in terms of a 'programme', of a father who has a thorough knowledge of the procedure of raising a child still in the mother's womb...?"

"I am not talking about the father *raising* his child, but about *giving birth*. The father does not do any 'raising' per se, but simply gives birth to the second, non-material self of his future son or daughter."

"I would say that we don't have any concept of that at all in our society. Our loss, no doubt. It is considered that the principal role of the father in a child's birth is finished after conception. Thereafter, in the best-case scenario, the father helps his pregnant wife with household tasks, makes sure all her needs are met."

"Unfortunately, that is all too often true."

"But, Anastasia, who then forms the Man's main spiritual component if the father doesn't understand his role in this?"

"Either circumstances, or someone who knows about it and uses it to forward his own agenda."

"So it turns out that men who are ignorant of the possibility of full participation in the formation of their future child right from conception are not raising their children in the fullest sense of the word?"

"Unfortunately, Vladimir, that indeed happens all too often."

It seems I have only just begun to understand the significance of what Anastasia has said, which in turn has showed me the whole absurdity of our way of life. It may be that all our social upheavals are the result of the fact that the overwhelming majority of us, even when we are together with our children, have little in the way of a relationship to them in practice. We abandon them to the whim of fate, hand them over to somebody else. But at the moment I was having my conversation with Anastasia on this subject, it was not societal but rather personal circumstances that were calling forth sad feelings in me — hopelessly sad, perhaps — feelings that will remain with me my whole life. I didn't even feel like continuing the conversation.

"You have gone pale, Vladimir," Anastasia observed, noticing my condition. "Your eyes have dimmed. Why?"

"I have no strength left to talk about it, Anastasia."

"I have a good idea of what has happened to you. But you will feel better if you can describe the cause of your unhappiness on your own."

"What is there to describe? It's perfectly obvious. When I realised the importance of the information you gave about childbirth, it made me realise, too, that I had not participated sufficiently in the birth of my own daughter, Polina. But back then neither my wife nor I had any idea of how we should relate to the question of childbirth.

"But *you*, Anastasia, had knowledge of this information. You bore a son, and a daughter, and I, it turns out, am once more on the sidelines. You knew this, and still, you didn't tell me in time what a father's supposed to do. Not only that, but I remember you telling me that I shouldn't see my son at all for some time, even after his appearance in the world. What did you do that for?"

"Yes, I did say that to you, Vladimir. But think about it yourself: what would you have begun to teach your son if you had stayed the nine months with me in the taiga? Do you want me to give you a hint as to the answer?"

"Go ahead."

"You remember, you asked me at that time to leave my family glade in the taiga, my Space of Love, which my parents had formed for me. You wanted me to give birth in a city, in a hospital. Then you said we had to send our son to kindergarten and the best schools, that you would make him into a businessman and that he would carry on your business."

"Yes, I did say that, but there was a lot I didn't know back then. Afterward I finally accepted that you would never be able to, or never want to, live in the city, but still, you did not invite me to stay with you in the taiga."

"If I had suggested it, would you have stayed?"

"I don't know, but quite possibly I would have."

"And what would you have done?"

"Like anyone else, I would have found some man's work to do around the home."

"But you should know, Vladimir, that I do not need any physical assistance. Everything here is all ready for willing service: the air, the water, the beasts and the grass. I asked about your activities in the hopes of finding out the most important thing, namely, where would your thoughts have been while awaiting the arrival of our son?...

"So, you have nothing to say. After all, your thoughts were just like your words back then.

"And you might have regretted that you did not succeed in persuading me to live in the city. You even had a plan in mind of taking me by force to give birth in a hospital. Yes? Admit it!"

"Well, yes, I did, but it didn't last very long."

"Now tell me, Vladimir, just how was our son supposed to react to such thoughts coming from his father? Such aggressive thoughts, besides."

"Yes, I see now, it wouldn't have been very good for him. And still, I'm sad that now I... In any case, it turns out that I'm not a fully-fledged father. And that means that you bore a son, and a daughter, too, who are not completely Man."

"Trust me, Vladimir, and don't be upset, and don't be sad. You *are* a fully-fledged father to our children. And our children have received everything in full measure. It turns out that our son is even a little overloaded with information and sensitivity — at one point my great-grandfather Moisey was not able to restrain himself and told him more than he should have."

"But how so? I wasn't with you during your pregnancy. I didn't compile any programme, I wasn't present at the birth, I did not invite my children to be born, yet you still say that I've come out a fully-fledged father. A moment ago, you were arguing quite the opposite."

CHAPTER FIFTEEN

A rite for a woman giving birth without a husband

"The Vedruss civilisation, Vladimir, had a great many rites. The word *rite*[1] is not entirely appropriate for such acts, but I simply cannot think of an alternative. Let us use it for the sake of brevity, only you must understand that in today's language the Vedruss 'rite' could easily be termed a scientific and rational act on the part of Man, one grounded in the knowledge of all the diverse energies of the Universe and their interrelationship with Man's soul. These rites, as you know, were thought out by generations of wise-men and enlightened thinkers, who also connected them with the stars. Subsequent generations checked their effectiveness in practice and perfected them as the years went by.

"One of these rites was for women who were carrying and giving birth to a child far from their husbands. Such situations did exist in the Vedruss civilisation, albeit rarely. It might happen that a woman's husband was obliged to go on a long trek somewhere. His pregnant wife left at home carried out an outwardly simple rite, but one which lasted a long time and was very complex in terms of the mind and will. If the woman's love for the child's father was strong, she achieved

[1]The Russian word for 'rite', *obriad* (pron. *abr-YAT*), is derived from the verb *obriazhat'* ('to dress, enrobe'), and initially signified 'to dress [a spiritual concept into a material form]', referring to an action (or symbol) based on deep spiritual insights and giving an actual physical embodiment to these insights.

her goal on her own and bore a fully-fledged child. She was assisted in this by the great energy of Love."

"What actions did this rite involve, specifically? In our modern-day society there are also women who are obliged to carry a child and then give birth without their husbands around. Maybe the rite you speak of would apply to them."

"Over the nine-month period, a pregnant woman whose husband is absent should spend at least three hours a day communicating with her child in the father's name — sometimes also conversing mentally with the father about the future child. They might argue, but under no circumstances should they allow any suggestion of aggression to enter in, even during an argument. The parents' dialogue should always proceed in a spirit of good will both toward each other and toward the child.

"The dialogue should preferably take place at the same time each day. The woman's communication with the child in the father's name may be divided into two segments — evening and morning. Approximately fifteen to nineteen minutes before engaging in this kind of mental dialogue, the woman should definitely take a small amount of easily digestible food or drink, which will be healthful both to her and to the child.

"The drink taken in preparation for the mental dialogue should not vary over the course of the nine months, and should not be used in any other circumstance or for any other purpose.

"I, for example, prepared a drink consisting of about a hundred grams of cedar milk, three drops of cedar oil and a pinch of pollen. I also took a little honey on a twig, mixed everything together in a wooden bowl and drank it in tiny swallows.

"The drink could also be made from other substances, only they must definitely be natural, ecologically clean and easily digestible by the mother's body, as well as healthful and pleasing to the child in the womb. This is very important. If the mother's drink is not healthful or pleasing to the child, he will associate the dialogue with his father with an unpleasant phenomenon and afterward reject his father and resist communicating with him.

"After the birth of the child the woman should take the same drink shortly before a feeding at which she plans to communicate with her nursling in the father's name.

"If the father does not return by the time the child ceases to take his mother's milk, the mother's drink should never be given to the child until the moment of his first contact with his father.

"The woman also needs to choose a star in the heavens through which to communicate with her beloved man. A star to think upon each time before initiating a mental dialogue with her child.

"In this mental communication, the woman should formulate as distinctly as possible a thought-picture of the child's father — his character, intonations and world-view — without falsification or embellishing any details. If she has a difference of opinion with him, she should try to explain her point of view, not aggressively but lovingly. Instead of blaming the *man* for the misunderstanding, she should point the finger to herself as incapable of setting forth thoughts understandably and convincingly.[2] Or possibly she should think more carefully about what her husband has said.

"In addition, during her dialogue the pregnant woman should stroke her tummy while cherishing an image of the father in her thought.

"And it is very important, while conversing mentally with her husband, to rule out all negative aspects that might have

[2]Compare Anastasia's dialogue with her great-grandfather in Book 2, Chapter 7: "Who's to blame?".

occurred earlier. It is vital to remember only the good while communicating with him.

"The woman should spend as much as possible of the nine-month period in real solitude. Then the child will feel both her and his father. And if the husband and father is not physically present, the child will still find himself in his father's aura.

"If the woman carries out the aspects of this rite, the man will come back to her and to their child. Even if earlier his love was weak, or was not there at all, love will flare up in him with unaccustomed strength, and provoke him to good deeds.

"Many Vedruss women knew the effectiveness and power of this rite. Later the wise-men tried to erase it from women's memories and turn to it only when they were confident that the woman was not harbouring any perverse feelings."

"What kind of perverse feelings, Anastasia?"

"A woman in love could, through the help of this rite, seduce a man who was not in love with her — even if he were living with another wife and even if they had not had intimate relations."

"But how could it happen if they had not had intimacy? Without intimacy a child could not have been conceived at all, and, in that case, who could she talk to about a father?"

"No matter what man she conceived with, she might try communicating with her child in the name of her most beloved, thereby drawing this man closer to herself. Not only that, but the child will even outwardly bear a greater resemblance to her most beloved, rather than the man who was actually with her. You should know that, Vladimir, from the phenomenon of telegony."[3]

"Yes, I know, Anastasia, but why are *you* giving out this information that the wise-men suppressed? Now some women

[3]See Chapter 5: "Conception involves more than flesh" above.

will start luring men they fancy away from their families with the help of this rite. It shouldn't be published."

"You needn't be concerned about publishing it, Vladimir. I purposely left one particular aspect out of my description. Now it will not destroy any happy families."

"But if you were able to leave out some aspect, why didn't the wise-men do the same?"

"The wise-men did not know what to put in its place."

"If the wise-men didn't know, how could you possibly know? Besides, Anastasia, you said that the wise-men always checked the effectiveness of their rites in practice. But you didn't have the opportunity to do that."

"I did."

"When? With whom?"

Oh, God! I remembered Anastasia's words from many years ago. I didn't pay much attention to them back then, but now... She said:

"I shall restore to you the respect of your daughter and the love of your wife."[4]

It's incredible, but she did it! But why, then, is my wife not jealous of Anastasia? And why does my daughter have such respect for her? I went back to see my family this year. Anastasia was able to perform the incredible! I don't know how she did it, but she did it.

All our earthly institutions taken together — institutions that pride themselves on their technological achievements — are incapable of solving the number one problem on the Earth: *how to restore love and respect to families.* But she can. Oh, Lord! What colossal, truly Divine knowledge mankind is losing! Why? Who can give an answer?

---

[4]Originally conveyed through Anastasia's grandfather. See Book 2, Chapter 26: "Anastasia's grandfather".

And what strength of love Anastasia herself is worthy of! What she has accomplished will probably be appreciated more by our descendants than by people today. I felt like doing something very nice for her. I went over to Anastasia, got down on one knee and kissed her hand. She also got down on her knees and embraced my neck. I heard her heart beating, and sensed the extraordinary aroma of her hair, her intoxicating breath, the fragrance of mother's milk as though it was coming from my own mother's breast, and I whispered:

"What can I do to be worthy of you, Anastasia?"

But she didn't answer, only pressed my head a little more strongly to her breast. My life has probably never been blessed with happier seconds, hours or days than these.

Chapter Sixteen

Where should we have our babies?

How hard it is to write in a dry style, and yet it is absolutely necessary to determine, without agitation or emotion, where the best and most comfortable place is for parents and infants to go through the birthing process. In a hospital operation room or a home setting?

As far as I know, the first maternity homes appeared during the period of slavery in Ancient Egypt and Rome, where they were organised for pregnant slaves.

A birthing slave-mother stayed from five to nine days with her baby before returning to work. She was allowed access to her child for nursing and at nighttime. This continued from six to twelve months. It was different in different places, depending on how the slavemasters treated their slaves. After being weaned from its mother, the child was taken care of by specially trained slave-nurses. Later, when the child had grown, he would go off to be raised by other slaves, depending on the function designated for him by the overlord.

For example, boys might be handed over to specialists to be trained as warriors. After going through special physical training and psychological conditioning, these warriors, who knew not their parents, proved to be the most loyal to their slavemaster. They were brainwashed from childhood to consider him as father and mother — in short, God. There was even a religion worked out especially for the purpose of this brainwashing.

How close seems this situation from antiquity to our reality today! A maternity home — nursery — kindergarten —

school — college — and presto, the slave is ready. But since the slavemaster is invisible, the slave thinks he is free and, consequently, will not rebel.

The *élite* of Ancient Rome and Egypt, and even their middle classes, couldn't begin to imagine, even in their wildest nightmares, the birth of their own children outside the home.

They would first call in midwives, later doctors and soothsayers.

In Russia the first huts for birthing mothers were designated for prostitutes. Sometimes this category of women went off to give birth in a gypsy camp, where they would leave their unwanted children to be raised by the gypsies. The gypsies accepted them.

A 'maternity home' — or a maternity ward in a hospital — is utter nonsense. It is clear testimony to the loss of women's instinct to continue the family line, as well as to modern Man's ignorance, not only of his pristine origins but even of the fundamental culture of feelings — his loss of feelings of true love for his wife and child as being a part of himself and his legacy.

A child born in an institution cannot be exclusively yours. He belongs to someone else besides. The birthing process includes conception, carrying to term and the appearance of the infant in the world. And the last stage is no less significant than the rest. If you hand him over to strangers who are completely indifferent to both you and your offspring, then you have less than a full relationship to the birth. Consequently, you will not have fatherly feelings for him in full measure, and he will feel this, and afterward requite it with an absence of strong filial feelings toward you.

More than that, the love will not be what it could. Such a child will not be able to love — not just his parents, but life itself, since life was never, right from the moment of his appearance in the world, presented to him as something attractive.

Of course this lacuna can be compensated for by means of certain behaviour toward the newborn, but that is by no means easy.

The birthing of children among different peoples of the world can be considered more and more perfect the farther we go back in history, and primitive in the absurd today. In our modern world it has become tantamount to removing the appendix from the body of a sick person.[1]

And so I should now like to switch to a brighter note. In spite of everything, mankind is beginning to ponder the meaning of what has been happening.

In Russia, America and France, so-called 'schools of spiritual midwifery' have sprung up. There is also an organisation known as the 'Association for Prenatal Education' active in a number of countries.

Courses on home births are being offered in Moscow and St Petersburg. People are trying to bring back the knowledge and traditions they have lost — the *love* they have lost.

Let us see how the birthing process took place in Vedruss families. According to Anastasia's account, it went as follows.

---

[1]An evident reference to a Cæsarean section, which in many Russian hospitals today is used in more than half of all births.

CHAPTER SEVENTEEN

The Vedruss birth

The birthing mother's mama and grandma would tell her what symptoms to expect on the eve of her labour. Liubomila's grandmother, in this instance, told her in detail how she gave birth to her own children.[1]

Vedruss women as a rule gave birth in their own homes, in a wooden tub, something like our bathtub, only shorter in length and not as deep. It was a container designed especially for childbirth. Afterward it served as a cradle for the new-born.

To start, it was filled with pure spring water, heated to body temperature. There were little ledges on the outside of the tub which served as footrests.

The edges of the tub were curved so that it was easy for the woman to support herself with her hands. The air temperature in the room was not measured with a thermometer back then. They said it should feel comfortable for a naked body in a state of repose, with no sensation of either heat or cold.

The tub for birthing mothers was placed on the floor and oriented so that the woman sitting in it would be facing toward the rising Sun. Another smaller container of water was placed beside it. On the bench next to the tub lay four plain, smooth-textured flaxen towels (without embroidery or designs).

---

[1]The first part of this chapter and the following two chapters are told in Anastasia's words, without identifying quotation-marks.

During a Vedruss birth only the husband was to be present in the room with a birthing mother. Even the couple's parents and close relatives, as well as experienced midwives, were excluded.

Just before labour began, the child's father would light a fire he had already prepared at the outer entrance to the domain, from which wafted sweet-smelling smoke. This was where the close relatives usually gathered, along with the midwife, and often a wise-man.

The birthing mother's and her husband's parents would bring in bundles and baskets of food and drink. They would sit down on benches under a tent-roof which had been set up earlier next to the fire-pit by the husband. Vedruss tradition forbade them from crossing the line into the domain. Nor was the birthing mother's husband permitted to go out to them, or even to talk with them at a distance.

Such rules were not the product of some kind of superstition, but the result of finely tuned psychological calculations. Nobody and nothing was supposed to distract the thought of the father, let alone the birthing mother, from the reception of their child.

The presence of the parents and midwife at the entrance to the domain, however, had a calming effect on the young parents-to-be. In case any abnormalities cropped up, they could always come in to help. But there was rarely a need for such assistance.

During the contractions the mother would constantly talk with her emerging child, giving him words of encouragement, helping him enter upon his new world without fear. The Vedruss people well knew how important it was to communicate both mentally and audibly with the new Man as he emerged into the world. As a result, all three — mother, child and father — were participants in the process.

It was also very important that the mother's first look at her newborn be without any fright at his appearance (a temporarily snubbed nose, for example, or the birth-colour of his skin), that her gaze be tender and joyous.

The father would pick up the baby out of the water he had been born in, use his own mouth right off to suck the mucus out of his little mouth and nose, and place him on his mother's tummy. The mother would then offer the baby her breast. This prompted the expulsion of the placenta, which the father placed in a specially prepared container, before cutting the umbilical cord with a knife which had been disinfected over a flame, and tying it.

Then the father took the baby and placed him on a towel. After washing him, he wrapped him up in a second towel and placed him on the bed. Then he washed his wife's body, using water from the other container next to the tub, dried her off with a clean towel and led her over to the bed where the baby lay.

Next the father, using either his mouth or his hands, strained off a small quantity of milk from the mother's breast and sprayed it over a flaxen sheet, with which he covered the new mother and the infant lying on her tummy or breast.

After that, the father sat down and gazed silently at his wife. If she desired, he would talk with her, but even if she were asleep, he would not leave the room.

About fifteen minutes later, he would light the wood-fire he had earlier prepared in the hearth.

He would then pour out the birthing water, as well as the water the woman had used to wash herself, between the two trees which had been planted soon after conception. Here, too, was where the placenta would be buried.

The relatives that had gathered at the entrance to the domain would see the smoke from the chimney and understand this, along with the father's actions, to signal that the birth had taken place successfully. At this point they began exchanging congratulations and partaking of the food and drink they had brought with them, after which they dispersed to their homes.

The Vedruss people understood that even in the womb the child could sense relatives' thoughts and feelings. And after coming into the world, he would continue to find himself in his parents' aura. If some kind of outsiders, even a relative with good thoughts about the child, happened to be in the birthing room, their feelings — even good ones — would be unfamiliar to the child, and put him on the defensive.

Besides, either deliberately or inadvertently, the relatives might distract the parents' thought from the infant. It was in the parents' mental field, after all, that the baby would feel the most comfortable.

A little experiment should help prove what Anastasia has said here.

Many women are aware that during breast-feeding they should not allow themselves to be distracted by random conversations and thoughts, especially on negative topics. They are concentrating their whole attention on their child, on his feeding, and mentally conversing with him.

For evidence that the baby really does feel the mother's thought, try entering the room where a mother is nursing her baby and strike up a conversation with her. The baby will at once feel uneasy, and may even stop his sucking and start to cry. He has become uncomfortable, and his Mama's thoughts about him have weakened or have wandered off somewhere.

But perhaps the baby was simply disturbed by the stranger's voice or odour?

I telephoned my daughter Polina. She picked up the receiver and started talking with me. Thirty seconds into the conversation I heard the cry of my granddaughter Mashenka.[2]

"Why is she crying?" I asked my daughter.

"I'm breast-feeding her, Papa," Polina responded. "She doesn't like it when I'm distracted."

I tried to end the conversation quickly. I did the same whenever I rang at an inopportune moment. My granddaughter would always start crying.

Many nursing mothers who are familiar with the culture of breast-feeding will confirm this phenomenon. But it does not happen, as a rule, with children of mothers who are unaware of the importance of mental contact with their nursling, who chat away at feeding time with all and sundry or spend the time thinking about their own problems. Why not? Because their child has no concept of mental contact with his mother. It is something he never had, and so has no point of comparison.

There's an old saying: *He took it in with his mother's milk.* What are our babies today taking in with their mother's milk?

Human society has learnt to create all sorts of satellites and intercontinental ballistic missiles. Yet at the same time it has lost something more important — the culture of giving birth to and raising Man. As a result, people end up aiming these missiles at each other.

Now what possible connection could there be between the culture of prenatal education, the breast-feeding of children and wars? A most direct connection, indeed!

---

[2]*Mashenka* (stress on first syllable) — an endearing variant of the name *Maria* (corresponding to *Mary* in English).

Many still remember the account of the Rostov serial killer Chikatilo.[3] He performed sadistic acts on young women and then killed them. Such maniacs have appeared in many other cities, terrorising the populace. Each time hundreds of policemen are despatched to hunt down and capture the killer.

But an interesting pattern emerges from this. It has been established that in the case of three Rostov maniacs, at least, their mothers had all made unsuccessful attempts to abort their fœtuses in the womb. As a result, when the fœtus was born and grew into manhood, it then began taking revenge against women.

Now tell me which is more important for high-school graduates: to get high marks in physics, chemistry and a foreign language, or to acquire a high knowledge of the culture of the conception, carrying and raising of a child?

I would say the latter is by far the more important. And yet the disciplines which present such knowledge are not even taught in the school curriculum. Hence there are graduates of schools, colleges and universities who give birth to children which they have conceived haphazardly. They often reflect on whether to give birth at all, or perhaps an abortion would be better?

They may end up giving birth, only what kind of babies are they giving birth to? The kind that not only should not be exposed to the achievements of physicists and chemists, but should even be kept as far away as possible from knives and sticks.

The birth of advanced spiritual thinkers is especially important in this age of scientific and technological progress.

---

[3] *Andrei Romanovich Chikatilo* (1936–1994) — a Russian serial killer in the city of Rostov-on-Don, who was convicted of murdering 52 women (mainly prostitutes) and children between 1978 and 1990.

It is a tragedy when a maniac like Chikatilo kills and tortures women. It is a blessing that nobody like him is sitting at the controls of nuclear missiles.

A blessing — a blessing, okay — but the caveat must be added: *for now.* The worst *will happen* if society does not change its attitude toward the culture of giving birth to Man.

Anastasia continued:

With their knowledge of this culture, Radomir and Liubomila effected the transition of their first-born son from his mother's womb to his new world quite smoothly and painlessly. Possibly, even joyfully both for themselves and for the infant.

Liubomila had an easy and fear-free birth, and a cheerful one, too. When the baby came, she let out not a cry of pain but a cry of joy, of welcome. She herself drew him out of the water and embraced him.

When Radomir washed Liubomila with pure water and then dried her off, he felt like kissing every corner of her body. He even wanted to get down on his knees before her. And he knelt beside the bed as his smiling Liubomila lay under the sheet with her newborn son. As he stood there on his knees, he said softly and penetratingly:

"Thank you, Liubomila. You have co-created a child, you are a goddess. You can make dreams come true."

"*We* have co-created a child, Radomir," Liubomila responded with a smile.

CHAPTER EIGHTEEN

Not Radomir's last battle

Many happy years went by. By now their children, grandchildren and great-grandchildren were living in domains of their own. But Radomir and Liubomila's love was as strong as ever. Even though their hair had gone grey, they grew happier with each passing year.

Radomir stood alone at the entrance to his domain. He looked at the road which led toward a little hillock and disappeared behind it. It was along this road that his sons and grandsons had headed off to battle two days ago. Even his teen-age grandsons had gone.

The enemy that lay ahead of them was most unusual. A prince had brought some sort of people from a foreign country who were all dressed in black and, for some reason, called themselves *monks*. In each settlement they visited, they declared that the entire populace had not been living a proper way of life, that their ancient beliefs and rites needed to be eradicated and that they should bow down to a different god.

The prince himself bowed down to it, as did his entourage and armed garrison. No sooner had the prince adopted a different faith than the men in black proclaimed his authority as coming from God.

Along with the men in black came soldiers dressed like those in the prince's garrison. They attacked each settlement in turn, demanding that everybody think differently about what they called 'God'. When they found people unwilling to bow down to the foreign 'God', they killed them with the sword and burnt their houses and orchards.

The tribal elders held a council to decide what to do. They called the monks and the prince before the council, but these only spoke to them of the 'higher good' their new 'God' would bring, thereby misleading them with a doctrine nobody could make head nor tail of. The elders were encountering a phenomenon they had never seen before. Whenever an out-and-out enemy had attacked the settlement before, men from all the families quickly formed a militia and collaborated in driving the foe from the land.

But here were monks carrying on about 'love' and 'meekness' — about 'blessings', and the marvellous life in Paradise awaiting anyone who submitted themselves to the new faith.

What the elders did not at first understand was that hiding behind the shield of these beautiful words was an entity which had definitely *not* been sent to them by God.

The God of the Vedruss people used no swords. The monks, on the other hand, were backed up by aggressive armed garrisons. Residents in some of the communities headed off to the woods, while others joined battle. Some immersed themselves in deep contemplation.

That day at dawn Radomir witnessed the departure of his grandsons from his own domain and his sons from neighbouring domains. They met at Radomir's domain early in the morning, as though they had planned it among themselves the night before.

Of course, they planned this, Radomir decided. After all, just the night before, his and Liubomila's eldest son had said:

"Tomorrow we're heading out for some war games. We shall learn how to keep enemies from invading our lands."

They departed, but still had not returned by the next day's sunset. And old Radomir kept watching the road.

Before long, a lone horseman emerged from behind the hillock, heading toward Radomir's domain at full gallop. On the spirited steed another grey-haired oldster, not unlike

Radomir himself, sat skilfully in the saddle. Squinting his eyes, Radomir recognised his old childhood friend Arga.

The grey-haired horseman climbed down from his steed with a groan and quickly began questioning Radomir:

"Who's left in your domain? Only talk fast."

"Liubomila's working on supper and our youngest great-grandson is after her with questions," Radomir calmly replied, adding: "It's strange, Arga, how you started asking me a question right off, without even saying hello."

"No time, I'm in a hurry. Get two horses right away, bring along Liubomila and provisions for three days, and bring your great-grandson with you, and come with me immediately."

"Whereto?"

"To the woods, to the Drevlians.[1] There's one family there I know fairly well that will give us shelter. No foe will find us there in the dense forest. Perhaps the people will come to their senses as time goes by. Save your great-grandson, Radomir, and you'll save your family line."

"And here I thought you'd galloped over to *help* me, Arga. I see two Vedruss swords tied to your saddle. What do you need them for, if you're planning to hide out from our enemies tonight in some place in the woods?"

"The swords are just in case. I'm not about to fight anyone. Besides, there's a whole horde of them — we'd be utterly routed. What's the point of dying thoughtlessly like that?"

---

[1]*Drevlians* (Russian: *drevlianye*, stress on middle syllable) — the name applied to a collection of East Slavic tribes from the sixth to the tenth centuries along the Pripiat River in what is now Ukraine. The name is derived from the root *drev-*, signifying both 'of the woods' and 'of ancient origins'. Following their armed resistance to the invading Kievan princes, which resulted in significant bloodshed and executions among the civilian population, by the mid-tenth century their territories had been absorbed into the Kievan Rus' empire, while their popular resistance to the 'authorities' and the Christian church continued for many centuries thereafter.

"Yes, I know, Arga. You never fought with anyone. You never even tried to join in any of the manly games at *Maslenitsa* time."[2]

"That's beside the point. You and I both know, Radomir, that Man's life may be eternal, that his soul may be reincarnated in turn in an earthly form. But for that to happen, Man must not reflect on death as death approaches, but instead direct his thought toward a marvellous future. Where his thought is to be found, there will Man be regenerated anew."

"I know all that, Arga. You and I were both taught together by the wise-men."

"Then you ought to recall, Radomir, that you can fall and be fatally wounded in battle, and be deprived of the opportunity to think about your reincarnation."

"I remember, but, again, Arga, I cannot leave my family domain. It is alive, and it won't understand if its friend and master suddenly betrays with disdain the Space which has given him its love and abandons it to be torn apart by an enemy."

"*'It is alive, and it won't understand!'* You've always been overly sentimental, Radomir, and you still are today. Well, then, stay if you like. Go ahead and stay."

Arga paced quickly back and forth, gave his horse's mane a bit of a tousle, and again came over to Radomir. The two grey-headed oldsters stood facing each other without a word. Nobody can ever say what made their hearts beat back then — perhaps each was immersed in a whole range of thoughts of his own. Once more it was Arga who was the first to break the silence, as he began entreating with noticeable agitation.

"Stay, if that's what you've decided, Radomir. But... but... do give me Liubomila and your great-grandson, and one of your steeds. At least let *them* depart and save themselves.

---

[2] *Maslenitsa* — see footnote 9 in Chapter 9: "The Creator's greatest gift" above.

Stay yourself, if you like, if you are unwilling to part from your living Space."

Radomir gazed at his friend and replied:

"You can ask Liubomila about that yourself, Arga. I know you've loved her all your life. That was why you could never marry any other girl and set up your own family domain."

"Who? Me? I loved her? That's utter nonsense!" Arga exclaimed, as all at once he started pacing again, as though trying to persuade himself of the truth of his claim. "I'm an artist, and all my life my aim has always been to draw designs and carve small statues. What would I need a wife for? I'm your friend, and my intent was to help you save and extend your family line. As for Liubomila, I'd quite forgot about her."

"You are an artist, Arga, and a great one. And an ace of a wood-carver — the best around. Your little statues grace many of the houses in these settlements. And doesn't everybody concur that all the women you draw have a face resembling Liubomila's! Your carvings, too, look like her."

"*Look like her?* So what of it? It's just that I've tried to perfect a certain type of face in my pictures."

"You've taken pains to hide your love all your life, Arga," Radomir maintained. "And now you're hiding it again. I was at the pine tree which remains all by itself at the edge of the forest. I know you often liked to sit beneath it and carve your little statues. I recently came upon your hiding-place there, where you've stowed away your latest unfinished work — the one that shows a beautiful maiden taming a hot-tempered steed. That is something only Liubomila could do, as is known to both of us, me and you."

"*I loved, I didn't love, I carved, I drew.* That's beside the point — it's not what we're about now, do try to understand." Then, after a brief pause, Arga exclaimed, almost shouting:

"Radomir! Radomir, all your sons have been slain in battle, and all your grandsons too!"

Radomir maintained his outward calm, looked at Arga but refrained from speaking.

"Save yourself!" Arga continued to exclaim. "I saw them before the battle. I tried to dissuade them from joining such an uneven fray. Your eldest son, your first-born, he's made just like you, an exact copy, in fact..."

"Stop beating around the bush, Arga!" Radomir entreated his childhood friend, though showing no outward signs of concern. "Tell me, what did my eldest son say?"

"He said: 'We'll join the fray. We'll manage to hold off those 'black monks' at least for an hour or two.' I asked your son: 'Why should *you* die in strife? What good are those couple of hours to you?'

"'Our whole family decided this in a council meeting,' your eldest son replied. He said: 'May our parents, Radomir and Liubomila, enjoy at least two more hours of a happy life.'

"Even though they were greatly outnumbered by the 'black monks' and their soldiers, your sons, along with some children from the next settlements away, managed to stave them off for a whole day. Eventually the monks slayed the children, hacking them to pieces, then went back to their lair again. Tomorrow morning they'll start heading for your domain."

Radomir listened to his friend but gave no response. Arga continued, agitatedly:

"I galloped over here to help you save your family line. You and I both know that reincarnation on the Earth is possible. But this way there will be a finer chance of being reincarnated in a body of a family member. Only your great-grandson this time is capable of extending the family line. Let me have Liubomila and your great-grandson, I'll help..."

All of a sudden Arga stumbled in his speech and paused. He began to peek past Radomir. Radomir turned and looked. Behind him, resting against a tree, stood Liubomila. Tears were rolling down her cheeks. A trembling hand was clasped to her breast.

"Did you hear what Arga said?" Radomir asked Liubomila.

"Yes, I heard," she replied with a trembling voice.

"So why are you crying, Liubomila?" Radomir went over to her and began stroking her hair and kissing her hand. "Our children have surrendered their lives so that we can thrive one more day here in gladness. It is not right for us to spend it in sadness."

"No, it is not," smiled Liubomila through her tears.

"You are bright, my dear wife. You have gained the wisdom of the wise-men more mightily than anyone else. Think about how best the remainder of the day, the night and the morning, should be spent."

"I think, so as to do right by the children, we should enter into our Space of Love. Our grandson is there in need — it is time to feed him."

And, taking each other's hand, they headed for the entrance to their family domain.

Arga climbed into the saddle and cried out as they walked off:

"You're both mindless, sentimental old fools! You ought to save yourselves. You're not in a position to fight with anyone. If you're wounded, it's possible you might not succeed in sending a thought into space about your reincarnation. I'm getting out of here. I'm going to save myself. I recommend you do the same."

At the entrance to the domain, Radomir turned around and responded to his old friend:

"Save yourself, Arga. Gallop off to your hiding-place in the forest. We are tracing a different path to salvation."

Arga spurred on his steed, which rose on its hind legs and galloped off to the forest at full speed.

CHAPTER NINETEEN

From the stars
will they return to the Earth

As they were walking toward the house, where their great-grandson Nikodim[1] was waiting for them, Liubomila said:

"I think, Radomir, that we should now begin a brand new game with our little great-grandson — the game of life."

"What kind of a game is that?" Radomir asked in surprise. "I've never heard of it."

"*I've* never played it either. But I learnt about it back in my childhood, when I happened to overhear two old wise-men talking with each other. The gist of the game is this: one person plays out all the different stages of life with a child, while the other recalls in detail, as fast as he can, everything he has known in his lifetime, and imparts this knowledge mentally to the child. And if the thought of the narrator is clear, the child memorises the story through his subconscious. And when he grows up, he finds all sorts of hints about life within himself."

"Who d'you think should lead the playing with our great-grandson, Liubomila?"

"You do that, Radomir, while I tell him the story through my thought."

"But how will you be able to impart to him all the wisdom of life in just one hour? After all, it'll be time to put Nikodim to bed in an hour from now."

---

[1]*Nikodim* (pron. *nee-ka-DEEM*) — a Russian name corresponding to *Nicodemus* in the Bible (see John 3: 1).

"I shall manage. You just start the game, and mark off the different stages of life with a clap of your hands."

Four-year-old Nikodim ran to meet them, his arms open wide. Radomir caught him and gave him a toss in the air. Then he set him back down on the ground and began to say:

"I recently heard tell of an interesting game. Would you like to play it?"

"I would," answered Nikodim. "But how is it played?"

"I shall name something from life in words, and you tell us what it's about without words, using actions and gestures. And Grandmother will watch you act it out."

"Terrific!" exclaimed Nikodim, as he started jumping for joy on the spot. "Let's start playing it right away."

"Okay, let's begin," said Radomir, clapping his hands. And he went on: "Once upon a time there was born into the world a little boy named Nikodim. He was just a wee little baby back then."

The boy at once lay down on the ground, flung out his hands and bent his little legs at the knees. "Waa, waa..." he bawled, imitating a baby.

Radomir clapped his hands and continued:

"In time the baby began to get up on his little feet and walk."

Whereupon Nikodim at once got up on his feet, and took a step as though it were his first, staggered a bit, and then dropped down to all fours. He crawled along for a metre or so and then got up again. But this time he was already walking steadily.

Another clap, and Radomir went on:

"The little one's interest connected with everything: he inspected the bugs, and the grass, and tried to detect how apples grew on trees. He reflected on why the Sun came up and why he felt so warmly affected by everything both in summertime and when winter came."

Little Nikodim bent over to inspect a bug creeping over the grass, he looked up at the sky and jumped for joy, then all at once ran over to his grandfather, put his arms around the old man's legs, then he dashed over to his grandmother, who was sitting on the grass. Clasping her around the neck, he pressed his cheek against hers and gave her a kiss.

Radomir again clapped his hands and said:

"One day it happened that all the people left their domains. They did not travel along the roads, and where they were going was not heard. Perhaps they flew away like the birds, on their way to the stars.

"Then into the domain, where the little one had been left alone, came a foe who burns houses and hacks down orchards with an axe."

Little Nikodim listened to his great-grandfather's frightening tale. This time he stood motionless, without attempting actions or gestures, and finally said:

"I don't like this game. That should never happen in life."

"Yes, in life it shouldn't, you are right," Radomir replied to his great-grandson. "But this is a game, after all."

"Well, I shan't play it!" The boy stamped his little feet and cried out: "*I shan't!*"

"I'll take over," declared Liubomila, getting up from the ground. "When the little one caught sight of the foe, he called over the bear that he had played with when still just a wee mite. He took hold of the nape of the bear's neck, just as he had always done. He grasped hold of the bear's fur with all his might, and the bear lumbered off with him into the woods."

With these words Liubomila called out in the direction of a little grove of trees where their household animals lived:

"Hey there, brown bear, come over to me! Come on, come on, as quick as can be!"

Out from the grove emerged the bear and bounded over to Liubomila. When he came up beside her, she began stroking its muzzle. Then she whispered something in its ear. She tousled the fur on its shoulder, then, grasping hold of it with her hands, sprang onto its back.

"Hey, giddy-up!" she called to the bear.

The bear ran around in a wheel formation with all his might, until halted by Liubomila.

"But why would our great-grandson go off to the forest on a bear, and not on a horse?" asked Radomir, and Liubomila replied:

"Of course, a steed could go faster than a bear over the fields, but a horse would be helpless indeed in the woods, while the bear will find food and shelter there. Besides, in the woods the bear will offer the best protection. So there's your answer. Let's go on with the game...

"So, the bear ran off into the forest and hid the child there from the foe. He took care of him until the boy grew up to be a man.

"When he had grown, one day the young lad caught sight of a girl in the forest, who had come to pick berries in a glade. They liked each other right off, and later got married. They found a spot on the ground which would be hidden from malevolent eyes, they built a domain and began to bear children. And all their relatives who had flown off to the stars long ago, came back to the Earth."

As he drifted off to sleep, little Nikodim thought about the game, but he did not find it entertaining.

During this time Liubomila and Radomir walked about their family domain and recalled the life they had lived there. It had been a thoroughly joyful experience.

Liubomila laughed like a child when Radomir tried to portray her as a little girl standing amidst the tall grass.

"D'you recall? You remember how you called out back then that I was a good-for-nothing, 'cause I had raised the hem of your dress? I dried your tears with your dress, and you talked about being dishonoured."

"Yes, I remember it all," his wife responded, laughing. "But I thought of something just now: you could have dried my tears with the edge of your shirt."

"I was a smart boy, I was. I decided: why soil and mess my shirt, when I was going to have to wash out your dress in any case?"

"Yes, you were a smart boy. But still, you did lift up the hem of my dress, you good-for-nothing!... Oh, look at our spot, the wedding mound! New flowers have come up. And look how tall and majestic the cedar has grown! It was so small when we planted it on our wedding day."

Liubomila pressed the palm of her hand to the trunk and rested her cheek against it. She stood there without saying a word. Radomir, as love-struck as ever, put his arms around her shoulders as before and said:

"Where shall we sleep tonight — here or in the house?"

"Wherever you say, my darling."

The next morning a detachment of fifty soldiers entered the domain. With them were two monks dressed in black. The soldiers saw an old man standing by the cedar, and an old woman beside him, her back pressed against his. Each of them held two swords in their hands.

"You see?" the elder monk called out to the soldiers. "You see the infidels standing there? These infidels have borne children. Don't use your arrows — hack them to pieces with your swords."

Two warriors approached the elderly couple from different sides, their swords raised. They tried to land a blow, but Radomir managed to turn back the foe and disarm one of the warriors with his sword. And Liubomila warded off the attack against her. Then the old people repelled a second attack, then a third. After that the soldiers began fighting with each of them by twos. But Radomir had two swords in his hands, which flashed like lightning. He warded off both attacks simultaneously, but did not shed the soldiers' blood.

The grey-haired Liubomila laughed as she, too, repelled both attacks on her.

"Everyone step back," shouted the elder monk. "They are being helped by an unclean force! Everyone step back. Everybody shoot at them with your bows."

Those wielding the swords retreated. Others prepared their bows, but as soon as they had reached for their bowstrings the old couple threw down their swords, turned to each other and embraced. Radomir whispered something to Liubomila, and she smiled in response.

"What're you waiting for? Shoot!" shrieked the monk. "*They* are infidels! *You* have been sent by God! Shoot or I'll curse you!"

One arrow went into Liubomila and two into Radomir. But as though they did not feel any pain, the old couple still stood there embracing as before.

The arrows flew. The ground was covered in blood. And Liubomila and Radomir slowly sank down, or perhaps they flew off to the stars. As their bodies lay on the ground, the elder monk, the priest's emissary, looked into their faces and said to himself: *They were not thinking about death as death approached. Their thoughts were of life. Their faces show no fear nor sorrow. What must be done to prevent them from being reincarnated again?* He stood there in fear, feverishly trying to come up with a solution.

All at once behind his back rose a murmur of agitation. The monk turned around and saw six soldiers lying dead on the ground beneath the apple tree. Each of their hands was clutching an apple core.

The monk knew right away what had happened. The high priest's emissary knew that the Vedruss orchards produced marvellous fruit, but it could only be eaten when the garden's owner gave it of his own free will. The Vedruss people treated their trees and flowers as living beings, which repaid them with their love. When the trees and flowers saw how strangers acted toward the people who had bestowed their love upon them, the apple tree called up other juices from the depths of its roots and infested its fruits with an extremely strong poison.

"Don't touch it! Don't eat anything here!" cried the monk. "I told you, this is a devil's tribe, and the place here is unclean. I command you in the name of the Almighty to cut down everything, but everything, here."

"Look!" yelled one of the soldiers. "Look over there!", waving his hand in the direction of the entrance to the domain.

Everybody turned to see a bear heading out of the domain by leaps and bounds. On top of it, clinging on to its fur, rode a little boy. The bear rushed out of the domain and made a headlong dash for the woods.

"After them! Go get them!" shrieked the monk. "Don't come back until you have hacked the little vermin to pieces."

He knew that if even one of the Vedruss people escaped, their whole line could be regenerated on the Earth. But he did not tell this to the soldiers. To them he simply kept referring to the 'will of God'.

"Go get 'em! God commands you to rout out everything unclean from the Earth! You see how unclean it is here?!"

The detachment's commander ordered a dozen soldiers to follow the bear, catch up to it and kill the boy. The soldiers jumped on their steeds and headed out after the bear at a gallop.

In the meantime the bear was bounding quickly toward the forest. But it could not keep up such a feverish pace for long. And the pursuers, galloping as they were at full speed, were gradually catching up. The distance between the bear and the horsemen slowly but surely narrowed. They were only about a hundred metres from the forest when one of the pursuers caught up. Racing alongside, he raised his sword to kill the child. But the bear suddenly rose on its hind paws and took the blow on itself. The horse with the rider struck out to one side and reared. In the meantime, the wounded bear continued streaking toward the forest. Now it had a mere fifty metres to go, but by this time the detachment of horsemen had almost caught up, swords in their hands at the ready.

But then all at once the soldiers noticed another horseman, this one all on his own, heading out from the woods directly toward them. An old man was sitting with ease in the saddle, his grey hair and beard waving in the breeze. Each of his hands brandished a sword, while he controlled his steed with his legs alone.

"Giddy-up! Giddy-up!" the old man called, and spurred on his horse which was already moving at an incredible gallop.

"He's ready to fight us. Make ready for battle with this crazy old man!" the detachment commander shouted to the rest.

"But he's all alone, and there're ten of us," a warrior protested. "He's just an old man, what's there to be afraid of? We need to get on with the chase!"

"Yes, he's alone, but he's a *Vedruss*! Make ready for battle, whoever's not a timid goose!"

The elderly attacker on his steed galloped around the detachment of horsemen. With his swords he managed to disarm the two outer warriors and cut the saddle-girth from two of the horses, at which point his own extraordinary steed was wounded by an arrow.

But the old fellow did not direct his wounded steed toward the forest, but galloped along the edge of the woods, causing the whole detachment to pursue this course as well. When they got to the lone pine tree at the edge of the forest, his horse stumbled and the rider fell. The old man jumped up from the ground and started running toward the pine. He was looking for something in the grass at the time the detachment caught up with him.

The pine tree took seven arrows in its chest, but the eighth pierced Arga's breast. The thrown Vedruss rider lay on the ground, but did not groan. A stream of blood flowed from his chest. The pine tree, being wooden, could not lament the wound, while Arga's thought rose to the heavens in a state of doom:

> *I don't ask for myself any reincarnation,*
> *But I give them my thought for their future creation,*
> *To add to their joy and their great inspiration.*
> *Get together, reincarnate, and live without end,*
> *Radomir, Liubomila: I'm no foe, but your friend!*

The Vedruss lay there on the ground, but did not utter a sound. Even in his weakened state, he was still able to press a little statue of his beloved to his breast.

"*Good shall prevail!*" he whispered to his beloved, almost in a wail. And the wooden pine tree wept. A rather strange-looking pitch began showing itself, flowing down its trunk.

All at once the Vedruss opened his eyes and his vision was clear. And, barely able to enunciate the words, he blurted out:

Don't be sad, little pine tree, it's all nonsense here.
My thought will break through these bad times of barbarity.
Once more there will flourish bright ages of clarity.
To all earthly goddesses the morn will give hail
And my thought will imply to them: Good shall prevail!

The soldiers on their steeds did not succeed in catching up to the boy on the bear. They tried to penetrate the forest, but the forest did not turn out to be a friendly place for them. Their steeds began snorting in fear, and no clear path under their feet remained. The soldiers returned and explained to the monk that the boy had been slain.

A few years went by, and people began to say that while they were mushroom-picking in the woods, they caught sight of a boy about ten or older. He would peer at them from the bushes, but seemed afraid to come near. And there was always an old lame bear with him.

Some time later, two young boys got lost in the forest and became frightened. A youth came toward them and gestured them to follow him. He led them to the edge of the woods, right to the road which led to their settlement, while he himself retreated once more into his forest hiding place. After this incident people stopped being afraid of the forest youth. And when, a year later, he headed out of the woods one day toward a group of young lasses gathering berries in the glade, the girls were not afraid of him and did not run away.

The youth was blue-eyed and of slender build. He was dressed in clothing woven from grasses. He stood at the edge of the glade. One lass in particular caught his eye, whose name was Praskovia. In truth, he could not take his eyes off her, and everyone suddenly stopped picking berries and stared at the youth.

Then very slowly, so as not to frighten them, he took several steps toward the group of girls, and stopped. Seeing that the maidens were not running away and were not afraid of him, he approached young Praskovia, stood facing her, smoothed out his hair and blurted out, though not without some stumbling:

"Together with you, my fair maiden, I could create a Space of Love to last forever!"

Praskovia had absolutely no idea as to what these words meant, but for some reason her cheeks flushed with a rosy glow and she began to talk with the young lad.

"Where do you live?" she asked. "Everybody says you live in the forest, all on your own."

"For the time being I live on the Earth alone," replied the youth.

"Alone? But where are your parents, then? No one exists without some kind of family."

"They are living. My father and mother, and elder brothers, and my sisters. And my grandfather Radomir, and my grandmother Liubomila."

"And where do they dwell? In the forest as well?"

"They have flown way up high to the stars in the sky. They will come back down to the Earth from afar when I have found my intended. I shall create and form a Space of Love all around, and this is where our children will be born."

"But how will you look for your intended in the forest?"

"I shall not need to look — she has already been found."

"And who is she?"

"*You*, my maiden — you are the most splendid of all. I ask you now to come with me to my Space, which I have already begun to create. I shall build a house, but... there are just a few tools I need to get. Not having them yet, I have constructed a shelter in the meantime. I have been observing from afar how it is done."

The maidens whispered amongst themselves and made fun of the youth. By this time they had become quite unafraid.

Praskovia did not answer his proposal right away, but withdrew to her group of maidens. The young man stood a little apart, looked to the sky and opened his arms wide, as though apologising to someone, then slowly turned and headed away from the glade.

A hush fell over the maidens. Praskovia watched him depart and then all at once called out loudly and confidently to the youth:

"Wait for me here tomorrow. I'll steal the tools you need from my father as a dowry."

The youth quickly turned around, and ran over to Praskovia. The maidens saw him smile for the first time. And all their cheeks flushed with a rosy glow. The young man's smile was extraordinary, and his eyes were beaming all the while.

"How handsome he is! Too bad he didn't pick me!" whispered one of the girls.

"I'm ready to go with him, too," another announced all of a sudden.

In the meantime the young man said to Praskovia, not seeing anyone around:

"You mustn't steal. That is not a kind deed."

"I was only joking. My father will be glad to give me anything I need."

From that point on, nobody ever again laid eyes on the pair — they saw neither the forest youth nor the maiden Praskovia, who had gone off with him to goodness-knows-where.

Chapter Twenty

Even in chaos there is a purpose

"Life continued on the Earth," Anastasia went on. "But it was not the same life as before. The great Vedruss civilisation, its traditions, rites and culture, which had existed for tens of thousands of years, were replaced by a chaotic, barbarian order of human society. In our state the period of slavery began with Kievan Rus'[1] and continues to the present day."

"But wasn't the Vedruss civilisation destroyed even earlier in other territories of the Earth? I remember you saying, Anastasia, that the Vedruss way of life was prevalent among the inhabitants of what is now Germany, England, Poland and the Baltic countries."[2]

"Yes, I did say that. It was all one people, one language, one culture. If you look closely, Vladimir, you will see that they all resemble each other even in outward appearance. This despite the fact that for more than two millennia there was a good deal of blood-mixing between them and Asian peoples."

"But why did things come about like that, Anastasia? You said it was a great civilisation and a great culture, yet in the blink of an eye this civilisation was destroyed by the sword, fire and arrows."

---

[1]*Rus'* — see footnote 4 in Chapter 5: "Conception involves more than flesh" above.

[2]A reference to Anastasia's declaration in Book 6, middle of Chapter 4: "A dormant civilisation".

"Not *destroyed*, Vladimir. That word is not really appropriate. As long as there are at least nine people on the planet who are striving for a conscious awareness of the Divine earthly being, the Vedruss civilisation is alive. But now, after all, there are not just nine people, but hundreds of thousands who are discovering more and more the truth within themselves and are changing their way of life at the core. They will soon number in the millions, but for now these hundreds of thousands should be seeking for the answer to the puzzle within themselves, for an understanding of how the disaster came about."

"But what if they don't understand? On our Internet site there's a whole lot of people who've been trying for several years now to determine what specific mistake mankind permitted to slip through in the Age of the Image.[3] There's a discussion forum there, known as "The mistake of the Age of the Image". But so far nobody's managed to make out what that mistake might be. There's a lot of variants, but no overall answer here. It may not come for another thousand years! Maybe nobody will ever be able to determine the mistake."

"They will. Perhaps in a day, or perhaps in five to nine years. They will find the answer."

"How can you be so sure?"

"Think about it, Vladimir. It was only a short time ago that people did not even talk about the subject at all, and there were not even any attempts to *think* along these lines. Now you tell me yourself that a whole lot of people are endeavouring to solve the mystery. Thought is switched on. Just like a little shoot from a seed, it will find its way to the light."

"It will find it someday, perhaps. People today are mainly involved in the routine of their everyday life. Your grandfathers and you have had the opportunity to do a lot more

[3] *Age of the Image* — see the section on "Vedism" in Book 6, Chapter 5: "The history of mankind, as told by Anastasia".

reflecting. Besides, you have access to a huge amount of information about the past, and then, naturally, you have your own view of things. Why not share it? At least give people a hint?"

"In other words, Vladimir, you are asking me to switch people's thinking off?"

"Now why would *I* be the one who wants to switch it off? Why would a simple hint have that kind of result?"

"If everybody who is trying to work out the solution today in their thought takes the hint as 'gospel truth', their thinking will immediately cease operations. Then they'll be expecting even more hints. And you may be sure that the hints will come — in fact they'll quickly pour down in showers upon them. That is precisely what is happening right now. People are getting hints right and left about what is healthy to eat and drink, how to dress, where the best resorts are, how to live, where to search for God. And what is the result? Life progressively gets worse. God created the order of the Universe with His thought, and He gave thought as a gift to Man. But somebody is constantly trying to bring it to a halt."

"Does that mean you know the answer, but you don't want to talk about it?"

"I do not know the answer, but I can presuppose."

"Well, what presuppositions have you come up with, for example, pray tell?"

"Perhaps a period of chaos was needed, a period of mistakes, so that mankind might have a complete account of it and not repeat it in the future. Similar phenomena have emerged in history when mankind is on the verge of a great discovery — a discovery of universal proportions."

"Now *that*, Anastasia, is what I call a good and encouraging presupposition. Your story about the Vedruss family, Liubomila and Radomir, had a very sad ending — quite unlike your usual optimism."

"Vladimir, why have you decided that the story has come to an end? Life continues, and so not a single story about life can ever be considered to have come to an end."

"I remember how the great-grandson, Nikodim, went off with Praskovia and continued the family line, but I still feel sorry for specific individuals like Radomir, Liubomila and others. The story about *them* cannot be continued. One can talk only about continuing the family line. If there's something more you can tell me, then please do tell me, Anastasia."

"Fine, I shall tell about events that took place in the very near future."

CHAPTER TWENTY-ONE

'Soulmate gatherings'

The time came when people started to realise the need of searching for their soulmates. Earlier they had been taught that the lovers themselves should find each other by the whim of fate. Of course that is true, but then Man may also control his own destiny. Or at least give fate a hint as to what Man desires of it.[1]

And so people in different towns began to organise special events to facilitate two soulmates getting to know each other. And they even applied some of the rites of the Vedruss period, with just a smidgen of adaptation to fit modern situations.

Every autumn, after the tasks of summer are completed, large gatherings take place in various towns, attended by young and old — anybody who has not yet been blessed with a happy home.

These are mainly your readers, Vladimir — those among them who have been endeavouring to build a domain to start up a happy family line.

These gatherings might go on in various towns over a period of two or three months. Your readers spread word of them ahead of time. And they come from different places and countries. Some might come for a week, some for a month. And your readers in particular have a significant advantage over others desiring to create a happy home. All the participants in these gatherings have a single goal — a conscious

---

[1]In the first part of this chapter, as well as in the following chapter, except as otherwise indicated, the narrative is presented by Anastasia herself.

awareness and concept of how to build a happy life for their future family.

"Wait, Anastasia, how is it that my readers specifically had a significant advantage? After all, many married couples apart from my readers have such a single goal in mind. There are often married couples, for example, among performing artists. But the majority of them get divorced, some several times over. They all have the same goal and aspiration, but there is no happy life for them."

"You and I are talking about *different* goals, Vladimir. One's profession cannot be — and should not be — a goal of life for a Man. In such cases, the Man would be debasing himself.

"Think about it — take a salesperson, for example. Is it in the nature of a son or a daughter of God to consider one's life goal to be simply selling things? Or driving a vehicle, or doing laundry, or going back and forth to a factory all the time to perform the same task over and over again?"

"Wait, Anastasia, you named off what may be necessary professions, but they're still not very prestigious. There are, however, some fairly prestigious professions — or, rather, professions everybody holds in high regard. For example, everybody knows about surgeons and cosmonauts, military commanders and marshals, or presidents of countries."

"But their significance, Vladimir, lies simply in the fact that they have created a bigger illusion of importance and significance than others. Who knows? Possibly *someone* has tempted one of them — a commander or a president, let's say — by the illusory significance of these particular professions or positions just so as not to allow his own spirit to develop — a spirit which is capable of accomplishing the acts of the Universe. The deeds such people have accomplished are not interesting to God. But when a Man builds his own corner of Paradise on the Earth and founds the happiest family line you can imagine, his deeds not only resemble those of God's — he actually becomes a god himself.

"And the readers who came to these gatherings had a noble goal, the same for both women and men. Their advantage was that both men and women were creating through their dreams a way of life for their future families. When they met together, they had a subject of common interest to talk about."

You know, after all, Vladimir, how often in modern families there is rarely a single topic of conversation of interest to both marriage partners. They have nothing in common, no common aspirations. Two people get married and live together in the same dwelling, but each of them thinks and dreams only of what is of interest to them individually. People like that become strangers to each other, and their cohabitation ends up in nothing but irritation.

The people who come to the gatherings are not married, but even those unacquainted with each other feel closer than many marriage partners.

They go on excursions together and organise fashion shows in which first women — and then men — of all ages take part. The clothes modelled at these shows have either been bought in stores or sewn by the women themselves.

The evenings are spent in playing wedding games in town squares or somewhere in one of the glades. One of them is *Rucheyok,* which I told you about before.

And there is no feeling of embarrassment, no concealing that they are seeking to find themselves a life companion. And women who are left to deal with life with children and no husband bring their children along to these nuptial gatherings. And they reveal the purpose of the trip to the children. The children's thought and participation help them a great deal in their search. Here, I shall show you a scene from one of these gatherings.

Look, a summer theatre in the open air. A full audience, comprised of adults and children of various ages.

See how they are introducing themselves from the stage. Those who are bold enough get up on stage, where they are each given five to ten minutes to talk about themselves and answer questions. Sometimes they introduce themselves in a humorous fashion, or sing and dance a *chastushka-govorushka*. They have full freedom in their choice of repertoire. Take a look.

A girl who looked to be in her mid-twenties came out on stage. She sported a fashionable hairdo and a skin-tight outfit. She had barely taken two steps in the direction of the microphone when she did a somersault and burst out laughing. After that she took a turn around the stage, strutting the catwalk like a professional model. Straightening her hairdo, she approached the microphone and purred teasingly:

"Hey, guys! Is this chick hot, or what?"

From the audience rang out peals of laughter and loud applause, and the girl went on talking about herself in a humorous vein.

"Hey, the way I look, you know, that's not even my greatest asset. I graduated from the Family Domain Academy with top honours. That means I'm tops at cooking, too. And I can rid your body of any ailment, you name it, and, hey, I can make one really coo-ool bed! And I can give you children that'll grow up big and strong...

"I'm not after anyone in particular, but here's a contest for you guys. But like they say, 'this ain't no cakewalk'. The contestants can do whatever they like to show what stuff they're made of. And the winner is... the one I fall in love with!"

After this a young boy came up the microphone and said:

"Hi! I'm Dima.[2] That's what they call me. And I'm eleven. Well, maybe not quite eleven yet, but I shall be very soon — this December... My Mama's name is Svetlana, or Svetlana Nikolaevna. She's a great restaurant cook. That is, she used to work in a restaurant, but now she doesn't... At first she cried when she stopped working there, but now she does fine catering for a whole bunch of rich people. She put an advert in the paper and they ring her up on the telephone...

"I'm in school. Mama says I'm not a very bright student, but I know I'm doing okay. It's just that I really don't need fives — threes[3] are perfectly good enough for me...

"My Mama and I are here to look for her future husband and my future Papa. Then we'll have a jolly friendly family... My Mama's a really nice person. She's pretty, even though there's no way she can lose weight. She's still pretty!... Mama and I have been spending lots of evenings talking about how we'll live as a complete family. Right now we're in a one-room flat for which we have a monthly rent to meet. But when we're a whole family we'll treat ourselves to a house and plant a garden...

"Mama's already been given land, and we lived there in a tent for a whole month this summer. It was really neat!...

"She — my Mama, that is — she didn't come up here with me on the stage, she's shy. But I've been tellin' her: you've got

---

[2]*Dima* (pron. *DEE-ma*) — an informal variant of the Russian name *Dmitri*.

[3]*fives* (piatyorki), *threes* (troiki) — part of the marking system in all Russian educational institutions: 5 — excellent (= A), 4 — good (= B), 3 — satisfactory (= C), 2 — unsatisfactory (= D), 1 — fail (= F).

to show yourself! If you don't show yourself, then why did we come all this way and waste a whole lot of money which we've been saving for a house?...

"Hey, there, Mama! C'mon up onto the stage!" the boy called out into the audience.

But nobody made a move toward the stage. Then the audience started clapping in unison, urging the boy's mother to go up to the stage.

Finally, a short, slightly plumpish woman of about thirty could be seen making her way to the stage. She stood beside her son, her cheeks flushed a bright red with embarrassment. She put her arms around the boy's shoulders and gave him a big hug, but couldn't bring herself to speak. Then the boy, in a very businesslike manner, took a crumpled piece of paper out of his trouser pocket, unfolded it and began to read what was written on it:

"My Mama and I live in the Briansk Oblast, in the city of Novozybkov.[4] There used to be a lot of radiation there, but now there's not so much, and there's going to be even less in the future. Here at the gathering we're listed under number 2015. If anybody wants to, they can write to us. That's all."

The boy's mother took him by the hand and they started heading over to the stage exit under noisy applause from the audience. But when they got to the edge of the stage, the boy suddenly released himself from his mother's grasp and quickly, almost running, went back to the microphone.

"I forgot to say — I mean, I didn't write it down, that's why I forgot. My Mama can play the guitar and sing really

---

[4]*Novozybkov* (pron. *na-va-ZIP-kaff*) — a city of some 45,000 people not far from Briansk, a major centre located 350 km south-west of Moscow, not far from Chernobyl, just across the Ukrainian border, where a devastating nuclear accident occurred on 26 April 1986, spreading radiation clouds for hundreds of kilometres around. An *oblast* is a territorial division similar in status to a state or province.

cool songs with it, even though they're sad. And my Mama can draw, too. She's drawn a house and a garden... And I, too, can help build a family. And even help build a house... When the elections were held in our town, I got hired to put up campaign posters. And we're gonna be having elections again soon."

Once more the audience thundered their applause, and the boy headed back to his mother. She took his hand, and they came down off the stage and took their seats in the audience.

Then four men got up from their seats at the same time and headed for the stage. The first looked around fortyish, and he walked with a bit of a limp. But the other three beat him to it, and he ended up last in the queue for the microphone. One by one, the men went up to the mike and said something about themselves, but they didn't make any public proposals of marriage. That simply wasn't done at gatherings like this. People were supposed to write notes. But the fact that they went up on stage was a good indication of their desire to get better acquainted with the mother and her son. When it came the lame man's turn at the mike, he said:

"My name's Ivan.[5] I have my own flat in Moscow. I'll soon be forty years old. I'm a former paratrooper, discharged as an invalid by a medical review board three years ago. I make something on the side in multi-level marketing, but I'm tired of it. I've still got a pup tent, an axe and a mess-kit, which my buddies gave me. Right now my dream is to set up this tent in Briansk Oblast around the town of Novozybkov. Next to your tent, Dima. I'll be glad to work in return for a place

---

[5] *Ivan* (pron. *ee-VAHN*) — considered to be one of the most common names in Russia, derived from the Biblical name *Ioann,* which corresponds to *John* in English.

to deploy my tent. I've been trained in bunker construction, and can put up a log house, only I'm not sure how to get an orchard or vegetable garden going."

"I know, I can show you!" cried out Dima, jumping up from his seat.

A day or two later Svetlana Nikolaevna, her son Dima and the former paratrooper Ivan left the gathering.

"Anastasia," I pleaded, "tell me, please, how did life turn out afterward for these three people?"

CHAPTER TWENTY-TWO

A nuptial rite for women with children

Their lives unfolded quite well. Ivan invited Svetlana and her son to come for a visit, and they stayed a week in his apartment. After that they corresponded with each other. When spring came, Ivan let his Moscow flat to tenants for a goodly monthly rent, while he himself went off to Novozybkov. He set up his pup tent next to Svetlana and Dima's tent.

The former paratrooper had everything needed for life in field conditions, including a camp stove that could be used for heating. Ivan eagerly set about digging trenches for the foundation of their future house. He was assisted even more eagerly by Dima, who visited with his mother on weekends. With the onset of the summer holidays, they all began sleeping in the tents. Each evening they would gather round a fire and talk about plans for their future domain.

One evening when it came time to go to bed and the fire was burning low, Dima said:

"In normal families a husband and wife sleep together in one room, and their children in another. Is it okay if I sleep in your tent, Ivan, and you and Mama in ours?"

"But we aren't husband and wife just yet," Svetlana protested.

Ivan rose to his feet and held out his hand to Svetlana, helping her up. Solemnly, with just a slight trembling, he pronounced:

"With you, fair goddess, and with our fine young son, I could co-create a Space of Love to last forever."

And Svetlana quietly responded:

"We are ready to help you in your grand co-creation."

Dima jumped for joy and clapped his hands. Then, under a starry sky, they performed the nuptial rite to become husband and wife, as well as the rite of adoption at the same time, whereby Dima became Ivan's own son.

"Maybe you intended to say, Anastasia, that the boy Dima became Ivan's *adopted* son?"

"He became his *very own* son. And Ivan became Dima's very own father."

"But how could that be, Anastasia? It goes against all the laws of biology!"

"But it does not go against Heaven. The Vedruss people knew the laws of Heaven. Ivan, Dima and Svetlana were familiar with the Vedruss nuptial rite for women with children. They performed it."

"What kind of rite is that? How did they know about it?"

"You described it."

"I never wrote about it."

"Don't forget, Vladimir, I'm telling you about events that will happen in the future. And you will describe this rite. I am going to tell you about it."

This rite derives its principal power from the thoughts and desires of three people who want to build a future together. Women play a central role in preparing for this rite. The woman should be able to explain to her child the necessity of living as a family, the necessity of having a father and creating a domain together with him, building a house and planting an orchard. When a child shows or generates an interest in such a project, he must be brought into the search for a future spouse and father. Every mother knows her own child better than anyone else. There is no single formula for achieving the desired result — it will be different for every mother. The main thing is to achieve one's goal.

Many children do not immediately desire to welcome some other person into their home. And in the absence of such a desire on the part of the child to have a father and join in the mother's search, it is better not to introduce anyone else into the home.

The mother plays a central role in preparing for the nuptial rite only at the beginning stages. At the moment when the rite is actually performed, the motive energy source will be the thought of the child.

If a man and woman have decided on co-habitation while the woman's child is still very small, they can live together without performing the rite until the child grows a little and acquires his own conscious awareness of what family life means. The man and woman should make joint efforts, too, toward this end. If the child grows up accepting his stepfather as his own father, the nuptial rite is still necessary, since it is able to transform an adopted son or daughter into the father's own — in terms of both blood and spirit. This rite can exert a tremendous beneficial influence only if it is performed on the ground of their future family domain, regardless of whether it was first started by the man or the woman. What is important is that it is to everybody's liking, especially the child's.

The rite should take place in the open air, under the stars. There should be a fire burning, or three candles. Svetlana and Ivan were lucky: after their mutual declaration of desire to co-create their life together, there were lots of stars in the sky, the fire was still burning, so they did not have to wait for another night, but got married right away. And they did everything just the right way.

Ivan and Svetlana stood in front of Dima. Ivan looked up at the stars and spoke first:

"Here, on the ground of our family domain, I wish a happy life for our family line. I wish to build a house and plant an orchard.

"I ask you, Dima, for your agreement to allow me to be wedded to your mother for ever, and for you to become my own son."

"I shall be very happy if you, Ivan, will live with my mother and me. Perhaps I shall even become a better pupil. And can I call you Papa?"

"Of course," replied Ivan.

Then it was Svetlana's turn to speak:

"Thank you, my son, for helping me find a husband. I agree to become his faithful wife. A wife should take care of her husband. With your permission, my son, I shall surround Ivan, your father, with loving care."

"Of course, Mama. You should most certainly take care of Ivan. And I shall take care of him. Let us buy Papa a new prosthesis. I saw him wrapping his old one around with insulation tape."

It is not important to pronounce the same words each time in this rite. The most important aspect is thought, which should be heard by the planets currently standing above the marital pair and their child or children. For this it is necessary to bring a wide-mouthed vessel of some sort — a glass, or a mug, for example — out of which each participant should take a drink of water (at least three swallows), and then pour water on their hands and wash their hair. Then all three should lie down on the grass for no less than nine minutes head to head, hold each other's hands and look up to the starry sky, mentally asking the planets above them to help them build a happy life for their family line, and requesting love to take up residence in the family domain. This will happen if the thought of all three of them is sincere and strong.

It is not necessary for the *love* to be strong at the moment of the wedding. A strong mutual sympathy or attraction is sufficient. Love will undoubtedly grow stronger with time. It almost always happened within a year or two among the Vedruss people.

This is a very powerful rite, but it is not occult. When astronomers and psychologists restore at least a part of the knowledge people used to have, they will understand its cosmic power.

Have you understood, Vladimir? This is something in which plants, water, the Earth, the planets and human thought all take part. As the people's aspirations merge into a single whole, they will harness the elements into forwarding their cause in accordance with Divine essence of the Cosmos.

You most certainly know already, Vladimir, the close interconnection between the faraway planets in the heavens and the blades of grass and flowers and bugs and everything else living on the Earth. The ebb and flow of the tides are governed by the planets.

Of course, there is a lot in human life which is influenced by the planets, but in this particular instance, the three people performing the rite, uniting into one, charge the planets with the task of making their union beneficially strong. Man's request to the planets, when his goal corresponds to God's programme, is treated by the planets as a great gift, giving them a feeling of pride in themselves and in Man. His conscious, earnest appeal sets many of the planets in the sky into a rousing, propitious acceleration. The heavenly bodies located at that precise moment above the people lying on the ground, form a wordless alliance to assist these people in their deeds.

This discovery was made by a wise-man, after a period of ninety years leading up to it, in which he observed the planets and compared them with people's deeds.

When the wise-men-scholars were endeavouring to understand this rite, they came to the conclusion that in some miraculous fashion, either the planets or the power of various cosmic energies can erase unpleasant reminiscences of one's past life from human memory, making room for new, bright sensations.

Not only that, but these energies unite three people together in ecstasy.

Remember, Vladimir, how you were telling me about telegony. Modern science has learnt that there is some kind of energy which participates in the formation of the physical bodies of animals and people. Note that these energies are invisible to the eye and are not contained in visible matter, but their power is effective. Besides, their participation comes about by the will of Man. When they act in accordance with human will, their effectiveness increases a hundredfold.

It is important to point out that the essence of the rite we have been discussing is such that, in contrast to telegony, there is no invasion of the old liaison into the new alliance, but that it completely extirpates the energies of the old alliance and endows the participants with new strength, and gives them new life.

"Wow! It's such a brief rite, and yet the results are extraordinary. It really creates blood ties among them."

"Brief, you say? Think about it carefully, Vladimir. The preparation for this 'brief' rite, as you call it, may take several years."

The rite must be preceded by two important customs.

Take the first — here is an example: the mother needs to prepare her child ahead of time, then — pay close attention, Vladimir — Ivan started by saying that he wanted a place to set up his tent and offered to do household work in return.

This point actually comes from a different rite. Every 'old stag' — as old or middle-aged bachelors used to be called — was supposed to spend one month a year working in a woman's home, either for a widow living alone or one living with children. He was not obliged to spend the whole month with the same widow. The bachelor could work a week for one, and then go on to another. This custom, of course, was not designed just to offer aid to single women. Its aim was to get people acquainted with each other and help them create a family.

A bachelor might come to a widow and say:

"Madam, I am looking for work, you see. Would you happen to have anything for me?"

If the woman did not like the man's looks at first sight, she might reply:

"Everything here's been done over and over again. Besides, I can't afford to pay anything right now."

On the other hand, if she liked the man, she might give him some sort of work to do for two or three days. Then she could offer him more work. It did not really matter how knowledgeable or skilful he was. The main thing was whether the two people liked each other or not.

If there was a mutual attraction, the woman might ask the man to stay longer than a month and, if he stayed, start calling him her *primak*.[1] And after a year of co-habitation they could either get married or go their separate ways.

"Tell me, Anastasia, after this rite, would the newlyweds still need to go to the Civil Registration Office?"

"People can go through with whatever formalities are necessary in life, but these can never interfere with what is most important."

---

[1] *primak* (stress on last syllable) — roughly equivalent to an 'associate' (a person one has tentatively joined with).

CHAPTER TWENTY-THREE

High-society ladies

As I was completing the preceding chapter, it came to me that a rite like this could be successfully applied in our day, too. People in many parts of Russia today, mainly readers of the Ringing Cedars Series, are gathering together in groups, each family taking a hectare of land, planting orchards, building houses and setting up their own little Motherland. They are doing this, by and large, as families. But these groups also include a significant number of single women.

The settlement I have visited the most often is the one near the city of Vladimir, which numbers at the moment more than sixty domains under construction. Already, children are growing up who have been born in them. But there are also single women who have taken a hectare and are building their domain, sometimes with the help of their children, but sometimes all by themselves. Can you just see it? A woman builds a house all by herself, and plants an orchard. It's not just a little dacha on a mere 600 square metres of ground that she is putting up, but an actual domain that she is building.

Is it hard for them? In a financial sense, yes. I know one woman who has rented out her Moscow apartment and is building a house in a field on the proceeds.

Because of insufficient funds, she is not always able to hire tradespeople, so she does a lot of the work herself. And she does it joyfully. She has a goal, and takes joy in progress toward that goal. The progress may be slow, but it still more than compensates for all the challenges, and makes them seem insignificant by comparison.

After collecting information from various communities, I came to the conclusion that I should write a book about them as soon as possible. This will be a truly historic book. Our descendants ought to know how their new and happy civilisation got its start, and who started it.

In the meantime I asked the wife of one of the founders of the Rodnoye[1] settlement in Vladimir Oblast to describe some of the unmarried women and what they were doing. Here are her brief descriptions:

Evgenia T. — born in Moldavia, 53 years old, a geologist, a real beauty, with a smile that would outshine Hollywood stars. She has an apartment in Malakhovka near Moscow, but she doesn't go to it. She says: "My home is here."

She first came to have a look around in 2003. She went mushroom-picking in the woods.

"They warned me," says Evgenia, "they said that's not your average forest! But I told them: 'I'm a geologist, I shan't get lost.' I spent twelve hours wandering within a three-kilometre radius! My legs were practically broken by the time I got back around midnight. 'This is my place!' I said. I rented out my flat in Malakhovka for 10,500 roubles a month.[2] I was able to start building with the money I received. I rented a house in Studentsovo, close to my plot. Turned out the furnace hadn't been lit in ten years, and the house was falling apart. I pulled out a nest from the chimney — I hadn't been able to light a fire.

[1]*Rodnoye* (pron. *rad-NAW-yeh*) — the name of the settlement in question, literally meaning 'one's own' or 'native', derived from the root *rod-* ('kin' or 'family'). For further information on this Slavic root, see footnote 1 in Book 4, Chapter 24: "Take back your Motherland, people!".

[2]Note that in terms of the then current official exchange rate, *one* thousand roubles would be roughly equivalent to US$35, but closer to US$70 in terms of actual purchasing power.

"I spent the winter in the village alone. Sometimes I would go visiting, to Koniayevo.[3] I was sparing with the wood, lighting a fire only every other time. In the fall I laid a foundation and put in a four-metre-by-four-metre log *banya*.[4] I spent the whole winter caulking the walls with tow. I now know the sound of falling snow.

"I would go about the house wearing three pairs of trousers and three sweaters along with a jacket and a *shapka*.[5] But when I worked outdoors I got by with not so much clothing.

"In the spring I took a knife and scraped the rest of the bark off the timber frame. I now have a house which looks as though each log has been finely planed. I can hear the snow melting.

"I needed someone to fix the furnace. So I got dressed warmly and took a fishing rod (with no hook) and went down to the pond where some men were fishing (God forbid they should see my 'tackle'). I got into conversation with the men and 'caught' myself a furnaceman. And whenever I needed a tractor, I just went out onto the road and stopped the first one that came along."

Evgenia's got herself a vegetable garden — it's all in order, everything's coming up. The first year she put in a lavatory and a summer kitchen made of wattle. When there's absolutely nothing left to eat, she makes up some porridge with fish oil. She's a marvellous cook. Her feverish activity has been giving everyone a pain in the neck — the locals

---

[3]*Koniayevo* (pron. *kan-YA-ye-va*) — like neighbouring Studentsovo, a village in Vladimir Oblast, close to the eco-settlement under discussion.

[4]*banya* — a Russian bath-house, similar to a Finnish sauna. For a more detailed description see footnote 20 in Book 2, Chapter 1: "Alien or Man".

[5]*shapka* — a warm hat, usually made of fur, with ear-flaps, to keep one's head warm in winter.

tend to shy away from us — but her house is already up! She says what she thinks.

Liubov E. — born in the Far East, 58 years old, lived 27 years in Perm[6] and 20 years in Tsimliansk in Rostov Oblast.[7] She's an ichthyologist, worked with fish conservation, now retired.[8] She has a mother 84 years old and a son, 30, who lives in Perm (two grandsons); another son, 18, lives in Tsimliansk.

This year she began counting time in reverse, says she's now 57. She began setting up her domain in 2003. She came for ten days, cut down the wild grass, planted a hedge (fir, pine, birch, aspen, linden, maple). An ideal plot indeed. In the winter she brought 50,000 roubles with her — all her mother's savings. She put up a house-frame and covered it with asphalt roofing... In the spring she arrived with her ex-husband; he dropped her off on his way to Perm. They worked on the plot together. She says if it had been like this before, she would never have left him. She arrived in the summer, on 6 July (she was hurrying to get here in time for the Feast of Ivan Kupala[9]).

She really loves holidays. She sings, plays the guitar and dances. She gets a pension of 2,000 roubles a month. She took a leave of absence from her work for the summer. She's got enough money, except for travel expenses... The

---

[6]*Perm* — a major city of over a million inhabitants 1,500 km east of Moscow.

[7]*Rostov Oblast* — a large territorial jurisdiction of just over 100,000 km² north and east of the Sea of Azov (north of the Black Sea). Its administrative centre is Rostov-on-Don. The town of Tsimliansk (stress on last syllable) dates from the construction of an electric power station on the nearby Tsimliansk Reservoir in 1961.

[8]*retired* — The normal retirement age in Russia is 60 for men, 55 for women.

community has helped her buy bricks, cement and timber. She herself spent a month laying the foundation under the furnace, then she put in the foundation for the house frame, put in uprights under the floor joists, caulked the whole house, made an awning and built a summer stove. She dragged around barrowfuls of rocks, sand and crushed stone. She thought she couldn't do it, but she could! She got stronger, lost weight, and began swimming across the lake and back (something she couldn't do earlier). She took off ten years (she dreamt of looking just a year younger). Her eyes sparkle, she's always smiling, and she's made friends and gets along with everybody... She's building the house for herself and her mother, and hopes the two of them can move in come spring. She wants her son and grandchildren to come and see her from Perm, and stay for a while so they can see whether they might want to live there... She's got no money, and no source of income. She does have an old Italian violin which her father brought back from the war. Fifteen years ago experts appraised it at between ten and fifteen thousand dollars minimum, without restoration. She really hopes she can sell it — it's

---

[9]*Ivan Kupala* — the ancient Russian Summer Solstice holiday, later adopted by the Orthodox Church under the name of a Christian saint, *Ivan Kupala* — the Russian name for St John the Baptist, whose official day of 24 June in the Orthodox Church's Julian calendar falls on 7 July by our modern (Gregorian) calendar. Even in their present form, the Ivan Kupala celebrations preserve key traits of the pagan festivities, including letting burning wheels run downhill into water (to symbolise the descent of the fiery, masculine energy of the Sun-god Yarila into the water — the feminine element of Mother Earth), jumping over a bonfire with one's intended mate, bathing in the lakes and rivers, searching for a 'fern's blossom' (symbolising a spiritual insight into the workings of Nature) and picking medicinal plants throughout the night. One of the main festivities of the pre-Christian era, the Summer Solstice was traditionally the day on which weddings were 'played out', more or less as a game.

a violin ready to be played, not just a museum-piece. If she pulls it off, the work will go faster; if not, she'll have to do everything herself. But you can't lay down a floor or ceiling without boards. She's very concerned over the lack of funds, but the house is getting built... She'll be coming again in September, for a month. This past winter she visited her grandchildren in Perm, and paid a visit to her new domain on the way back — just for one day, to walk around, and stand in her own place, even though she could have taken a direct train to Rostov...

Natalia D. — born in Vologda,[10] came here from Moscow, has two children — daughters two and five years old.

She's been living in a tent since the end of May. She's divorced, and wants to take her children out of the city to avoid having them turned into puppets of the system. The summer's been cold and rainy, but not a single complaint from Natalia. They brought in an old trailer for her. She's peeled off all the old wallpaper and given it a thorough cleaning. She wants to cover it with board siding and put in insulation, so she's buying up boards... She has no money. Her husband provides enough to feed the children. She's now living with them, and earning a living by working in the old field, helping the men put in the foundations. She dreams of staying on in the domain — even if not for this winter, then at least for the following one. She's studying all the different house plans that she can build herself (including an adobe and a dugout). The children have become calmer and more cheerful.

---

[10] *Vologda* (pron. *VAW-lag-da*) — a city of more than 300,000, located 400 km north of Moscow. Like Moscow, Vologda's first recorded mention was in 1147.

When she drops by Liuba[11] E.'s house and sees what *she's* managed to do, she says: "Well, if you can do it, I can, too. After all, I'm younger and stronger than you." *She'll do it!*

She's always smiling, and has a terrific singing voice. She's got a college-level education. A beautiful soul!

Sorry to be so emotional, but I just love them all so much...

Nadezhda Z. — a farmer from Belarus. After the Chernobyl disaster they lived near Azov,[12] then spent a year at Paretskoye in the Suzdal area (while waiting for a field), and this past year they've been living in someone else's house at Koniayevo.

This summer she began construction on her own house. Two grown-up children are currently living in Moscow. Her daughter and sister have also taken plots. They all want to get together. The husband and children work. Nadezhda looks after the household, supervises the construction, and works on building the house herself... For many years she was part of a professional dance ensemble. She has the poise of a ballerina, even when she's pushing wheelbarrows full of manure... You can't help but admire her! The family has two dogs, four cats (mousers), rabbits, hens (Smirnov breed, preserved in homesteads during revolutionary times), a goat, and pigeons.

The house is awash in all sorts of flowers, both plain and exotic. She has an encyclopædic knowledge of everything she needs to know about. Her husband and children support her, but she has to do everything herself; they're

---

[11] *Liuba* — an informal variant of the name Liubov, a name which literally signifies 'Love'.

[12] *Azov* — a port on the Don River, not far from Rostov-on-Don.

leading their own lives for the time being. She is firmly and confidently building the future.

She recently broke her right arm (falling off a bicycle which her children gave her as a fiftieth-birthday present, so that she could get around everywhere). She took one day off. The very next day she was back forking hay (winter fodder for the animals). Now she's painting and planing the boards. When I asked her how she does it, she smiles: "With one hand tied behind my back!" She's always smiling, she loves to sing, she's the life of any party, she's everyone's darling, a real storehouse of knowledge, and our consultant to boot. She's tiny and slender, a support for the whole family. She's successful in everything she puts her hand to — house, construction, animals, vegetable garden, canning preserves, and what fruit liquors she makes!!! She hasn't any apartment or house to go back to, and by the fall she'll have to vacate the house in the village, as the owners are returning. She'll be spending the winter in her new house!

This information I obtained a year ago. Now all the heroines described have already finished building and none of them plan to retreat from their goal. No doubt it was women such as these the poet[13] had in mind when he said:

> *She'll stop a wild horse on the gallop,*
> *And enter a hut all in flames.*

---

[13] *the poet* — These lines dedicated to simple Russian village women (particularly their bravery in saving others) are taken from the epic poem *Moroz, Krasny nos* ('Frost, Red-nose'), written in 1864 by the celebrated Russian poet Nikolaj Alekseevich Nekrasov (1821–1878). Later he would write another epic poem (in two parts), entitled *Russkie zhenshchiny* ('Russian women').

And I would add: *She'll build the domain herself, and take her man into eternity.* But where is this man of hers? When will she have a chance to meet with him if she's engaged in such a big undertaking from morning 'til night?

How many bright young women in various parts of the country dream about co-creating a family domain! And it would be good if they could find their life partner before creating it.

I've thought about the possibility of organising a data bank where such women could register, and men could pay them a visit as temporary workers. Maybe the women could even choose themselves soulmates. It shouldn't be that the men choose them, but that they should choose the men.

We have an expression: *a high-society lady,*[14] meaning a woman who is 'in' with the élite crowd of the rich and famous. But what is this 'high society', if the in-crowd has nothing better to offer society at large than spread gossip in the tabloids? But if you marry one of these ladies, as many men have noted, you get nothing but caprices and unreasonable demands thrown at you.

It has come to me that the real 'ladies of high society' are the married and unmarried women of today who are building their family domains and are getting ready to give birth therein to healthy children, or pass along what they have built to their children already born.

Good can come only from them — good which will benefit not only single men but the nation as a whole. The children they bear will be the face of our future civilisation.

And Anastasia's grandfather could not have been more right when he spoke of the vital importance to resolve

[14]*a high-society lady* (Russian: *zhenshchina iz vysshego sveta*) — literally, 'a woman from a higher world'. Note that the Russian word *svet* (world) can also signify 'light'.

questions of the family on the national level. How they are being resolved today, the Russian families themselves know better than anyone — and not just *Russian* families.

Somehow we have got to resolve the question of organising events which will be able to assist these women, or rather assist the men to get acquainted with women who are setting up their own little Motherland.

I hereby request the administrators of the *Anastasia.ru* website to consider ways to better facilitate such acquaintanceships on-line. Perhaps each unmarried woman or man among my readers could post their address and contact co-ordinates on the site. I would remind anybody who doesn't have a computer that there are Internet clubs in almost every city, where they can read information from websites, as well as post offices which offer Internet access services.

For my part, I shall formulate here the text of my greeting to men of all countries where my books are available, and would ask all the translators in Europe and America to highlight it.

Gentlemen! I know that many of you, and especially those who are not yet involved in family life, would love to meet that unique woman with whom you could find joy in a lifetime companionship. But where to find such a woman? Just about the only recourse you have is to apply to one of the many marriage bureaus around. Beware, however, that almost all of them give priority to outward characteristics, as well as age, with only a little attention paid to character and life-goals. And even this 'little' has not been confirmed for certain. But what *is* for certain?... Women have shown up offering their youth, beauty and smiles, all ready to sign a marriage contract with you on the condition that you are rich and can guarantee them an abundance of material benefits. Already in Moscow there are cafés where beautiful women gather to offer themselves to rich suitors. This is no new phenomenon.

"But what's wrong with it?" certain men might think. "I'm a man of some means and I can afford to sign a marriage contract with a young and beautiful girl. All she has to do is take care of my needs in bed and make me the envy of everyone at social gatherings. After all, if you have relationships with young people, you'll become younger yourself."

All this is fine and dandy, but there is one *but*. What does your young cohabiter think and dream about? She is, after all, a living being and capable of attraction and affection, only the object of her affections is by no means *you*. So along comes the desire, sooner or later, to free herself from you, whom she sees as an obstacle on the road to happiness. So then, even if she doesn't resort to putting out a contract on your life (such things occasionally do happen, as you know), or to slipping poison into your morning coffee, it doesn't take much more than a thought — a subconscious thought at that — to get you permanently out of the way. And even though you may think you are bringing into your home a kind and tender beauty, in fact you are bringing home a poisonous serpent. The distinction between the two is only in external appearance, and so, instead of placing this serpent in an aquarium behind impenetrable glass, you are putting her beside you in your bed.

Perhaps, as a counter to the destructive phenomena of our life, some women have shown themselves to be harbingers of a new and happy civilisation. In building a family domain, they are not merely putting a roof over their head, they are actually laying the foundation for a whole new life. *An actual foundation!*

A dying billionaire, for example, will be revivified and will regain his youth upon meeting a woman like that. A prosperous businessman will flounder without her. It is not money that prolongs life, but the thought of your beloved and the Space of Love which the two of you have co-created together. And insofar that it guarantees the conditions requisite for a quick and conscious reincarnation, it not only prolongs life, but makes life eternal.

No matter what words I have written, no matter what arguments I have put forward, they will not succeed in touching your heart the way an acquaintanceship with such women can. I would urge you to make every effort to get to know these earthly goddesses of eternity.

And it is quite possible that this encounter will be similar to the one Anastasia told me about.[15]

---

[15]The whole of the following chapter is narrated by Anastasia.

CHAPTER TWENTY-FOUR

Millennial encounter

One day a girl in her mid-twenties by the name of Liuba came to one of the 'soulmate gatherings'. She was wearing an embroidered linen blouse and a plain skirt whose hem reached just below the knees. A small travel-bag was slung on a strap over her shoulder, but it contained nothing more than a few rather plain outfits.

The girl walked up and down the street in the hopes of finding some sort of privately run lodging for the night. During the gatherings all hotels (both for Russian and foreign visitors) and *pension* rooms had been booked up in advance. Besides, Liuba could not afford an expensive hotel room, and so she was looking for plainer lodgings. But there was no chance of finding any privately-run accommodation during the nuptial gatherings. With little hope of success, Liuba asked a woman who happened to be coming out of the gate in front of a private house:

"Hello, there. Could you tell me please, whether you might have any rooms available in your house for overnight accommodation? I'm looking for something not too expensive."

The woman replied:

"Not much chance of that, dearie. Everything's been booked up for ages. All the visitors make arrangements in advance through the housing office. You're just wasting your time. You'd better head for the railway station, or you won't find a place to sit down even there."

"Thanks for the advice. I'll probably do that," Liuba responded and headed down the street in the direction of the terminal.

"Wait a minute, dearie. Come here," the woman called out, and Liuba came back to her.

"I'll tell you what you can do. Try knocking or ringing the bell five houses down. There's a doorbell right at the gate — try ringing it. Maybe an old woman will come out — one that looks like Baba-Yaga.[1] She's Greek, and has a hooked nose. My husband says that all Greek women are beautiful when they're young, but when they get old, they all end up looking like Baba-Yoshkas.

"Anyway, dearie, you can ask and see if she's got any rooms. Before, when her husband was still alive, she used to have all sorts of people stop over, but he died, and she hasn't let a single person in these past three years now. Anyway, you can always try asking — she just might give you a room."

"Thanks, I'll try," replied Liuba. And she went along to the house the woman pointed out. She rang the bell once, and a minute later she tried it again, right at the gate, but nobody came out. Finally, after ten minutes had gone by, the door creaked open, and a bent-over old woman came out. She came down the grapevine-lined path and opened the gate, groaning at every step. She started in speaking without any formalities of saying hello.

"What you knockin' at my gate for, girl?" she asked with a tone of annoyance.

"I wanted to ask you about a room. A kind lady, your neighbour, suggested I should."

"She was not bein' no kind, she was laughin' at you. I haint had no roomers for ages."

---

[1] *Baba-Yaga* (stress on final syllable), also known as *Baba-Yoshka* — a witch (usually portrayed as an old hag with a hooked nose), who, despite her threatening looks and habits (in the Christian period her image was often demonised to represent evil), actually offers help to the good and punishes the evil in traditional Slavic folk-tales.

"I know, she told me that too. But I've been looking all day and I haven't found anything, so I decided to ring your bell, just on the off-chance."

"Just on 'off-chance', eh? Well, you won't find any 'off-chance' with me. You've *all* come here just on 'off-chance'... So, just like everyone else, you have come here to find yourself 'a bloke'?"

"I want to meet my intended. Please, forgive me for bothering you. I'll head down to the station and spend the night there."

It began to drizzle, and the old woman grumbled:

"To hell with these girls! To hell with them! And now — it's started: rain. Fine, I will set you under this tent-roof in my garden. There is this hammock there, and this bench, and nails for you can hang your clothing up. And for this you will pay me five hundred roubles each night."

"Five hundred?!" exclaimed Liuba in surprise.

"And just how much was you thinkin' it will be? What, you imaginin' that you are come to visit your relations?"

"Okay, I'll give you five hundred. Only I wanted to stay here ten days. Never mind, I'll just stay for five. I agree to your terms, Granny."[2]

"Then come. You can see where you will sleep and pay me this money each day in advance."

Five days went by. On the fifth morning Liuba began neatly packing her plain-looking clothing away in her bag. The old woman approached her, groaning and leaning on her cane.

"So you already start packin', eh, girl? You leavin'?"

"Yes, Granny. It's been five days now."

"Five days. You got your ticket?" the old woman asked, sitting down on the bench.

---

[2]*Granny* (Russian: *babushka,* pron. *BAH-boosh-ka*) — a more or less respectful term of address to senior women.

"Yes, I bought a single/return ticket before I left home. The return is actually for five days from now, but I think I'll be able to exchange it at the station and get one for today or tomorrow."

"No chance of that — not with everyone and her dog comin' and goin' around here these days. I will tell you something, girl, you stay with me five days more until your ticket will be good."

"I can't. I've got no money left to pay you."

"No worry. No need to pay, you just stay."

"Thanks, Granny!"

"'Thanks,' she says... Only your stayin' will not do you any good!"

"Why d'you say that?"

"I been watchin' you. That is no good way to look for 'a bloke' these days. Why you are up at dawn each day? What is the use? All 'a blokes' are still asleep that time of day. But *you* — you go to bed right early. Right when all this partyin' begins, this is when you decide to go to bed for each night! All those 'a blokes' keep partyin' 'til midnight, while you are in bed at ten. Besides, you dress like a nun, no makeup. That is no good way to find 'a bloke' today."

"I'm preparing my body, you see, Granny, for my encounter with my intended. And so I try to maintain a strict daily routine. I don't make myself up so that he can recognise me."

"Recognise?! You, girl, you sound like you are 'a mite daft in the head'!"

"That's what my Mama says, too. But there's nothing I can do about it. I often have dreams about him looking for me all over the globe and not being able to find me."

"Dreams? You have been dreamin'? Here too?"

"Yes, twice already. Once it seemed I was walking in a huge garden, and he was there, too, only there was no way we could approach each other. And it seemed as though I could hear his voice, calling to me over and over: 'Where are you? Where are you?'"

"You heard? A voice? You know, you probably ought go see a doctor, girl. What is all this about an 'intended' bein' pounded in your head? To a point where you even hear voices, in your dreams?!"

"Sometimes I dream that I lived with him once a long, long time ago. And we had children and grandchildren."

"Once upon a time? Well, girl, next thing you be tellin' me you can say what he look like!"

"Yes, I can: he's half a head taller than me, with light brown hair. And hazel eyes. And a kindly smile, only a little gap between two of his teeth. And he walks in a proper, dignified fashion."

"A gap between his teeth? His walk? But what if someone else should come?"

"They've come. My Mama's always after me about that at home, saying that my dreams will keep me an old maid forever."

"'An old maid'? Of course, 'an old maid'. You will never find your 'bloke' that way, not with those dreams of yours. You know, girl, I will tell you something. Here, take my rainbow shawl. Put it over your shoulders, and tie it just little more fashionably. And go walk along the embankment later tonight."

"Thank you, Granny, for your concern. But I can't cover up my blouse with a shawl. You see, I did the embroidery myself. It came to me in a dream. And it seems as though at some time in the past I was wearing this embroidered blouse when I was taking a stroll with my intended in the garden."

"Embroidered? Takin' a stroll? Well, girl, you... Well, God be your judge. There is some milk there on a table, and I have made scones. Have a bite to eat! I will just scoot to my neighbours' for a bit."

The old woman hobbled off with a groan, muttering all the while to herself: *She will put me in my grave yet. I must be daft. I took her in, and now I cannot help worry about her. I will go talk to my neighbour's son, see if he will show her some attention. Yes, he will show her some attention. He is dark-haired, and she wants light brown with a gap between his teeth, but there is nobody like that among my neighbours. She will put me in my grave!*

That morning Liuba began wandering around the public garden. She picked up a *pirozhok*[3] with potato filling for lunch. As she was walking past a restaurant, a group of men were just coming out of the door. They were laughing and chatting away in some foreign tongue. When they saw Liuba, they spoke to her in their own language. Liuba didn't understand and walked on past. Right off the men began talking with other girls.

Then, all of a sudden, without turning around, she could feel someone detach himself from the group of cheerful foreigners and come after her. She knew for certain that *she* was his specific target. She even counted his footsteps without quickening her own pace, and for some reason her heart started to tremble. She could feel his breath behind her, and all at once the foreigner began addressing her in a language she couldn't understand:

"*Mit dir, die wünderschöne Göttin, dürfte ich den ewigen Raum der Liebe schaffen.*"[4]

Liuba could not decipher the German words. But for some reason she found herself whispering:

[3]*pirozhok* (pron. *pee-ra-ZHOK*) — a Russian pastry with a meat, vegetable or fruit filling, akin to a Ukrainian pierogie. See footnote 2 in Book 2, Chapter 11: "A sharp about-turn".

[4]*Mit dir ... schaffen* — German for: 'With you, marvellous goddess, I could create an eternal Space of Love'.

"I'm ready to help you in your grand co-creàtion!" and she turned around to look at the stranger.

There before her stood a young man, half a head taller than she. Light brown hair, hazel eyes, a kindly smile and a small gap between two of his teeth. He held out his arms to Liuba, and without realising quite what she was doing, Liuba snuggled her head against his chest. He hugged her trembling body as though he had known her for an eternity.

The unseen planets in the heavens began to quiver for joy. Oh, how many events did they need to create to arrange the threads of destiny for the ages! But it worked! They met and they embraced!

Radomir with his marvellous Liubomila! And even if they don't remember the past, their souls will create a future to marvel at.

People on the beach couldn't figure out why the young couple were creating some kind of design or sketch in the sand. They were speaking different languages, but it seemed as though they understood each other. First they would discuss the drawing, then argue a bit, and then all of a sudden come to an ecstatic agreement.

Carried away as they were with the drawing, Liubomila and Radomir did not know, either, that they were sketching in the sand a design of the splendid family domain which they had created just before their wedding five thousand years earlier.

"There should be a pond here, a round one," said Radomir in his own language, and dug a little round hole in the sand to represent the pond.

"But not that shape," whispered Liubomila. "It should definitely be oval," she countered, changing the round hole to an oval shape.

"Yes, exactly, an oval pond is much better," Radomir agreed, as though suddenly remembering something.

That evening they came back to the house where Liubomila was staying. She asked her elderly landlady permission for her companion to drop in for the evening. The landlady agreed.

With a smile on her face, Liubomila drifted off to sleep in the hammock, while he sat on the bench, gently rocking the hammock and delicately fending off flies with a small tree-branch. And he sang something very, very soft.

From a window in the house, the old woman peered at them through a crack in the curtain, until just before dawn.

In the morning on the little table in front of the house stood milk and scones, covered with a white linen tablecloth. There was also a note, written in an ageing hand. Liubomila read it aloud:

"I have gone away on errands. Will not be back for couple of days. Look after house. To look after it, stay in my big room. There is food in a fridge..."

Liubomila and Radomir left town together. But where did they go? The ages will show where their family line will be reborn.

CHAPTER TWENTY-FIVE

Anastasia's wedding

As I bade farewell to Anastasia's grandfather, I said to him:

"You'll have to forgive me for my misunderstanding back in the taiga, when we were talking about the party's goals and activities. Now I realise that the stronger the family's role in the State, the more loving families will be living in it, and the more order there will be in the nation as a whole.

"We must restore the customs and rites which our ancestors thought through. They only need to be somehow adapted to our modern age. Anyway, I'm beginning to realise that they are not even 'rites' in the traditional sense of the word. They constitute the great science of life. And the wise-men were the greatest scholars and wisest teachers of all.

"Apart from that, you know what I'm regretting right now? I'm regretting that I knew nothing of these rites back before my first encounter with Anastasia. About how they help in using the planets for the benefit of families. I didn't know that, and so Anastasia had to bear a son, and then a daughter, without being wedded."

Anastasia's grandfather gave me a sly look and, smiling through his grey moustache, said:

"And so, now you know that, you're concerned as to whether Anastasia bore her son and daughter by you?"

"No, I wouldn't say I'm terribly concerned. But still, it wouldn't hurt for Anastasia and me to go through the appropriate rite."

"It's a good thing, Vladimir, that you have these regrets. It means you're beginning to understand the essence of being, and where human society finds itself at the moment. But you need not feel regret when it comes to Anastasia. She was married before you spent that first night with her."

It was several minutes before I could get over the shock and regain enough composure to speak. Finally I sputtered:

"To whom? I didn't go through any wedding ceremony. I remember that for certain."

"You didn't. It was enough for us that she went through it alone. For three days my father couldn't get over her weird behaviour. It was the kind of gaffe that not a single man of wisdom could have thought up in a million years. But the upshot is, she's married."

"To whom?"

"Maybe, to you."

"But I never went through a wedding. And what's this about 'maybe'? What, you don't know for certain?"

"What she did, Vladimir, nobody can evaluate, at least not yet. It's entirely possible she created this magnificent rite herself and thereby offered all women the opportunity of making their illegitimate children legitimate. It's entirely possible she created something in Heaven, besides. What she has created, perhaps only a wise-man would be in a position to evaluate. I'd better tell you everything in order."

And Anastasia's grandfather recounted to me the following:

That first time you came with Anastasia to her glade and were getting ready to go to bed in the dugout, *we* had to come to our granddaughter's glade, too.

"Why?" you might ask.

She summoned us. We felt her summoning us and my father and I came to the lake.

Anastasia was standing on the shore, holding in her hands a crown of flowers woven together. She was all prettied up in her very best, just like a bride. As we approached, my father asked her in a rather severe tone:

"Anastasia, what events prompted you to prevent the flow of our evening thoughts?"

"Oh, Grandpakins and Great-Grandpakins, I have no one else to present myself to but you. You alone are capable of comprehending me."

"Then speak," allowed my father.

"I am now about to get married, and I've summoned you as my witnesses."

"Get married?" I queried, "*get married?* And where is your bridegroom?"

I was not supposed to speak when Father was leading the dialogue. He gave me a stern look. She didn't respond to *me*, but to him as the elder:

"When the wedding rite is performed, the young couple are first asked how they will set up their life, what Space they will co-create."

Father knew about that, and agreed, without violating any rules. But here, it seems, our granddaughter somehow managed to 'switch off' our consciousness, as you say in your language — either that or she charmed us as in a marvellous dream.

Anastasia began talking about her future neighbours. You know how she can create holograms with her thought, don't you, Vladimir?... Yes, I thought so.

Only this time over the surface of the lake she changed the pictures of the future of the Earth at an incredible rate of speed. Her pictures were incredibly clear and involving.

In one scene there were people walking along flower-lined allées, self-confident and with dignified smiles. Another portrayed angelic-looking children running through a meadow to a river. In a third, we seemed to be looking down on a lake from a great height and seeing the reflection of the whole planet.

And there were a great many scenes and episodes showing marvellous landscapes of extraordinary beauty.

And all at once a single Man appeared over the lake, as though out of a mist. And everything else suddenly disappeared. This Man stood in the middle of the lake all by himself, looking at us. Presently, another man approached from his right, then a maiden of extraordinary beauty, then a second, and a third. After that they were joined by two little twin boys holding hands. A whole lot of people were standing around, all tall and slim. They looked at us with kindly smiles, which made a pleasant feeling of warmth run through our bodies. At that very moment we heard the voice of our granddaughter:

"Grandpakins and Great-Grandpakins, look: these are your descendants thinking about you with warm smiles on their faces. Look, Great-Grandpakins Moisey — you see the boy standing at the end, he looks like you and his gaze is radiant with your soul."

When all the holograms disappeared, leaving us standing there with extraordinary feelings, Anastasia all at once said:

"What do you think, who can place the crown upon my head?"

And my father, feeling absolutely no sense of subterfuge, enquired (as was customary in the wedding rite):

"Maiden, who may place the crown upon your head?"

And she replied:

"I place the crown upon my own head in the sight of you, of Heaven and of my own destiny." And with that she placed the crown upon her own head.

"And where is the one you have chosen to wear the crown?" Father asked.

"He is getting ready to go to sleep. But even when he is awake, he is sleeping, too. He knows nothing about our rites. You will need to ask him again, after several years sweep by."

"You have violated the rules, Anastasia," said Father, stern-ly. "The ancient science of the wise-men. Two people ought to take part in the rite. People can only get married to each other. The wedding rite has not taken place."

"Believe me, Great-Grandpakins, it has. I am now married in the sight of Heaven. Two people *should* take part in the rite. But, after all, it is customary to ask one first, and then the other, as to their desire to be wed.

"*I* was asked, and I gave *my* consent for all to hear. My cho-sen one is still thinking about his, and he can think for as long as he likes as the years go by. Nobody has ever defined how much time is permitted between the two questions. It could be a moment, it could be ten years. But even if in the nega-tive might be his reply here, I shall remain married in my own sight. And the covenant of the ages I shall not defy."

Father wanted to say something more. He had even start-ed speaking when a huge peal of thunder resounded from the sky, drowning out all his words. And he turned and started walking off, paying no attention to the path under his feet, as he was wont to do when he got agitated about something. I could just barely keep up with him as he walked, but I heard how fast he was talking, as though to himself:

"She's a stubborn lass, cunning and clever, not an easy one to countermand. It seems that she is being eternally pandered to by Heaven itself. She is changing the very correlation of the planets. Does that mean women now have the opportu-nity of wedding themselves and begetting their children on a lawful basis? We must figure out what Anastasia has done, but first, all ought be returned to the existing laws of being. They have not endured these many ages for nought. To do this, we must come up with a weighty objection. But I was not able to: she's greatly cunning and clever, but I... Aha, I've discovered a way to object and make her wedding rite of none effect."

All at once Father did a sharp about-turn and headed for the lake. As we approached the shore, but had not yet emerged from the bushes, we saw over the lake an extraordinary light, albeit barely noticeable — and the stars reflected in the water. It looked as though they were falling into the lake in a shower. And there was our granddaughter, sitting all by herself on a fallen pine log, wearing her floral crown. She was looking in the direction of the dugout where you were sleeping, and softly singing.

My father did not emerge from the bushes. He listened to her song, and then said:

"She is wedded." And he tapped with his staff on the ground, adding: "Nobody has the power now to annul her marriage. In terms of strength it knows no equal, and... whether she was married by Heaven or by herself on her own, it makes no difference."

"And what did Anastasia sing?" you ask, Vladimir. "What song?" It was this one:

> By my own hand in wedlock I am crowned —
> And now to be your woman I am found.
> You are, you know, the only man for me.
> Our dreams shall all be brought to life, you'll see.
> On Planet Earth, our Terran world of blue,
> Our son will happy be with me and you.
> Our daughter will be fair and quick of mind,
> To many a Man they will be good and kind.
> By Heaven I am joined with you together.
> You know I am your woman now for ever.
> The grandchildren we have will live afar —
> We'll see them on that big, bright, distant star.

To be continued....

A voyage of self-discovery
Translator's Afterword

> *And the Lord said unto me,*
> *Arise, take thy journey before the people...*
> — Moses (Deut. 10: 11)

It has been a long and interesting journey indeed. This journey began for me in the autumn of 2004 — in a manner of speaking, aboard ship. The ship was the *Patrice Lumumba,* and belonged to one Vladimir Nikolaevich Megré, a seasoned entrepreneur who traded up and down the Ob River in Western Siberia, selling produce and manufactured goods brought from southern cities to northern villages and buying up local handicrafts in return. As with the vast majority of Megré's readers, the description of the *Lumumba* in Book 1, Chapter 1 ("The ringing cedar"), served as my first introduction to the much more powerful (mentally speaking) literary vessel known as the *Ringing Cedars Series (RCS).*

I was invited on board the *RCS* by its editorial 'Captain', Leonid Sharashkin, who had in turn been commissioned by 'Admiral' Megré to sail across the seas and bring the ship's precious cargo of ideas to the land of Anglophonia. I was hired as an English-speaking 'navigator' familiar with this new land's linguistic waters, and equipped by forty years' experience in Russian-English translation to present these ideas in a format capable of reaching the hearts and minds of Anglophones. The adventure sounded promising, and, admittedly impelled by a sense of divine guidance, I gladly signed on, eager to set sail with a *Yo-heave-ho!* (or *Ey-ukhnem!* — as the Volga boatmen were said to chant). Eight times (count them!), no sooner had we delivered a shipment to its destination than we went back for more.

Now, as we approach a layover of indefinite duration (following the completion of our ninth voyage), I can look back and honestly say that the experience really has delivered on its promises — these trips have been truly rewarding in terms of both excitement and education,[1] and I am actually going to miss the many ups and downs that my editor and I have been tossed about by in this particular venture in literary navigation. Part of me will be sad, at last, to disembark onto terra firma (safer, perhaps, but not nearly as exciting), but I shall content myself with the 'glad' part — watching from afar as the nine shipments of ideas we helped deliver begin bearing fruit in the consciousness and lives of Americans, Australians, Britons, Canadians, New Zealanders, South Africans and countless others who for some reason have had the English edition of the *RCS* land in their hands.

From a translator's point of view, each of the linguistic shoals, sandbanks and icebergs we met along the way (not to mention the occasional.typhoon!) offered a particular challenge. Some of these challenges were more formidable in appearance than others. My editor and I soon discovered that the task at hand was not just a matter of translation, pure and simple, for we were soon confronted in our journey by a whole host of cultural phenomena (references to people, places, institutions, historical events and cultural traditions) that would not be as familiar to Westerners as they were to native Russian readers of the Series, and hence required (sometimes substantial) research and documentation.

---

[1] One of the 'educational' rewards was a 'side-trip' around to the other side of a 'mountain', which provided fresh insight into my own beliefs and faith. See Translator's Afterword to Book 6.

Mindful of the lessons of the *Titanic,* I hope we were at least moderately successful in resisting the temptation to place too much trust in technology or to become over-confident and over-reliant on our own previous professional experience.[2] The above-mentioned challenges, both large and small, were met through constant reference to both paper-published and on-line 'charts' (Russian and English dictionaries, thesauruses, encyclopædias and Google searches) — sometimes it came down literally to 'phone a friend', and on several occasions to a prayer for more of that 'divine guidance' that had urged me to climb aboard in the first place! Not only that, but results were checked over and over again before being entered into the final 'log'.

On occasion we even found ourselves exploring hitherto uncharted waters and had to navigate, as it were, by the seat of our pants. For example:

How to describe a Russian *dacha* and its primary function as a vegetable-raising centre to North Americans (and other anglophones) raised on vacation cottages with their swimming, boating and sundry recreational facilities?[3]

How to select a suitable English equivalent for the word *chelovek* — a Russian word that still designates a human being of either gender — when faced with a choice between (a) *human,* derived from words associated with lower concepts (like the ground) and (b) *man,* which originally (like *chelovek*) described a 'thinking, intelligent being' of either gender but has since become narrowed in meaning to include (in popular parlance, at least) only half the human race?[4]

---

[2]Certain aspects of technology, I admit, were most definitely a time-saving boon. Thank goodness for e-mail and the Internet!

[3]See Translator's Preface to Book 1.

[4]See Translator's Preface to Book 1 (especially the 2nd edition).

How to portray *dolmens* and other 'sacred sites' to a culture more accustomed to high-rise construction sites and Internet web sites?[5]

How to put across the concept of one's millennia-old *Rodina* ('Motherland') to readers whose roots in their current place of residence may go back no more than a few years or even mere months?[6]

How to express concepts of the pre-Christian Vedic Russian culture in an intelligible manner to English-speakers, when such concepts are still unfamiliar to many Russians themselves in their native tongue?![7]

How to reproduce the author's plethora of writing styles (from 'choppy novice writer' to authentic-sounding 'blue-collar dialogue' to the 'poetic prose' of Anastasia's metaphysical descriptions — not to mention poetry itself) in such a way as to convey to the reader not only the semantic meaning, but, just as importantly, the *literary feeling* of the original work?[8]

It is the *RCS*'s readers (even more than its literary critics) who will be the ultimate judges of our success in meeting these challenges.

Then, beyond the translation questions (which, after all, can sometimes get bogged down in the nitty-gritty of historical etymology and psycholinguistic nuances), lies the broader issue of how the Series as a whole is reaching an anglophone readership far more attuned to Gene Roddenberry's *Star Trek* or J. K. Rowling's *Harry Potter* than to the *Holy Bible* or the

[5]See Translator's Preface to Book 2.

[6]See Translator's and Editor's Afterword to Book 4.

[7]See Book 6, Chapter 5: "The history of mankind, as told by Anastasia".

[8]Again, see Translator's Preface to Book 1.

Bhagavad Gita[9] — a readership that is only too ready and willing to embrace phenomena that lie outside traditional physical perception, provided that the works presenting them are duly confined to the 'Fiction' or 'Occult' shelves of their local library, bookshop or video store.

After all, one doesn't have to read too far into the *RCS* before encountering passages that look as though they might be right at home in a *Star Trek* episode or a sci-fi novel — Anastasia's telepathic ray,[10] for example, or the "fiery sphere" described to the author as watching over Anastasia as a baby.[11] Or her later reference to the not-so-mythical fire-breathing "Gorynytch Serpent".[12]

It is all too easy, on the basis of such examples, to dismiss the whole Series as just another (albeit very intricately woven) sci-fi yarn. It is all too easy, *upon first glance*, to classify Anastasia's descriptions (in this present volume, for example) of so-called 'pagan' rites in the pre-Christian Vedic Russian civilisation as just another fanciful foray into the esoteric, or the occult. Or to pass off the *RCS* as yet another entry in the 'wishful thinking' category, where a number of critics have pegged recent 'feel-good' films such as *The Secret*.[13]

What distinguishes the *RCS* from science fiction (or, at least, from the vast majority of science fiction works) is the

---

[9]*Bhagavad Gita* — a sacred Hindu text written in Sanskrit; the name literally means 'Song of the Divine One'.

[10]See Book 1, Chapter 7: "Anastasia's ray".

[11]See Book 2, Chapter 27: "The anomaly".

[12]See Book 4, toward the end of Chapter 3: "The first appearance of *you*".

[13]*The Secret* — a film produced by Rhonda Byrne for Prime Time Productions, directed by Drew Heriot. Since its release in 2006, the film has stirred up a good deal of excitement along with a heavy barrage of criticism. In my view, this work does indeed hint at a great truth, but one with much deeper ramifications than suggested by the superficial treatment presented on screen (which seems to be focused more on effects than underlying causes).

fact that it attempts to show how even such 'far-fetched' accounts as those mentioned above could actually refer to naturally occurring, scientifically explainable phenomena rather than just mere literary inventions or the occult fantasies of the human mind.[14] After all, in 1865, Jules Verne's *From the Earth to the Moon* was written and received as a science-*fiction* classic, only to turn into scientific reality a little more than a century later with the success of the Apollo XI Moon mission on 20 July 1969.[15] As for the charge of 'occultism', Anastasia (through the author) takes great pains, especially in Book 6, to distance her concept of the Universe from any kind of occult phenomena. These only lead mankind, she says, to being "completely disoriented as to the Space created by God".[16] And in regard to the "rites of love" in particular (described in

---

[14]See, for example, the technical explanation of the 'flying saucer' phenomenon presented in Book 1, Chapter 16: "Flying saucers? Nothing extraordinary!". The above-mentioned Book 1, Chapter 7, includes a reference to experiments on 'rays' by the Director of the Russian Academy of Natural Sciences' International Institute of Theoretical and Applied Physics. And the account of the 'fire-breathing serpent' in Book 4, Chapter 3, also includes a logical explanation for what is generally dismissed as a mythical phenomenon.

[15]It is interesting to note, too, that a number of *Star Trek*'s 'inventions' have already become 'science fact', within mere decades of their presentation as 'science fiction' — the 'medical tricorder', for example — a *Star Trek*-inspired device under development at the University of Alberta. See: Jodie Sinnema, "Scientists test 'tricorder' to root out disease". *The Edmonton Journal*, 16 September 2005, p. B1. In fact, a whole array of books may be found dealing with the factual aspects of *Star Trek* — e.g.: Lawrence M. Krauss, *The physics of Star Trek*. With a Foreword by Stephen Hawking. New York: Harper Collins, 1995. Still another 'science fiction' TV series of the 1990s (this one all too short-lived) — *SeaQuest DSV* — featured a commentary at the end of many of its episodes by Dr Robert Ballard, Scientist Emeritus in the Department of Applied Ocean Physics and Engineering at the Woods Hole Oceanographic Institution, relating the series' science fiction to science fact.

[16]See Book 6, Chapter 8: "Occultism".

the present book), Anastasia's grandfather assures the author: "None of these rites was characterised by occult superstition, as today. Each one served as a school of higher learning, an examination by the Universe."[17]

'Anastasia says...' 'Anastasia's grandfather does...'

Yes, in almost any discussion of Vladimir Megré's *Ringing Cedars Series* among its readers, phrases like these tend to trip off the tongue without a second thought, leaving many outsiders (and even some 'insiders') to wonder: *Who is this Anastasia?* Which brings us to what may be the most frequently asked readers' question of all — one which Québec writer Mado Sauvé chose as the opening sentence of her review of the Series in the Spring 2007 issue of *Le Journal Vert*: *"Anastasia existe-t-elle?"* (Does Anastasia exist?)

I have a feeling Sauvé expresses what is on many readers' minds as she continues:

> Does she really live in the Siberian taiga or was she born of the imagination of a clever entrepreneur? Even after reading the first four [books] of the Series ... it is still difficult to answer this question.[18]

A broad range of opinion on this issue has indeed been expressed to date by *RCS* readers collectively — from those who dismiss her as a mere figment of the author's imagination to those who see her as the reincarnation of some ancient

---

[17]Quoted from Chapter 1: "Love — the essence of the Cosmos".

[18]Original: "Vit-elle vraiment dans la taïga sibérienne ou est-elle née de l'imagination d'un habile entrepreneur? Même après avoir lu les quatre premiers [livres] de la série ... il est encore difficile de répondre à cette question." — Mado Sauvé, "Le mystère de la déesse russe". *Le Journal Vert* (printemps 2007).

prophet. But to me this only begs a further set of questions: *What does it mean, to 'exist'? Is 'existence' an objective or a subjective state? Is 'existence' confined to material perception, or can it be determined by non-material criteria (faith, for example)?* Megré quotes Anastasia herself as saying:

"I exist for those for whom I exist."[19] What could that possibly mean?

In pondering the question of the existence of Megré's Anastasia and her family, it might be worthwhile considering a few other personages whose existence has been a subject for questioning over the ages — names like Shakespeare, Santa Claus (Father Christmas), Job in the Old Testament and even Christ Jesus in the New. In a civilisation so reliant upon physical, material evidence as the primary, if not the only criterion for proof of existence, perhaps it is little wonder that sometimes figures with a larger-than-life reputation fall prey to public suspicion as to their very existence. Are we not almost globally educated to be sceptical about anything that departs from a society-defined, materially determined norm?

Such is the case with the man considered to be the greatest writer the English-speaking world has ever produced. No simple village-dweller, some have said, could have possibly produced all the time-tested plays and sonnets credited to the Bard of Avon.[20] And yet few today would deny that the

---

[19]Quoted from Book 1, Chapter 26: "Dreams — creating the future".

[20]For a sampling of the controversy surrounding Shakespeare's authorship, see: George McMichael & Edgar M. Glenn: *Shakespeare and his rivals. A casebook on the authorship controversy.* New York: Odyssey Press, 1962; H. N. Gibson, *The Shakespeare claimants: a critical survey of the four principal theories concerning the authorship of the Shakespeare plays.* Oxford & New York: Routledge, 2005; Mark Anderson, *'Shakespeare' by another name.* New York: Gotham Books, 2005.

writer universally known as *Shakespeare* actually existed in some form. After all, his masterpieces did not magically appear one day out of a vacuum![21]

Many people today, not only in America but elsewhere in the world, are familiar with the appeal of a little eight-year-old girl named Virginia O'Hanlon to the editor of the New York's *Sun* newspaper in September 1897:

"Some of my little friends say there is no Santa Claus. Papa says, 'If you see it in THE SUN it's so.' Please tell me the truth: is there a Santa Claus?"

And few can forget the key phrase (italicised below) from veteran newsman Francis Church's memorable reply, even if they are not as familiar with the writer's name or his remarkable justification for this reply:

Virginia, your little friends are wrong. They have been affected by the skepticism of a skeptical age. They do not believe except [what] they see...

Yes, Virginia, there is a Santa Claus. He exists as certainly as love and generosity and devotion exist, and you know that they abound and give to your life its highest beauty and joy...[22]

---

[21]The thought has often come to me over the past few years that, given the powerful ideas and intricately crafted literary structure evident throughout the *RCS*, if it should somehow turn out that the whole story of Anastasia was entirely the author's invention, then Vladimir Megré would have to be considered one of the world's cleverest and most gifted writers since Shakespeare! Even if most of his information were drawn from a variety of secondary sources, weaving them all together into a plausible plot-line over two-thousand-plus pages of text could be considered nothing short of a major literary feat. On the other hand, it would be no denigration of Megré's writing skills to accept that he has simply described pretty much what he actually witnessed, *in some form,* from experience.

And lest anyone hasten to dismiss Santa Claus (in contrast to Shakespeare) as a completely mythical figure, it should be remembered that St Nicholas was indeed a real human being in the flesh. He was the Bishop of Myra in what is now western Turkey, back in the 3rd century C.E. It was his reputation for secret giving to the needy that eventually evolved into the popular story of the world's ultimate holiday gift-giver.

A similar question hangs over the Old-Testament character of Job in the Bible. According to Dummelow's Bible commentary:

> It has always been a question whether the book of Job is to be regarded as history or parable. Among the Jews themselves the prevailing opinion was that it was strictly historical, though some of their Rabbis were inclined to think that the person of Job was created by the writer of this book in order to set forth his teaching on the problem that was vexing human thought. ... The opinion of Luther is probably the correct one, viz. that a person called Job did really exist, but that his history has been treated poetically.[23]

---

[22]Francis Pharcellus Church, editorial in *The Sun* (New York City), 21 September 1897 *(italics—JW)*. (The full text of the editorial is available in many on-line sources.) Many books and cinema films have echoed Church's thesis in different ways, notably director George Seaton's 1947 film classic *Miracle on 34th Street*. In the 1994 re-make under the same title (this one directed by Les Mayfield), Santa's existence is 'proved' in a court of law by reference to the phrase *In God we trust*, which appears on the reverse of every American one-dollar banknote. This is cited as evidence of the United States government's endorsement of the existence of an entity based on faith alone.

[23]Rev. J. R. Dummelow, *A commentary on the Holy Bible*. New York: Macmillan, 1908, p. 292. According to Dummelow, *Daniel* is another biblical figure whose historical existence is a matter of some controversy (see *Commentary*, pp. 525–526).

Can we expect a similar commentary to be written about the person of Anastasia a millennium or two hence?

While *Job* may indeed have been mainly an allegory written for moral instruction, what of that most celebrated among the human figures of the Bible — namely, *Christ Jesus*,[24] whose life and works form the very foundation of the whole movement of Christianity? Many Christians believe Jesus to be the earthly incarnation of God Himself; others accept him, rather, as God's Son and messenger to mankind, but there are few indeed who deny his historical existence. And yet the authenticity of the Gospel records is occasionally called into question, and not just by atheists.

It is instructive to examine the writings of two late-nineteenth-century spiritual thinkers on this point — one of them a peasant philosopher in Russia and the other the founder and leader of a world-wide Christian movement headquartered in America. While neither of them actually question Jesus' existence themselves, both shed a non-traditional light on the ultimate significance of that 'existence'.

On 12 May 1888 the Molokan[25] peasant writer Fedor Alekseevich Zheltov (1859–1938), a deeply committed Christian, sent a treatise he had just written to Leo Tolstoy (whom he regarded as a mentor), entitled "On life as faith in Christ".

---

[24]While *Christ* and *Jesus* are often used synonymously, the two words are quite distinct in meaning. *Jesus* (*Iesous*) is a Greek adaptation of the Hebrew first name *Yhôwshûa* (lit. 'Jehovah saves'), identical to the Old-Testament name *Joshua*, while *Christ* (*Khristós*) is the Greek translation of the Hebrew *Mâshîyakh* ('Messiah', or 'the anointed one'), and can be thought of more as Jesus' title, or the spiritual, immortal idea he embodied (the message itself as distinct from the messenger). For a further explanation of the distinction, see: Mary Baker Eddy, *Science and health with Key to the Scriptures*. Boston: Trustees under the will of Mary Baker Eddy, final English edition 1911, p. 333.

Toward the end of the treatise he makes a rather startling declaration:

> None of the actions and events accompanying Christ's sermon are a stumbling-block for me — I do not rely upon them as a basis for understanding truth, and it makes no difference to me whether they happened or did not happen, or how they happened, whether they were imaginary or real, whether the Gospels were written by the apostles or by someone else — none of that makes a difference nor is it dear to me. What is dear to me is only the truth which Christ imparted — it in itself is a precious jewel and my task is to know its price and to know why it is so precious.[26]

About two decades later, on 1 December 1906, the discoverer of Christian Science,[27] Mary Baker Eddy (1821–1910), published a statement[28] in the weekly magazine she had

---

[25] *Molokans* — a Christian sect which broke away from the Russian Orthodox Church in the mid-16th century, rejecting ecclesiastical hierarchy and its alliance with government and militarism and insisting God must be worshipped primarily in one's heart and mind. They left their initial alliance with the Doukhobors, who, unlike the Molokans, preferred oral Scriptural traditions over written texts. Toward the end of the nineteenth century many Molokans went to America, while large numbers of Doukhobors emigrated *en masse* to Canada, their trip financed largely by Leo Tolstoy and his followers. Interestingly, like the Doukhobors, the Vedic 'wise-men' Anastasia describes also favoured an oral method of teaching; they were able to sum up volumes of detail in just a few words and a single easily remembered rite — see the first section of Chapter 6 ("Into the depths of history") in the present volume.

[26] In: Ethel Dunn (ed.), *A Molokan's search for truth: the correspondence of Leo Tolstoy and Fedor Zheltov.* Translated by John Woodsworth. Original editor: Andrew Donskov. Berkeley (Calif.), USA: Highgate Road Social Science Research Station and Ottawa, Canada: Slavic Research Group at the University of Ottawa, 2001, p. 48.

[27] *Christian Science* — see footnote 1 in Book 6, Translator's Afterword.

founded, the *Christian Science Sentinel,* detailing her professional relations with Rev. James Henry Wiggin (whom she had
hired as a publishing consultant) and refuting public allega-
tions that he had had a hand in the authorship of her seminal
work *Science and health with Key to the Scriptures.* In this statement she reports Rev. Wiggin as asking her the question:
"How do you know that there ever was such a man as Christ
Jesus?"
To which she replies (in part):

> I do not find my authority for Christian Science in history,
> but in revelation. If there had never existed such a person
> as the Galilean Prophet [i.e., Jesus], it would make no dif-
> ference to me. I should still know that God's spiritual ideal
> is the only real man in His image and likeness.

It is evident that for both Zheltov and Eddy it was not the
person of Christ Jesus that was sacred and significant, but the
ideas (the 'Christ ideas', one might say) that Jesus presented
to the world — ideas which could be effectively practised in
our age and their practice taught to others, as Eddy proved
not only by her own remarkable works of healing, but, more
importantly, by the thousands upon thousands of spiritual
healings brought about by her students, their students and
students of their students, right up to the present day.[29] For

---

[28]Reproduced in: Mary Baker Eddy, *The First Church of Christ, Scientist, and Miscellany.* Boston: The First Church of Christ, Scientist, 1925, pp. 317–319.

[29]Many of these healings have been verified by the medical profession or other eye-witnesses and published as testimonies. See especially: Yvonne Caché von Fettweis & Robert Townsend Warneck, *Mary Baker Eddy: Christian healer.* Boston: The Christian Science Publishing Society, 1998; *A century of Christian Science healing.* Boston: The Christian Science Publishing Society, 1966; Robert Peel, *Health and medicine in the Christian Science tradition: principle, practice and challenge.* New York: Crossroad, 1988.

these students, textbook study and class instruction, while an acknowledged help, inevitably have taken second place to individual prayer, to their own direct mental and spiritual connection to God as their ultimate Teacher and ultimate Healer.[30]

And, lest there be any doubt as to how Eddy viewed her own role as a presenter of the science of spiritual healing to the world, in her later years she stated unequivocally: "Those who look for me in person, or elsewhere than in my writings, *lose me instead of find me.*"[31]

So now, perhaps, we can look at the *Journal Vert* reviewer's question "Does Anastasia exist?" in a new light.[32] It was the same question Sauvé had put to me in an interview in preparation for her review, where she quotes my reply (in French) along these lines:

---

[30]Eddy also makes some very similar statements to Anastasia's regarding occultism and mysticism. In *Science and health* (p. 569), she foresees an occult-free future for mankind: "The march of mind and of honest investigation will bring the hour when the people will chain, with fetters of some sort, the growing occultism of this period." And in the same work (p. 80), she observes: "[Christian] Science dispels mystery and explains extraordinary phenomena; but Science never removes phenomena from the domain of reason into the realm of mysticism."

[31]M. B. Eddy, *The First Church of Christ, Scientist, and Miscellany,* p. 119 *(italics—JW)*. Similar sentiments are expressed in other places in her writings — see especially the article "Deification of personality" in her *Miscellaneous Writings* (Boston: The First Church of Christ, Scientist, 1925, pp. 307–310). Note also Eddy's statement in *Science and health* (p. 82) in her discussion of the importance of writers' thoughts and ideas over their personages: "Chaucer wrote centuries ago, yet we still read his *thought* in his verse. What is classic study, but discernment of the *minds* of Homer and Virgil, *of whose personal existence we may be in doubt?*" *(italics—JW)*.

[32]For one thing, in the 'club' of those with a questionable historical existence, these 'Siberian recluses' appear to be in pretty good company.

I believe that Anastasia certainly exists in some form, but not necessarily in a fleshly body visible to our material eyes, even though I would not rule that out. As I see it, there is no doubt that she exists as a very powerful idea and that she is a force of inspiration. She exists in the words, in the rich thoughts of feelings and promises as transcribed by Megré.

And today I would add (in the spirit of Zheltov): "She exists in the hearts of them who are ready to seek out and apply for themselves the ideas she presents, and this is what is truly dear to me."

Does that mean that the author's portrayal of Anastasia as a living human being is irrelevant or unimportant? Not at all. For some readers, accepting her as a bodily personage, at least to begin with, may be extremely helpful. By identifying with a figure who expresses what seem like incredible qualities of the Divine and yet still affirms "I am Man",[33] many readers may get their first glimmer of awareness of their own innate capacities. But the more they read — especially in a second or third examination of a text they have read before — their initial impressions may gradually evolve away from personage and more into idea.

When Francis Church identified the real Santa Claus with the spiritual qualities of "love and generosity and devotion", he did not thereby obliterate the image of a jolly old man in a sleigh from a young child's mind, but enriched her temporary image of 'Santa' with a new dimension, a new idea. As the child grew older and developed her reasoning capacities, she would have been able to retain this new idea in her thought even when she no longer clung to the old image of a personal gift-giver.

[33]See (for example) the middle of Book 1, Chapter 26: "Dreams — creating the future".

In each of the cases we have looked at, we can witness the *evolution of an image* at work in individual human thought.[34] In Book 6, Chapter 6 ("Imagery and trial"), Anastasia describes the *image* as "an entity of energy invented by human thought, ... created by a single Man or by several together", and further likens it to an actor's portrayal of a dramatic *persona* on stage — a portrayal in which "the invented image acquires a temporary embodiment". Note that the portrayal of one and the same *persona* will vary from actor to actor, and even from performance to performance by the same actor, especially as the actor gains new insight into the deeper dimensions of the character he is portraying.[35]

But just as Zheltov's image of the central figure of the New Testament evolved into one focused more on the truth itself than the person of its human embodiment, just as Eddy (a real-life historical figure who frequently found herself targeted by both adoring worshippers and malicious critics) finally urged her followers to stop looking to her as a person and start practising the truths she revealed by healing their own

[34]Note also Megré's observation in Book 7, Chapter 3 ("You create your own fate"): "*the power of the energy of thought has no equal in the Universe: everything we see, including ourselves, is created by the energy of thought.*" Yet he also relays Anastasia's warning that the 'energy of thought' which we all possess is vastly underutilised. In Book 5, Chapter 12 (poignantly entitled "Do we have freedom of thought?"), after taking account of all the distracting subjects on which people tend to waste their thinking capacities, Anastasia concludes: "All told, the average Man spends only 15 to 20 minutes of his life reflecting on the mystery of creation."

[35]Anastasia goes on (in the same chapter) to show the effects of collective images held by members of a society — images of others, of themselves and of the world as a whole. And in Chapter 3 ("Why does love come and go?") of the current book she points out the vital role played by *image* in finding (and keeping) one's soulmate and how one's image may change or stay the same independently of the real person (see especially the section entitled "False images").

and others' mental and physical ailments, so Anastasia, whatever personal form she may possess, urges (through Megré) a similar charge upon her would-be followers.[36]

In Book 2, for example, in reply to the author's query as to whether *she personally* might have been helping him in a particular situation, Anastasia tells him:

Everything in the Universe is interrelated. To perceive what is really going on in the Universe one need only look into one's self.[37]

And in Book 3 when Vladimir expresses curiosity as to the extent of her abilities — "Can you answer any question confronting science today?" — Anastasia offers the following reply:

[36]Does 'practising the truths' revealed by Anastasia mean that every single reader should start looking for a plot of land in the country with a view to setting up his or her own 'family domain'? Anastasia herself recognised that this would not be feasible for everyone at the present time, although she does promote this option as especially suited to providing an ideal nurturing-ground for discovering one's inner being, even if it starts off with just a simple flower-pot on the window-sill (see Book 5, Chapter 15: "Making it come true"). In Book 8 she outlines the benefits which the 'domain' movement will have even on those still living in the city (see the section "Let's create" in Book 8, Chapter 10: *"The Book of Kin* and *A Family Chronicle"*). While I can definitely see the logic in Anastasia's own recommended vehicle of expression for the ideals she shares, I would think there may be as many avenues for putting these ideals into practice as there are individual readers of her books. The important thing is to keep in mind that these ideals *are eminently practicable* in some form — i.e., they are like seeds destined to push their way above and beyond one's mental soil into the fresh air and sunshine of one's whole life (see Translator's Preface to Book 2 for one small personal experience along this line). In many cases this will bring joy to others as well as to one's self.

[37]Quoted from Book 2, Chapter 6: "The cherry tree".

Many of them, perhaps. But every scientist — *indeed, every Man* — can find the answers. Everything depends upon the purity of one's thoughts, and the motive for asking.[38]

Over and over again she emphasises that the ideas and powers she possesses are within the grasp of every individual on the Earth, because they all come from the same source, i.e., the Creator (God). Over and over again both she and her grandfather keep urging Vladimir (and, by extension, every reader of the *RCS*) to resist the temptation to rely upon *them* as a personal source of wisdom and seek instead to find and utilise the ideas within themselves.

"Try not to wallow in all your information and contemplations, Vladimir," Anastasia's grandfather exhorts in Book 4. "Decide what's real for yourself."[39]

And in Chapter 1 ("Love — the essence of the Cosmos") of the current volume he accuses Vladimir of "laziness of mind" for constantly pestering him with questions when he should be looking for the answers within.[40] Subsequently he admonishes:

"I speak, and you listen, and instead of working out your own conclusions in your thought, you are merely taking note of mine."[41]

Similarly, time and again Anastasia urges Vladimir not just to accept her conclusions at face value, but to reason things through for himself by logical thinking — a capacity which (as

---

[38]Quoted from Book 3, Chapter 6: "Forces of light" *(italics—JW)*.

[39]Quoted from Book 4, Chapter 33: "School, or the lessons of the gods".

[40]He teases Vladimir on this point: "So, there's not enough information out there and you've come to me to get it, eh?" Note also his advice to Vladimir regarding the problem of getting legislative approval for setting up family domains: "You ought to be deciding your own course of action, without any kind of advice" (Book 8, Chapter 9: "A fine state of affairs").

[41]Quoted from Chapter 6: "Into the depths of history".

her grandfather points out), when not actively cultivated, is in danger of being lost by mankind.[42]

She, too, warns the author against "laziness of mind". In Book 8, Chapter 5 ("Divine nutrition"), when Vladimir confesses: "It's still not too clear to me just how I should be thinking", she gently assures him: "It will become clear if you are not too lazy to think."

Again in Book 8, Anastasia cautions Vladimir to be wary of relying on words alone. When asked by Vladimir about the role of words, she replies:

...it is not the words that are important, but, rather, people's conscious awareness. Words, of course, are necessary to bring it forth. A conscious awareness of eternal life will help perfect Man's way of life.[43]

Words are similar to outward appearances: they often play an important role in shaping one's initial conscious awareness of an idea. But, like one's early person-focused impressions, they tend to fall away as the image evolves in the direction of the Divine.

Hence, if one is truly to follow Anastasia, it would seem wise to heed her own advice and start seeking her out (as many readers are already doing) not in person, and not just in words about her (as fascinating as those may be), but in *idea* — the idea which, she says time and again throughout the Series, exists in every single one of us, if we are only alert enough to harness our mental capacities to discover our own innate

[42]See the middle of Chapter 7 (in the present volume): "Russia erased".

[43]Quoted from Book 8, Chapter 13: "A new civilisation". See the Editor's Afterword to the present volume for a delightful illustration of the dangers of putting too much stock in printed books and words at the expense of one's own logical thinking and feelings.

purity and power of thought in the likeness of our Creator. And then to start applying this idea to renewing and improving our day-to-day lives.

And because the evolution of an image is primarily an *individual* phenomenon (although yes, it may at times be collective, i.e., a shared individual experience), we shouldn't be surprised if our own discovery of Anastasia and her idea appears to evolve in a different way or at a different pace from that of other readers, or is different from the perception we ourselves had in a previous reading.[44] Like an actor honing a portrayal on stage from performance to performance, each one of us is evolving our own image of her as a *persona*. But the more we seek and find her not so much "in history, but in revelation" — the more we focus on the message rather than on the person of the messenger — and within our own hearts and minds, the stronger a position we shall be in to discover harmony within ourselves and with others, and the more deeply we shall be able to comprehend and appreciate her own beautiful self-declaration: *I exist for those for whom I exist.*

The power of the 'Anastasia idea' presented throughout this Series was certainly one of the reasons I signed on to these 'voyages' three years ago, and the fascinating concepts that have multiplied therefrom have indeed made the whole venture most worthwhile.

[44]In a remarkable little book entitled *The five clocks,* former University of Toronto linguistics professor Martin Joos (pron. *Yose,* rhyming with 'dose') states that one of the hallmarks of great literature is the capacity to convey a variety of different meanings to different individuals, or to the same individual upon each successive reading. The dedicated writer, he says, can enable the searching reader "to educate himself indefinitely far beyond what the writer put into the text in the first place". — Martin Joos, *The five clocks.* New York: Harcourt Brace, 1967, p. 42. There is no question, to my mind, that this 'capacity' Joos describes is eminently inherent in the writings of Vladimir Nikolaevich Megré concerning Anastasia.

Anastasia's (and her grandfather's) emphasis on the need for logical thinking and a conscious application of universal ideas to one's life-practice is a clear example of how the *RCS* eminently transcends what is popularly classified as *science fiction.* In my Translator's Preface to Book 1, I described the work (and, by extension, the Series) as a *chronicle of ideas* — a metaphysical treatise

> ...set forth with both the supporting evidence of a documentary account and the entertainment capacity of a novel. In other words, it can be read as any of these three in isolation, but only by taking the three dimensions together will the reader have something approaching a complete picture of the book. And all three are infused with a degree of soul-felt inspiration that can only be expressed in poetry.

Having completed the whole Series, I would now add that it is a chronicle which touches upon very many of the disciplines traditionally defined as 'academic', but in the context of their interrelation with each other and their application to our daily human life. As I look back over the *RCS,* apart from its obvious focus on ecology and environmental science, I can think of references to astronomy, biology, chemistry, physics, forestry, agriculture, horticulture, geology, archæology, engineering, architecture, medicine and the healing arts, psychology and psychotherapy, sociology, criminology, political science, economics, philosophy, religion, drama, literature, music and poetry, linguistics, foreign languages and quite possibly several more — all presented with a view to their application to everyday life, including work and leisure activities, along with love, marriage, family and other interpersonal relationships. The voyage of the *RCS* has taken in all these 'ports of call' along the way, and not just from a sailor's point of view (try an astronaut's perspective!). The voyage, indeed, reaches unto the very stars!

In line with the 'Moses' epigraph above, I have now taken my journey. And by the time you read this, you may well have already taken yours, at least once. But I trust the ideas you have *taken in* along the way will stand you in good stead for many ages yet to come.

As your English-speaking 'navigator', I salute you and wish you a hearty *Bon voyage!* as you set out on (or continue) your own voyage of self-discovery in the likeness of the Creator.

See you on a star! *On a star see ya!*[45]

Ottawa, Canada
31 December 2007   John Woodsworth

---

[45]An approximation of the Russian pronunciation of *Anastasia* — see footnote 5 in Book 7, Chapter 28: "To the readers of the Ringing Cedars Series".

The Book of Happiness
Editor's Afterword

"Papa, which do you like better — your computer or us, your family?" my daughter Lada enquired of me one morning as I was sitting at work in my home office.

"What? Of course I like *you* better. Why?" I replied, still glued to the screen.

"It's just that you spend all day long in front of computer, but I'd rather you played with me, or come see the pumpkins Mama and I've planted. Even when we go for a walk all together, all you do is think about your work — you barely notice us!"

"Well, that's true" I admitted. "But I do need to earn money, too — to pay for the piece of land we plant our garden on, for example. In other words, to afford things that are important in life."

"Nonsense!" she protested. "It's all arranged like that on purpose — so as to make you think that everything important in life you can buy for money — to make you think money's the most important thing of all."

As I turned to face her, Lada looked me straight in the eye and added, tugging at my sleeve:

"You know, Papa, I really feel you need to come with me to my tree house. I'll teach you three lessons on how to live happily ever after... without money."

Seeing the seriousness of the issue, I rose from the desk. Lada took me by the hand and escorted me to her green 'classroom'.

Half an hour later, as she finished delivering her three lessons and made sure I grasped their key concepts, Lada surprised me with a fresh demand:

"And now, before you go, you must promise me that you shall never ever share what I have just taught you — with anybody."

"How come?" I queried. "If the path you outlined to me can really lead people to happiness, I thought you would encourage me to tell others about it!"

"Don't you know about what happened with *The Book of Happiness?*"

"What *Book of Happiness?* Never heard of it."

Lada crossed her hands on her knees, sighed, and began telling me the story.

Once upon a time, in a large city with dirty, polluted air, there lived a man who had lost his happiness. It seemed as though he had searched for it everywhere — including behind the sofa and under his desk — but happiness was nowhere to be seen. It occurred to the man that his cat might have taken his happiness outside and hid it somewhere — so he searched all around his apartment block, but found nothing.

Exhausted by the search, he decided to spend the following day — his day off — in the woods, picking mushrooms. And so he did — he put on his big rubber boots and his backpack, took a knife and a large basket woven out of willow twigs — and headed off.

He had a very good day, and even forgot his grief over the lost happiness. By the time the Sun was setting, his basket was so full of beautiful large mushrooms it was hard to lift off the ground. The man was ready to go home, but now he couldn't find his way out of the forest. There was no visible path. He tried going in one direction — which he hoped would lead him out onto the paved road — but ended up in a swamp. He had no electric torch, no flashlight, and in the fading twilight it was hard to see the way, so the man decided to spend the night in the forest, and try to find his way home the following day.

He made a bed out of dry pine needles under a tall pine tree, put his backpack under his head for a pillow and tried to go to sleep. But the mosquitoes attacked him, putting sleep out of the question. So he just lay there, immersed in his thoughts. Finally he drifted off into a dream.

The man awoke suddenly in the middle of the night. The forest was dark and quiet all around, but far off in the distance, over to one side, he could make out what seemed to be a light glistening midst the branches. Thinking it could be a house, or a lamppost on the road, the man picked himself up and walked in the direction of the light, slowly making his way through the darkness.

After a while he found himself emerging from the dense bushes into a glade. There was no house or lamppost anywhere in sight, but in the centre of the glade there was a moss-covered hillock radiating a soft, golden light. As the man approached the hillock, he saw an old book in a leather binding lying on the top. The light was coming from the book!

The gold lettering on the cover read: *The Book of Happiness*. He opened it and began to read.

The book opened with a promise to show the reader how to find his happiness.

Wow, this is exactly what I need! thought the man as he hefted the heavy tome from the moss and hurried out of the glade, taking the book with him.

Perhaps it was the light coming from the book, or perhaps his own insight, but he now felt confident as to which way he should go. And, indeed, it wasn't long before he found the path, then the paved road, and began walking along the empty night-time highway in the direction of the town, his mushroom-filled basket in one hand and *The Book of Happiness* in the other.

Dawn was breaking in the sky when he reached the outskirts of the city and, soon afterward, his home. Despite his heavy load he felt neither tired nor sleepy. He put the basket down by the front door, took off his rubber boots, plunged onto the sofa and immersed himself in reading.

He finished the whole book that same day and it delivered on its promise. It brought him his happiness back. His happiness turned out to be lying behind the bookshelf — the only place he had not looked when searching for it. Presently he remembered that at one time he had indeed put his happiness on top of this bookshelf to save space in his small flat. Then he had added more books on top, which had apparently pushed the happiness over and caused it to fall behind.

When the man — following the instructions from the Book — regained his happiness, it was all covered in dust, hair and cockroach feces, but he wiped it clean and it began to look like new once more.

So as not to lose it again, he decided to carry it with him all the time. He attached it to a watch chain he bought specifically for this purpose, and now carried his happiness in his pocket.

For days and weeks he found himself in a state of bliss and joy. But seeing the unhappy people all around him — on the sidewalks of the streets, in offices and shops — he could not help but go back in his thought to the very last statement contained in the Book, namely:

You shall not show this book to others.

But just why, he thought, *can't I share* The Book of Happiness *with others to make them happy? This can't be fair — seeing how much suffering and injustice there is in the world!*

Gradually, as he contemplated the world around him, his feeling of happiness began to give way to a sense of disquietude, which over time became unbearable. Eventually the man resolved to try sharing the Book with just one man — a fellow-worker who had spent his week compiling some sort of production reports on his computer and who looked particularly lean and unhappy.

And so one day he brought the Book with him to work and, toward the end of their shift, entered his workmate's cubicle. Explaining its significance, he lent the Book to him for just one night, on his earnest promise that he would return it the next morning. That night, as he was going to sleep, lying in his bed and clasping his chained happiness to his chest, he felt blissful and fulfilled once more at the thought of sharing the path to happiness with even one fellow-human being.

The next morning, however, a sticky feeling of unease crept into him when he saw that his workmate he had lent the book to the night before was not in his office. The man managed to bear this uncertainty until noon, trying to console himself with the thought that his friend must be finishing the last page of the Book at home and would appear at the end of the corridor any moment.

As this did not happen by the lunch break, the man obtained his colleague's home address from the manager (who had been trying to reach him by phone the whole morning, without success) and ran over to his place. There, he found the door of the apartment wide open, and his workmate gone. With him was gone, too, *The Book of Happiness*.

At first the man found it hard to live with the nagging thought that he himself had not heeded the Book's warning and was now to blame for its disappearance. But as the days turned into weeks and weeks into months, the sensation of loss gradually wore down, and life returned to normal.

Then one morning a year later, as the man was walking to the office, he sensed a strange agitation in the air. Everywhere people could be seen shouting and running, and a huge queue had formed in front of the neighbourhood bookstore. With a dark feeling of foreboding the man made his way through the crowd to the bookshop window where, lo and behold, a hundred copies of the latest sensational release were on display. He gasped as he read, in large golden letters on the cover of each book — *The Book of Happiness.*

At this moment the store window lost its ability to withstand the pressure of the human bodies leaning against it and it shattered. Pieces of broken glass showered down on the crowd. A moment later a flood of people rushed to the display case and emptied it. Dozens of people were now running away from the bookstore, each clasping a volume to their chest. One of these people was the man who had found this book more than a year ago in the forest.

He rushed back to his apartment and leafed through his prize. There was not a shred of doubt left — this was an exact reprint of *his* Book, apparently made from the copy stolen a year earlier by his workmate. Strange as it may seem, though, the man did not feel angry at him, but rather quivered in excited anticipation as to what would come next.

For the next few days the whole city was caught up in a reading frenzy. Nobody seemed to go to work or even go outdoors. The whole populace, young and old, were staying home and reading the amazing yet simple revelations of *The Book of Happiness.* And yes, more than one soul puzzled over the last sentence in the Book:

You shall not show this book to others.

They questioned themselves as to why this restriction was imposed and, more importantly, why the Book had gained such tremendous circulation despite this reservation. But the general welfare resulting from the wide distribution of the Book and its ideas was so palpable that these questions were soon forgotten.

For the next two weeks, few businesses were open in the city, as all citizens joined in a spontaneous festival to celebrate their new awareness and congratulate each other on the new era that the discovery of this remarkable book had ushered in upon them.

And when the people did return to their workplaces, they were so overfilled with happiness that they took to their routine tasks with joyous enthusiasm. The bakers were baking tastier bread, the builders were laying stronger foundations for new buildings, and the policemen became more polite than ever before (!) — while not just crime, but even traffic accidents seemed to completely disappear overnight.

Weeks passed, and the whole city and the surrounding countryside were transformed in such a remarkable, beneficial fashion that everyone was going to bed with smiles on their faces in excited anticipation of what new joys the next day would bring. And only the man who had originally discovered the Book seemed to have any recollection of the warning it contained in its final line. Yet the warning, even for him, seemed to pale into insignificance.

Months went by. As he came out of his apartment block one morning into the blossoming of the Spring, his ears were blasted by the sound of nearby police-car sirens, which no one had heard for a very long time. He hurried around the corner just in time to see two policemen shove an arrested felon into a patrol car and take off. The elderly lady left standing on the pavement was explaining to passers-by that a young delinquent had assaulted her and tried to wrench her happiness from her. Her attacker had complained that she possessed more of it than he himself...

The next day similar incidents started to take place all over the city, as more and more people began to suspect their neighbours, colleagues or just passers-by of usurping a larger portion of happiness than they were entitled to.

Before long, all hell broke loose. Shooting began in the streets and neighbourhoods. People were murdered for the tiny pieces of happiness they were desperately trying to cling on to. The police department was overwhelmed. Days later, the police themselves joined the trend and raided homes to carry out whatever happiness remained — "for government needs". Rumours had it, however, that police were keeping the confiscated happiness for their personal greed, and even fighting over it amongst themselves.

A large portion of the populace fled the distressed city, most of the businesses closed, and of the few individuals who remained, nobody so much as cared even to remove the rotting corpses of the slain men, women and children from the streets and squares that just a few weeks ago had been home to — as it had seemed at the time — boundless happiness.

As the man who had originally found *The Book of Happiness* in the woods was making his way stealthily along a completely deserted avenue leading to the city's main square, he suddenly heard the squeaking of brakes, a lone gunshot, the clapping of car doors, and the receding noise of a motor. When it finally died away in the distance, he mustered his strength and turned the corner into the plaza where the incident had happened only moments earlier. There, by the fountain, lay the man who had stolen the original of the Book a year ago and — in a pool of fresh blood nearby — the hefty leather-bound volume, opened to the last page.

You shall not show this book to others — read the final line.

Centuries went by. Wind and water had eaten away stone, concrete, and metal; paved streets and squares had given way to trees and meadows. Virtually nothing now betrayed the traces of the former city, concealed as it was in a lush, dense forest. The few ruins that remained had been fenced off and designated as historical monuments, occasionally drawing the odd tourist group from a faraway urban centre.

One day a visitor with a basket woven from willow twigs separated from his group and, lured by the most beautiful mushrooms he had ever seen, wandered deep into the forest, off the beaten path. Late in the afternoon, as he was crossing a large glade on his way back to the tourist camp, he stumbled over something in the high grasses. He reached down and brought up a thick book in a leather binding with gold lettering. *The Book of Happiness*, read the title.

Wow! thought the man. *This must be a real oldie — and probably worth a fortune.* Hiding it from his companions, he returned to the camp and when alone in his tent, took out the book, opened it and started reading.

He read all through the night, feeling no drowsiness nor fatigue. When he emerged from his tent in the morning, the world presented itself to him in a new and happy light. *There's only one thing I cannot grasp*, he thought as he watched his fellow-campers busying themselves around a fire. *Just why does it say: "You shall not show this book to others"?*

Lada finished her account, and we spent some time sitting there quietly without saying a word, listening to the breeze ruffling through the treetops and the crickets chirping in the grass.

"Do you know what the surest way to keep a secret is?" Lada finally asked, breaking the silence.

"No idea," I confessed. "What is it?"

"*To forget it!*"

Then she opened the palm of her hand in which, it turned out, she had been clasping all the while three little round clumps rolled from some kind of herb.

"But I have an even better solution, one especially for you," she continued. "This is a special kind of grass that helps keep secrets. You go ahead and eat these clumps. If you eat enough of them, you will still be able to remember the three lessons I taught you, but you will not be able to share them with others. But if you eat too many of them, you will forget everything I told you — either way you won't be able to share them with others."

"And how much is 'enough'? If I eat all three, will I still remember the lessons myself?" I enquired.

"That," Lada observed, "you will find out for yourself after you've eaten them!"

Noticing our prolonged absence, my wife Ira came looking for us in the far corner of the garden.

"And just what might you be doing here?" she asked with a smile, finally spotting us under the tree.

"We... ah..." I hesitated, looking at my wife and daughter by turns as I swallowed down the last bit of the third clump. "We... were playing tree house!"

"Aha, I see," Ira gave me an understanding look and started on her way back to the house. "Come when you're hungry, lunch is ready. Though I gather you've just had some snacks!"

"Hey, Mama!" Lada called out after her. "D'you happen to know, what's the most important thing in life?"

Ira turned and confidently replied:

"*Life is!*"

"Wow, you got it right this time!" Lada jumped up and clapped her hands for joy. Then she turned to me, beaming with pride and delight at the degree of mutual understanding our family had achieved.

I hope the three clumps were just enough.

Maui, Hawaii, USA
19 December 2007   Leonid Sharashkin

THE RINGING CEDARS SERIES AT A GLANCE

Anastasia (ISBN 978-0-9801812-0-3), Book 1 of the Ringing Cedars Series, tells the story of entrepreneur Vladimir Megré's trade trip to the Siberian taiga in 1995, where he witnessed incredible spiritual phenomena connected with sacred 'ringing cedar' trees. He spent three days with a woman named Anastasia who shared with him her unique outlook on subjects as diverse as gardening, child-rearing, healing, Nature, sexuality, religion and more. This wilderness experience transformed Vladimir so deeply that he abandoned his commercial plans and, penniless, went to Moscow to fulfil Anastasia's request and write a book about the spiritual insights she so generously shared with him. True to her promise this life-changing book, once written, has become an international bestseller and has touched hearts of millions of people world-wide.

The Ringing Cedars of Russia (ISBN 978-0-9801812-1-0), Book 2 of the Series, in addition to providing a fascinating behind-the-scenes look at the story of how *Anastasia* came to be published, offers a deeper exploration of the universal concepts so dramatically revealed in Book 1. It takes the reader on an adventure through the vast expanses of space, time and spirit — from the Paradise-like glade in the Siberian taiga to the rough urban depths of Russia's capital city, from the ancient mysteries of our forebears to a vision of humanity's radiant future.

The Space of Love (ISBN 978-0-9801812-2-7), Book 3 of the Series, describes the author's second visit to Anastasia. Rich with new revelations on natural child-rearing and alternative education, on the spiritual significance of breast-feeding and the meaning of ancient megaliths, it shows how each person's thoughts can influence the destiny of the entire Earth and describes practical ways of putting Anastasia's vision of happiness into practice. Megré shares his new outlook on education and children's real creative potential after a visit to a school where pupils build their own campus and cover the ten-year Russian school programme in just two years. Complete with an account of an armed intrusion into Anastasia's habitat, the book highlights the limitless power of Love and non-violence.

Co-creation (ISBN 978-0-9801812-3-4), Book 4 and centrepiece of the Series, paints a dramatic living image of the creation of the Universe and humanity's place in this creation, making this primordial mystery relevant to our everyday living today. Deeply metaphysical yet at the same time down-to-Earth practical, this poetic heart-felt volume helps us uncover answers to the most significant questions about the essence and meaning of the Universe and the nature and purpose of our existence. It also shows how and why the knowledge of these answers, innate in every human being, has become obscured and forgotten, and points the way toward reclaiming this wisdom and — in partnership with Nature — manifesting the energy of Love through our lives.

Who Are We? (ISBN 978-0-9801812-4-1), Book 5 of the Series, describes the author's search for real-life 'proofs' of Anastasia's vision presented in the previous volumes. Finding these proofs and taking stock of ongoing global environmental destruction, Vladimir Megré describes further practical steps for putting Anastasia's vision into practice. Full of beautiful realistic images of a new way of living in co-operation with the Earth and each other, this book also highlights the role of children in making us aware of the precariousness of the present situation and in leading the global transition toward a happy, violence-free society.

The Book of Kin (ISBN 978-0-9801812-5-8), Book 6 of the Series, describes another visit by the author to Anastasia's glade in the Siberian taiga and his conversations with his growing son, which cause him to take a new look at education, science, history, family and Nature. Through parables and revelatory dialogues and stories Anastasia then leads Vladimir Megré and the reader on a shocking re-discovery of the pages of humanity's history that have been distorted or kept secret for thousands of years. This knowledge sheds light on the causes of war, oppression and violence in the modern world and guides us in preserving the wisdom of our ancestors and passing it over to future generations.

The Energy of Life (ISBN 978-0-9801812-6-5), Book 7 of the Series, re-asserts the power of human thought and the influence of our thinking on our lives and the destiny of the entire planet and the Universe. It also brings forth a practical understanding of ways to consciously control and build up the power of our creative thought. The book sheds still further light on the forgotten pages of humanity's history, on religion, on the roots of inter-racial and inter-religious conflict, on ideal nutrition, and shows how a new way of thinking and a lifestyle in true harmony with Nature can lead to happiness and solve the personal and societal problems of crime, corruption, misery, conflict, war and violence.

The New Civilisation (ISBN 978-0-9801812-7-2), Book 8, Part 1 of the Series, describes yet another visit by Vladimir Megré to Anastasia and their son, and offers new insights into practical co-operation with Nature, showing in ever greater detail how Anastasia's lifestyle applies to our lives. Describing how the visions presented in previous volumes have already taken beautiful form in real life and produced massive changes in Russia and beyond, the author discerns the birth of a new civilisation. The book also paints a vivid image of America's radiant future, in which the conflict between the powerful and the helpless, the rich and the poor, the city and the country, can be transcended and thereby lead to transformations in both the individual and society.

Rites of Love (ISBN 978-0-9801812-8-9), Book 8, Part 2, contrasts today's mainstream attitudes to sex, family, childbirth and education with our forebears' lifestyle, which reflected their deep spiritual understanding of the significance of conception, pregnancy, homebirth and upbringing of the young in an atmosphere of love. In powerful poetic prose Megré describes their ancient way of life, grounded in love and non-violence, and shows the practicability of this same approach today. Through the life-story of one family, he portrays the radiant world of the ancient Russian Vedic civilisation, the drama of its destruction and its re-birth millennia later — in our present time.

Vladimir Megré
The Ringing Cedars Series

Translated from the Russian by **John Woodsworth**
Edited by **Dr Leonid Sharashkin**

- Book 1 **Anastasia**
  ISBN: 978-0-9801812-0-3

- Book 2 **The Ringing Cedars of Russia**
  ISBN: 978-0-9801812-1-0

- Book 3 **The Space of Love**
  ISBN: 978-0-9801812-2-7

- Book 4 **Co-creation**
  ISBN: 978-0-9801812-3-4

- Book 5 **Who Are We?**
  ISBN: 978-0-9801812-4-1

- Book 6 **The Book of Kin**
  ISBN: 978-0-9801812-5-8

- Book 7 **The Energy of Life**
  ISBN: 978-0-9801812-6-5

- Book 8, Part 1 **The New Civilisation**
  ISBN: 978-0-9801812-7-2

- Book 8, Part 2 **Rites of Love**
  ISBN: 978-0-9801812-8-9

**RINGING
CEDARS
PRESS**

Published by **Ringing Cedars Press**
www.ringingcedars.com